POLITICS OF
TRANQUILITY

POLITICS OF TRANQUILITY

The Material and Mundane Lives of
Buddhist Nuns in Post-Mao Tibet

Yasmin Cho

CORNELL UNIVERSITY PRESS   ITHACA AND LONDON

First published 2024 by Cornell University Press

Library of Congress Cataloging-in-Publication Data

Names: Cho, Yasmin, 1977– author.
Title: Politics of tranquility : the material and mundane lives of Buddhist
    nuns in post-Mao Tibet / Yasmin Cho.
Description: Ithaca : Cornell University Press, 2024. | Includes bibliographical
    references and index.
Identifiers: LCCN 2024015917 (print) | LCCN 2024015918 (ebook) |
    ISBN 9781501778803 (hardcover) | ISBN 9781501778810 (paperback) |
    ISBN 9781501778827 (epub) | ISBN 9781501778834 (pdf)
Subjects: LCSH: Yarchen Gar. | Buddhist nuns—China—Tibet Autonomous
    Region. | Buddhist nuns—China—Tibet Autonomous Region—Social
    conditions. | Monastic and religious life of women—Political aspects—
    China—Tibet Autonomous Region.
Classification: LCC BQ6160.C6 C46 2019 (print) | LCC BQ6160.C6 (ebook) |
    DDC 294.3/657—dc23/eng/20240604
LC record available at https://lccn.loc.gov/2024015917
LC ebook record available at https://lccn.loc.gov/2024015918

For the Buddhist nuns in Tibet

Contents

Preface

Throughout this book, I want readers to envision an encampment or a Buddhist shantytown instead of a strict monastery when they imagine Yachen Gar, the Tibetan community that is the focus of this work. For various reasons, Yachen has come to resemble more and more a formal monastic complex rather than the haphazard encampment it once was. First, the majority of its residents are robed monastics who adhere to vows and rules that are typical for a Buddhist monastery. Second, their daily activities consist mostly of practicing Buddhism—chanting, meditating, and attending rituals. Thus, it is fair to say that Yaqingsi, the Chinese term for Yachen Gar, also means "Yachen Monastery."

I have no objection to this way of thinking about Yachen. I also don't dismiss the fact that the term "gar" has been used for a type of traditional monastic community that has existed on the plateau throughout Tibetan history. But I would nonetheless like to offer a caution to readers who may fixate on the term "monastery" as referring to a site with very specific functions, regulations, and roles. For such readers, certain facts about Yachen that I share in this book may be puzzling. Some of what I and some other disciples were able to do in Yachen would normally be impossible in a formal monastic complex in Tibet, which is why I hope that readers will remain open-minded about Yachen and treat it as a continuously evolving Buddhist shantytown on the plateau. One of the startling things about Yachen, if the reader thinks of it as a formal monastery, is that I, a foreign national and a layperson, was able to roam the community freely and even to stay with the nuns in their rooms for long periods of time without meeting any institutional barriers. I entered Yachen just as I would enter any village, and I stayed with the nuns almost as if I were staying with friends.

In 2010, I arrived in Yachen as a solo traveler. Before arriving, I had contacted a lay Chinese woman who was staying in Yachen at the time. She was visiting her teacher and attending his lectures in Yachen for several months. Many dozens of lay Chinese like her were residing in Yachen to receive teaching from their Tibetan teachers (*lamas*). I was led to her teacher's hall where some other monastics and lay Chinese were sitting and talking. It was late afternoon, and the lama's lecture had just ended. I approached a group and explained my purpose in coming to Yachen as a researcher and said that I wished to find a place in the nuns' area to stay for an extended period. None of them knew how to find a place for me on such abrupt notice. In fact, if I hadn't insisted on staying on the nuns' side of Yachen, I could have quite easily found a place to stay in the monks' area. Many Chinese lay disciples, regardless of their gender, stayed in the monks' area because there were lots of empty huts that could be rented; furthermore, the monks' area was the same area in which the teachers' lecturing halls and houses were located. Therefore, it was not unusual to see a young Chinese lay woman living next to a young monk. These kinds of mixed gender and mixed lay-monastic residential arrangements might shock those who see Yachen strictly as a monastery.

From the beginning, I strongly felt that the success of my research depended on my staying in the nuns' area. As I talked to more people that afternoon, one Chinese nun cautiously told me that she had an abandoned meditation cell in her yard where I might be able to stay at least for that night. (I describe this first night in Yachen in detail in the introduction.) From then on, I moved from one hut to another for my first six weeks in Yachen in the summer of 2010. During my visits to Yachen in the years that followed, I stayed with different nuns for a few weeks or a few months at a time, in different huts and in different parts of the encampment.

At one point, just like the nuns did, I built my own tiny hut in a corner of a nun's yard. My hut was so tiny that I couldn't even stretch out my legs at night, and without a proper piece of lumber for its beam, the roof was extremely vulnerable. Whenever wild dogs would run across the roof at night, my rickety hut would begin shaking, and I thought it would crumble in that moment. But it lasted for much longer than I expected: I spent the entire 2012–2013 winter season in this hut. The winters in Yachen are cruel, especially because the huts have no heating systems. In winter, I went to bed wearing three pairs of pants, a sweater, and a winter jacket, and buried myself under three thick, heavy blankets. I nearly suffocated under those three layers, but this was still better than being exposed to the freezing air in the room at night. I placed my contact lenses under my pillow so that they wouldn't freeze during the night. Yet I often forgot to put my toothpaste under the blanket and would find it completely frozen the next morning. Nonetheless, I was happy with my already decaying hut and the idea of my own living space in this massively overcrowded encampment. I could understand how important it was to a nun to have her own space in Yachen. When I got back to Yachen after a trip in the spring of 2013, I found my roof had finally fallen. I went looking for other nuns who could take me in again. In this way, like a true nomad, I resided in Yachen for a total of nearly two years. I shared meals with Tibetan and non-Tibetan nuns, talked with them day and night, fetched water every day with them, traveled and visited their hometowns, and talked to their family members.

The nuns embraced me instantly. I introduced myself as a researcher, but this didn't seem to make sense to many of the Tibetan nuns at first. They wondered more often about whether I was married and had children than about what I was studying. But some older Chinese nuns with whom I worked told me that they understood what I was doing, and they willingly provided advice about my research. Their prime advice was that I should talk to their illustrious teachers in Yachen because these great beings would know everything and answer everything I asked and would guide my research in the right direction.

My East Asian appearance and my Chinese speaking ability often gave me a free pass because people assumed that I was a Han Chinese disciple visiting her teacher. When I did my main field research between 2010 and 2016, many Chinese pilgrims visited Yachen and stayed for weeks or months paying homage to their teachers. Most of the time, the Chinese authorities did not stop me to check my ID, and I did not deliberately reveal who I was to them when I was not asked. In those years, reaching Yachen was treated more as a matter of faith and even the result of karma rather than as an issue related to police restrictions. Because of the high-altitude environment, some non-Tibetan disciples had a hard time reaching Yachen, let alone staying there; when this happened, other disciples often interpreted such difficulties within the frame of karmic maturity. In other words, karma hadn't ripened yet for the unsuccessful traveler or karmic sins had hindered them from reaching such a holy place as Yachen. I don't know whether I have such karmic maturity; but fortunately, I have never failed to reach Yachen when I have decided to visit. For high-altitude sickness, I simply take pills before the trip and for the first few days after I arrive in Yachen. The pills expand my blood vessels so that my body can adjust quickly to the depleted level of oxygen.

In recent years, however, visiting Yachen has become more and more a political issue. When the encampment was reduced by half in 2017, both Tibetan and non-Tibetan nuns left (some of them did so against their wishes) and are not able to return. The encampment was also closed off from outsiders' reach; only those Tibetans who hold an ID from Sichuan province (where Yachen is located) can visit and do the pilgrimage. The Tibetan teachers in Yachen were no exception. Many lamas were asked (or ordered) to return to their hometown monasteries in other provinces. Only those lamas from the same province as Yachen could remain and continue serving as teachers in Yachen. The Chinese government has not only reduced the size of Yachen but has also restructured it as a monastic compound that serves only local needs.

What Yachen will become in the next decades remains to be seen. This book is a record of one of the most vibrant times in Yachen, when it was full of potential and hope for the nuns who joined it daily. I know that the reason I could roam freely in Yachen and stay with the nuns in their huts is not only about Yachen's lack of formality. Without the nuns' unfathomable generosity and hospitality that I received over the years, from my first day in Yachen throughout the following years, my rich experiences there and this book would not have even been possible. They invited a stranger, a layperson, into their most intimate spaces and shared their food, bedding, and stories. I hope this book does justice to their incredible compassion.

Okahandja, Namibia
April 2024

Acknowledgments

Doing fieldwork in Tibet was one of the toughest challenges in my life—enduring the freezing winter of the plateau with temperatures of −30°C or below with no heating system, getting bitten by a wild dog and being hospitalized for over a week, and remaining on constant alert for possible government surveillance of my whereabouts and what I was doing. But my memories of the people I met in Tibet made my fieldwork one of the most blessed experiences in my life. I would like to express my most sincere gratitude to the Buddhist nuns I met on the Tibetan plateau and in Chinese cities for their enduring compassion toward me. I never felt lonely or insecure when I was around them. They always welcomed me wholeheartedly, even though I am sure that my presence was an interruption in their secluded lives. Without them, this book would not exist today.

Outside the Tibetan monastic compounds, I also received invaluable help and assistance from scholars and experts on Tibetan Buddhism and Tibetan studies. I want to express my special appreciation to Bo Chen (Chengdu), Laxianjia (Beijing), Tashi Tsering (Dharamsala, India), Dan Smyer Yü (Beijing), Ming Zhang (Chengdu), and Deji Zhuoma (Beijing) for sharing their experience and knowledge about potential interlocutors and about how to navigate Tibetan regions in China during the initial years of my research. I deeply thank the circles of Chinese lay devotees whom I met in cities and monasteries over the years. They shared with me their experiences and knowledge about Buddhist practices and their devotion toward their Tibetan teachers. I am grateful to my Tibetan language teachers, Gen Tseten la and Gen Chok la, for their patience and guidance through the intensive Tibetan language program I took in the summer of 2012 at the University of Virginia. With their help, I was able to acquire a firm grasp of the Tibetan language in a short time.

I appreciate the Social Science Research Council for its general support through the fellowship that enabled my field research in Tibet and China. I would like to thank my mentors at Duke University for their comments and feedback on some early chapters, which became the basis for this book. My special thanks to Anne Allison, Hwansoo Kim, Louise Meintjes, David Need, Rebecca L. Stein, and Katya Wesolowski for reading drafts of every chapter many times and giving me productive feedback that allowed me to sharpen my arguments. I also thank Venerable Karma Lekshe Tsomo, who served as an external reader of my work. Through her insights as a monastic-scholar, I was able to deepen my overall understanding of the lives of Buddhist nuns. My mentor, Ralph Litzinger, guided me through the critical phases of my research and helped me to see the value of my book when I was struggling. I truly appreciate his trust and encouragement both during and after our time working together. I would also like to express my gratitude to my colleagues at Duke, Layla Brown, Tamar Shirinian, and Cagri Yoltar, who watched me develop my book from the beginning and gave me endless support. I also thank Jennifer Bowles from the University of Michigan who became a trustworthy writing partner. I had a group of Korean friends at Duke, Enyoung Kim, Junhee Kwon, Youngji Lee, and Juhyung Shim, with whom I could talk in my first language and from whom I received both valuable insights on my book and moral support. I thank them for their presence and help.

I greatly appreciate the two external readers of this manuscript (who graciously allowed Cornell University Press to reveal their names to me): Gray Tuttle and Nicola Schneider. I admire their thorough reading of the earlier version of this manuscript and deeply appreciate their insightful feedback and comments, which have led to a much-improved final version. I am deeply grateful to Jim Lance at Cornell University Press for his firm support of my manuscript and for his ongoing patience and understanding about my haphazard fieldwork situation in Namibia while I was completing my revision. I want to express my thanks to Amy Holmes-Tagchungdarpa and Kalzang Dorjee Bhutia, whom I met at a conference several years ago. They became steady readers of my work over the years, and I admire their knowledge of Buddhist studies and appreciate their input on my work. I would like to thank Erik Mueggler, who was my mentor at the University of Michigan when I began my first postdoctoral program there. His support and guidance allowed me to adjust to a new campus life and to focus quickly on this manuscript. I deeply appreciate Richard Balme from Sciences Po, France, for his enduring support and mentorship over a decade spanning my research career from China, US, and Europe. I also thank my colleagues and mentors, Trine Brox, Jane Caple, Beata Switek, and Elizabeth Williams-Oerberg at the University of Copenhagen, who read chapters over the years and offered productive comments.

I express my special thanks to the Tibetan friends I met—at Duke, in Tibet, and elsewhere—who have supported me throughout my journey to become a junior scholar: Tsering Dolma, Dondrub Dorje, Sangyi Drolma, Drolma Gadou, Tsem Gonthar, Palden Gyal, Gesang Lamu, Thupten Norbu, Tsering Samdrup, Geshe Sangpo, and Namgyal Tsepak. A particular thanks goes also to Jongbok Yi, who helped me to revise the Tibetan transliteration in my manuscript. I thank my friends in South Korea and elsewhere, Enjung Cho,

Hyebyeol Choi, Hee-en Chung, Joo-Youn Chung, Jiyoon Kim, Kyenglim Kim, Soyeon Kim, Soyoung Kim, Gumlan Lee, and Heymi Lee, who have shown their unshakeable support for and trust in me over the past decades. I express special gratitude to Susumu Kawata at Osaka Institute of Technology for his pioneering and painstaking work on Tibetan Buddhist revival in contemporary China and for his insight. I appreciate Kazuko Kawata for her fascinating drawings of Yachen over the years and her generosity to use her work for the cover of this book.

Last but not least, I am deeply grateful for the help and support from Christopher Ahn, who is my dear friend and has been an enthusiastic advocate of my work over the years. His linguistic gifts and ability to read between the lines has helped me clarify and refine my prose. I really appreciate the careful manner with which he treats my writing and the integrity of my manuscript. Several Tibetans I met in Tibet and China gave me invaluable information and guidance, but I cannot name them here for political reasons. I send my sincere appreciation to them, and their help allowed this book to come to fruition today.

Notes on Transliteration and Treatment of Names

I provide the names for Tibetan towns in both Tibetan and Chinese when they appear for the first time in each chapter or section of the text. The order in which I present the terms is based on the frequency of usage at the local level. For example, I use "Ganzi" in Chinese pronunciation first and provide the Tibetan phonetic spelling in parentheses. The order itself does not matter very much, however, because the names of towns and cities, whether in Tibetan or Chinese, are easily understood by the people of the region. I use pinyin for Chinese terms and, for Tibetan terms, I use the Tibetan and Himalayan Library's (THL) Simplified Phonetic Transcription of Standard Tibetan (Germano and Tournadre 2003). The THL system does not always accurately reflect the sounds as they are spoken by local Tibetans, but I have adopted this system (for most, but not all, Tibetan terms) because it approximates the local sounds to some extent and provides legibility for a general readership. For the spelling of some frequently accepted terms in the field of Tibetan studies that do not correspond to the THL system, such as *tulku*, which means "reincarnated lama" (in the THL system, it is *trülku*), I have chosen to follow the more widely accepted spelling to maintain the overall consistency of terminology in the field. Throughout the book, I prioritize phonetics over written forms; in most cases, therefore, when a term first appears, I place its Wylie transliteration in a note (italicized in square brackets following the phonetic spelling) rather than in the text. I do not use a space between the syllables of a word when giving its phonetic spelling (for example, *tulku*), but I include a space between syllables in the Wylie spelling to make it easier to recognize the Tibetan characters that make up a word (for example, *sprul sku*).

I use pseudonyms throughout except for public figures such as Achuk lama, Tulku Asong, and Khenpo Jigme Phuntsok. I have also minimized or changed personal characteristics, including places of origin, village names, ages, and workplaces, to protect the identities of my interlocutors.

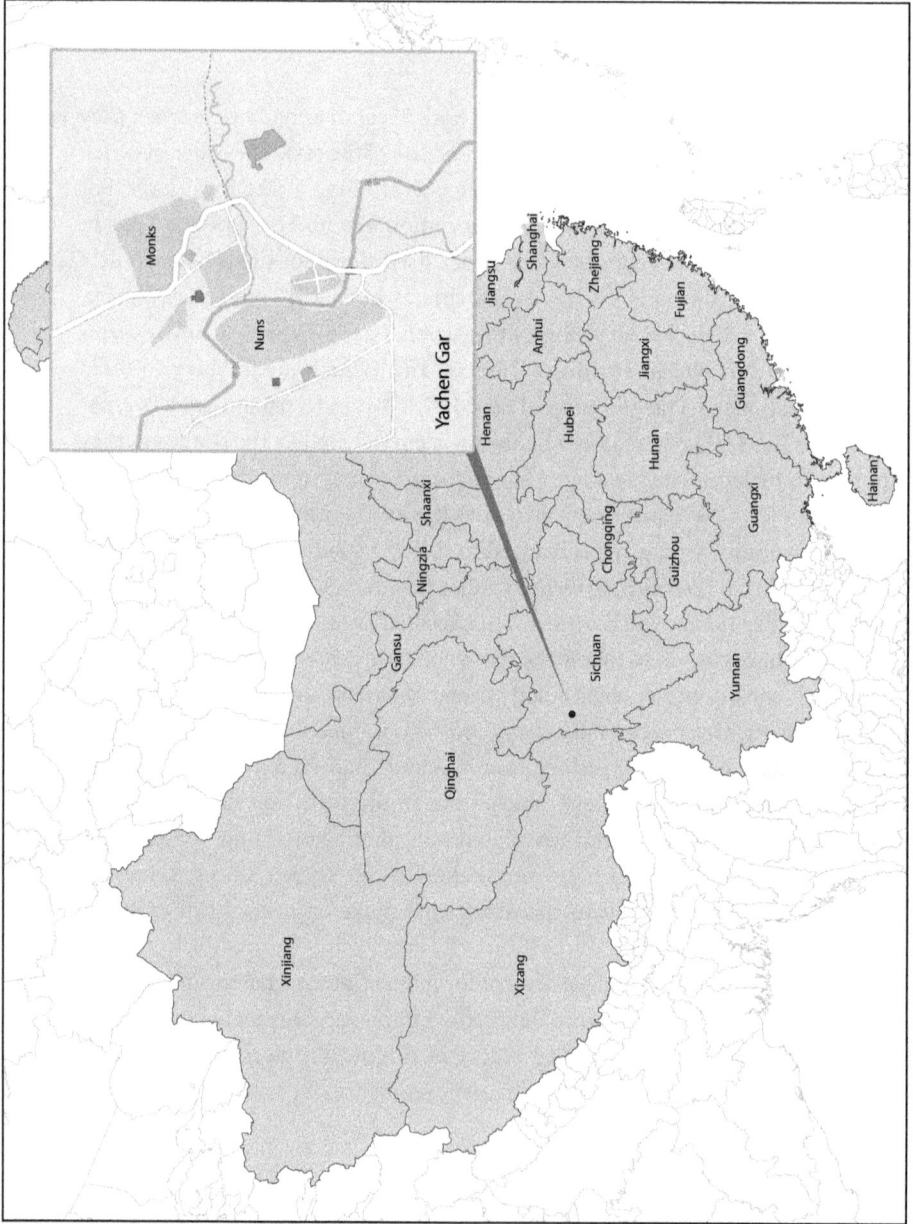

FIGURE 1. A map of Yachen based on data from the Geographic Information System. Map designed by Christopher Ahn.

POLITICS OF
TRANQUILITY

INTRODUCTION

Politics is not made up of power relationships; it is made up of relationships between worlds.
—Jacques Rancière (1999, 42)

Early in the morning in Ganzi (Kardze), a small Tibetan town in northwest China, Tibetan Buddhist nuns and monks crowd onto a shuttle bus. Their destination is Yachen Gar, a mega-sized Tibetan monastic encampment (*gar*) with the largest concentration of young Tibetan nuns in the world.[1] While the passengers are cramming their bags, sacks, and themselves into the vehicle, the driver ties the oversized luggage on the roof, raising a small mountain on the top of the already burdened bus. The trip will take six or seven hours westward through the unpaved, notoriously meandering Ganbai road across the eastern Tibetan plateau, a region broadly known as Kham.[2] Because more than half of the passengers on board do not have seats, any space on the bus that can possibly be occupied—hood, aisles, steps—is shamelessly taken. Once the bus begins moving, the journey becomes intensely multisensory: the scent of barley flour blended with homemade butter fills the air; the mumbled chanting sounds of passengers mix with high-pitched Tibetan folk songs blaring from the shuttle's poor audio system; people jostle up and down to the uneven rhythms generated by the bumpy surface of the roads; and shoulders, torsos, legs, and luggage aggressively tangle and press against each other.

In this chaotic scene, it would be pointless, if not almost impossible, to locate a clear order, hierarchy, or center; neither distinctions nor distances between humans, nonhumans, smells, sounds, chanting, folk songs, self, and others can be meaningfully discerned. The laws of perspective break down and even gravity seems momentarily suspended when bodies are constantly bouncing in their seats because of the bad road conditions. It is similar to what Kathleen Stewart

1

(2014, 556) describes as "the strange and prolific coexistence of word and world." There are intensities but no depth; senses, objects, laws, situations, and subjectivities register all at once in one dimension and are equally expressive. Or as Gustave Flaubert (1979, 79) said of his first impression of a Cairo street in 1850, "Each detail reaches out to grip you; it pinches you; and the more you concentrate on it the less you grasp the whole." Whether on a street in Cairo or in a crammed bus to Yachen, there is little that can be neatly singled out for interpretation. The objects reach out to grip the interpreter and merge her into the scene. They are all (in) this very materiality and all (in) the very details that constantly emerge.

This kind of material intensity is deeply embedded in the seemingly uneventful lives of the Tibetan Buddhist nuns in Yachen Gar, one of two mega-sized encampments that have emerged in the Kham region of Tibet in the past four decades. Through its examination of Yachen and the nuns living there, this book challenges two common assumptions about Tibetan Buddhist communities in contemporary China. First is the assumption that a Buddhist monastic community is best understood in terms of its esoteric qualities—as meditative, otherworldly, and spiritual. This book shows how starkly material and mundane such a community is in its very existence and in its daily operations, and how deeply gendered these material conditions are. Second is a less common yet still powerful assumption that Tibetan politics toward the Chinese state is best understood as rebellious, incendiary, or centered on Tibetan victimhood. This book shows how it can be otherwise: that Tibetan politics can be unassuming, calm, or self-contained, and yet still elicit substantial political effects, even during times of dreadful political turmoil such as the cycle of alternating self-immolations and brutal crackdowns in the early 2010s. The Tibetan nuns in Yachen Gar, who are located at the intersection between spiritualized, male-centered Tibetan monastic arrangements, on the one hand, and a volatile Sino-Tibetan politics, on the other, have called forth an alternative way of living and expressing themselves as Tibetans and female monastics despite a repressive context. This book is committed to addressing their lives as Tibetan Buddhist nuns at this particular intersection.

This book is thus about politics and also about "resistance," yet neither of these is the kind of politics or resistance that focuses on seeking organizational power, collective agreement, or procedural legitimization. Instead, they are, to borrow Jacques Rancière's (1999) notion of politics, attempts to break down the existing distribution between bodies and their allocated place and time. In other words, they are the redistribution of the unseen and the seen, the unsaid and the said, and thus the uncounted and the counted. Political activity, as Rancière defines it, "is whatever shifts a body from the place assigned to it or changes a place's destination. It makes visible what had no business being seen, and makes heard a discourse where once there was only place for noise; it makes understood as discourse what was once only heard as noise." Throughout this book, I show how the nuns' bodies are often not properly counted, how their work is taken for granted, and how their words are heard as "noise." In Rancière's terms (1999, 30), the nuns are those who "have no part" in the existing system of distribution.

The lives of the nuns in Yachen both highlight and disturb the allocation of nuns (their bodies) and their "proper" tasks in patriarchal society, Tibetan monastic systems, and Sino-Tibetan politics. As girls from rural Tibetan regions, they were supposed to help with household chores until they were married off; after marriage, they were expected to fulfill the roles of mother and wife. As minority women and as female Buddhist monastics, they are expected to carry out their allocated roles as docile, even invisible, monastic members and ethnic minorities. As I will elaborate in detail throughout the book, however, the nuns in Yachen are constantly eluding their assigned places and tasks, disturbing the presuppositions about their supposed roles as daughters, female monastics, and ethnic minorities in Tibetan, Buddhist, and Chinese societies.

What is important is that, in reassigning themselves to new tasks and places, the nuns do not aim at engaging in a grandiose (or any) subversion of power relations, nor do they have centralized goals and agendas for acting against the authorities. Rather, they exert "minor forces"—small actions and daily tasks—that prioritize ensuring their lives as nuns in Yachen and ultimately lead to larger possibilities. Over the course of fieldwork between 2010 and 2016, by interacting with the nuns in their rooms, kitchens, and huts; going to assembly halls and construction sites; learning about the nuns' secret journals; and visiting their natal villages and homes, I came to see how the material qualities, possibilities, and limitations of the nuns' mundane lives in Yachen constantly and unexpectedly led to political outcomes and changes through what I call the *politics of tranquility*. In this book, I show how Yachen's growth into a large, lively Buddhist community has occurred through the persistent, material engagements of the nuns as they strive to "get by" in their daily lives. Instead of reacting to the state policies and changing political situations on the plateau, the nuns are committed to and prioritize their own personal and spiritual goals as fully as possible. Their "indifference" to the patriarchal structure of the state and society is precisely why the politics of tranquility is not a strategy against domination in a narrow sense. It is not an instance of the resistance of the weak against oppression that focuses on shifting or overturning power relationships (Scott 1985). Rather, it is the nuns' sovereign attempt to redistribute or place alongside (not against) one another the following oppositions: the unseen and seen, the unsaid and said, "noise" and "discourse."

Yachen Gar as Political Effect

In summer 2010, after sitting for three days on a rattling bus coming from the provincial capital of Chengdu, I finally arrived in Yachen Gar for the first time. Yachen appeared to be nothing but a giant shantytown, rather than a formal monastic complex, built on the grasslands and populated mainly by a large number of Tibetan nuns—over ten thousand, as I was later informed. On the first night, I ended up unpacking my luggage in the heart of the nuns' residential area. Led by a nun whom I'd just met, I walked into a deep labyrinth of thousands of tiny self-made huts. The pathways between them were narrow, curving, and muddy. I bumped my head a few times along the way on pieces of wood jutting out from the coarsely finished huts. I was taken to a long-abandoned meditation cell that had only enough space to contain one sitting body. It was pitch dark and rainy. Water began dripping into the hastily built structure. As I tried to sleep in the leaky cell by folding my body almost in half, I faced a more urgent problem. The door was broken and would not stay closed unless I held the doorknob from inside. A couple of wild dogs, sensing the presence of a stranger, began barking outside. I feared that, if I lost my grip on the door for even a second, the dogs would jump inside and kill me. I spent a long night in the damp cell, desperately gripping the doorknob as if my life depended on it. Crouching in that dark wooden box, I sighed and drowsed in turn all night, pondering what on earth was this field I had arrived in.

The field that is Yachen Gar is inherently contingent and dynamic with unexpected events and components unfolding on a daily basis. Although it is filled with Tibetan monastics whose primary focus is their regular monastic activities, Yachen is not a fixed monastic compound; it is not a stable container for the nuns and other practitioners. It is both "more" and "less" than a formal Buddhist monastery. I am not the only or the first person to see Yachen as something other than a monastery; the group that founded it also seems to have imagined Yachen as different from a formal monastery, as indicated by their choice to call it a "gar," an encampment, rather than using the more straightforward "*gönpa*,"[3] whose meaning in Tibetan is much closer to "monastery." Some might say that Tibetan monasteries have been designated historically by a variety of names, and it is not useful to be too meticulous about these terms. But I disagree, especially in the case of Yachen Gar. I would argue that this kind of blunt treatment of the term "gar" reflects the tacit and broad acceptance of the invisibility of the nuns in Tibetan Buddhism in general. In an architectural sense, an encampment, unlike most formal monasteries, is not a predetermined structure based on an architectural blueprint. It *evolves* into an encampment as it grows in response to the contingent flows of people and their particular needs at different times. The term "encampment" therefore suggests the inherently ad hoc, unruly, or even "poetic" (Larkin 2013). In Antonio Terrone's (2010, 29) pioneering study on Yachen Gar, he calls Yachen a "quasi-monastic religious encampment (*chögar*)."[4] By adding "quasi-," he perhaps also notices something "more" or something "less" about Yachen Gar when compared to other formal monasteries in Tibet. Indeed, Yachen's distinctiveness was clearly impressed upon me on my first night there when, instead of being immersed in a meditative and sanctified monastic ethos, I had to grab the doorknob of a damp, narrow cell and hang on to it for dear life all night long.

Yachen's history is short; it emerged when a small group of practitioners gathered in a remote pastureland on the eastern Tibetan plateau in the mid-1980s. The name Yachen seemed to bear no special meaning at the time; it has been used by local nomadic groups to indicate the nearby area where the first group of practitioners settled. Since then, the disciples of Yachen have constructed and sanctified a history of Yachen that incorporates a longer lineage and prophecies associated with the founder Achuk lama. But Yachen's humble and rather abrupt beginning cannot be denied.

The major contributors to Yachen's unusual growth are the young Tibetan women who have been drawn to it, taken up permanent residence there, and become nuns. Without modern facilities, infrastructure (roads, transportation, electricity, tap water, etc.), or state involvement at its beginning, the evolution of Yachen has been extremely disorderly, but the encampment has flourished at the same time. It is filled with what seem to be poorly built residential shacks lined up one after the next, each equally shabby and ad hoc, creating a giant hut-maze in which even the residents can sometimes find themselves adrift (figure 2). Yet, through this improvisational hut building by newcomers (largely the nuns), the very boundaries of Yachen, if its boundaries were ever clearly defined, are constantly redrawn and enlarged.

Life in Yachen, especially in these early years, was utterly rough and wild. Water and food were not easily available, and medical and toilet facilities were either insufficient or simply absent. The long winters were deadly cold, and there were no heating systems. The pups of wild dogs often froze to death in this harsh season, and vultures would gouge out the still-soft intestines of the dead animals. Since its early years, the wilderness and the material unruliness of Yachen have posed challenges not only to the nuns living in it, but also to the Chinese authorities who are supposed to monitor and control it. A group of Buddhist practitioners who live in an isolated place and focus only on Buddhist practices would usually not be considered a threat to the regime. It was only in the 2000s, when the population of Yachen grew to over ten thousand, with no signs of stopping, that the Chinese state began to consider

FIGURE 2. The nuns' residential area in Yachen. Photo by the author, 2010.

embarking on more active monitoring measures by arranging police stations around Yachen and posting a work team (*gongzuozu*) within it.[5] At this time, the state also recognized Yachen as an independent town. Even so, neither the police force nor the work team seemed very motivated to "control" the practitioners who were peacefully meditating all day, were self-sufficient, and not demanding anything from the government.[6] It was also physically challenging for Chinese government personnel to remain in Yachen for an extended period. A former work-team member told me that when he was stationed in Yachen, the members there received an extra bonus added to their regular salary and generous subsidies for buying meat and coal every month from the government, and that without this extra compensation, not many people were willing to stay in this harsh living environment for the purpose of controlling docile Buddhists.

In the context of the Chinese state's ongoing controls of Tibetan Buddhism and Tibetan affairs in general, as well as Yachen's genuinely challenging living environment, the emergence and development of Yachen as a large and thriving Buddhist community can be considered a political achievement in and of itself. I want to argue that the nuns are crucial but forgotten contributors to this outcome. The ongoing growth of the nuns' population in Yachen has forced the head office to begin investing in systematic education for the nuns and to allow them direct access to high-level teachings (something that has been rare in Tibet). This higher educational standard for the nuns, even at this beginning stage, is a concrete change that Yachen has introduced to contemporary Tibetan Buddhism, and this change requires a redistribution of the existing allocation of resources and a retooling of the usual ways of seeing, thinking about, and talking about the nuns in Tibetan Buddhism generally.

Minor Forces

Before my arrival in Yachen, the information I had gathered from Buddhist disciples uniformly emphasized both the head lama's and Yachen's unusual spirituality. They described the journey to Yachen as a sacred path toward receiving great blessings, and spoke about Yachen's physical hardships—its material and environmental rawness—as a necessary price to be paid for experiencing pure spirituality.[7] Meanwhile, the scholars and friends I met warned me about the volatile political situation on the Tibetan plateau. My foreign presence and my association with a Western institution might attract unnecessary attention from the local Chinese authorities and create problems for the people or for my research in China.[8] Among the various pieces of advice that I received about Yachen, however, one obvious fact had been left out: on almost no occasion did anyone, whether scholars or disciples, Tibetans or non-Tibetans, mention the strikingly large number of Tibetan nuns living and practicing in Yachen. How had the existence of these nuns, who made up nearly 90 percent of the entire population of practitioners in the community, been so widely ignored?

In studies on the Tibetan Buddhist revival in post-Mao Tibet, and in the Kham region in particular, the focus is largely on the pivotal role of a handful of heroic figures such as Tibetan male lamas (*tulkus*, *khenpos*, etc.)[9] and especially their extraordinary spirituality, compassion, and personal charms that have attracted an enormous following of not only Tibetans but also non-Tibetans around the globe.[10] Other studies pay attention to the slightly looser political climate that has existed on the plateau since the 1980s after the draconian Cultural Revolution era. These studies interpret the Buddhist revival as a projection of submerged Tibetan nationalism or cultural pride that has been severely suppressed since the Chinese army's takeover of Tibet in the early 1950s and the decades of political, cultural, and economic deprivation in Tibet that followed under the rule of the People's Republic of China.[11] Studies of

Tibetan nuns and female practitioners have been produced but only rather sporadically and largely with different objectives not associated with the current Tibetan Buddhist revival in China.[12] None of the studies done so far on Tibetan Buddhism, or on the revival in particular, offer a satisfactory approach for answering my initial question regarding the "absence" of women in Yachen and in the revival, much less consider the material intensities of their lives that I observed and experienced throughout the entire course of my fieldwork.

My focus on the mundane and the material aspects of the nuns' lives in Yachen is not meant to downplay the spiritual aspect of life there. Yachen is indeed a place where the highest teachings in Tibetan Buddhism (of the Nyingma sect) are actively transmitted. The nuns' main purpose in joining Yachen, after all, is to practice Buddhism and to attain enlightenment. I also fully acknowledge the existential uncertainty attached to Yachen as a burgeoning ethnic religious community in China. No matter how spiritual and law abiding it is—in other words, how calm and uneventful it is—a town like Yachen can be shut down or even destroyed in as little as a day with one governmental executive order. Certainly, spiritual liveliness and political precariousness are part of what characterizes Yachen and the revival in general. Yet such characterizations alone can be reductive, serving to nullify other perspectives that are not subsumed into that original framework. The expectations and warnings about Yachen expressed by scholars, friends, and disciples capture legitimate concern indeed, but these perspectives fail to account for the changing, contingent, and chaotic realities of Yachen that do not fit into a neat, abstract, and homogenized worldview.

In the dominant framework, the Chinese state, the high-ranking male lamas, the sacred teachings, and the sacred geographies are easily seen as fixed and abstract essences that unilaterally exercise power over disciples and ethnic Tibetans who are perceived as equally static and unwavering subjects. While the Chinese state apparatus and Tibetan male religious authorities certainly shape the macropolitics involved in the survival and surveillance of an ethnic Buddhist town like Yachen, I argue that they can do so only by relying heavily and constantly on contingent events and on the unassuming activities and endless material engagements of the nuns. To put it differently, they rely on the "minor forces" that fill in and stealthily intersect this macropolitics. Borrowing from Erin Manning's (2016) "minor gesture," I use the notion of a minor force for thinking through the other-than-"major" elements affecting the emergence of Yachen and the revival in China. Although treated as being secondary and negligible, minor forces constantly open up possibilities and experiences that are not given to the major—that is, to the conventional course of macropolitics, its existing structures, and its normative standards—but appear as tendencies or gestures that initiate a shift or a change. As Manning says, "While the grand gestures of a macropolitics most easily sum up the changes that occurred to alter the field, it is *the minoritarian tendencies* that initiate the subtle shifts that created the conditions for this, and any change" (2016, 1, emphasis added).

Even though the small actions and minor daily practices of the nuns in Yachen would appear to be irrelevant to macropolitics, they nonetheless infiltrate, affect, and make possible the very conditions of both the religious and the political in this domain. To be specific, whereas the reputations of Yachen's lamas and Yachen itself have been built through the constant pilgrimages and donations of those who support the encampment, such grand gestures cannot be carried out without the endless daily work of the nuns. After all, the Tibetan nuns (never the monks) are mobilized in nearly all construction projects and any labor-intensive activities in Yachen. The nuns' minor gestures, unrevealed yet ubiquitous, in fact, create the very conditions in which grand gestures can shine in the ways they are intended. More crucially, minor forces are intrinsic to the political transformations that macropolitics claims to achieve. Ordinary Tibetan nuns, through the minor force of their most common and repeated daily physical activities, generate meanings and changes that are manifested in, and attributed to, macropolitics.

By paying attention to the minor forces, small actions, material engagements, and contingent and improvisational events that saturate the lives of the mostly invisible majority, I provide an alternative understanding—one that is more inclusive and material—of the ethnic religious revival occurring in China. I argue that the Tibetan nuns in Yachen practice a politics of tranquility that emerges from their way of living, acting, and expressing, and that it is not beholden to the existing Sino-Tibetan political modus operandi in particular or to a rigid dichotomous framework of oppression and resistance in general.

Indifference

The Tibetan nuns with whom I worked in Yachen, including most of the high-ranking female teachers there, did not appear to show a deep interest in exhibiting extraordinary spirituality, knowledge, or personal charisma, at least not in the same way that male Tibetan lamas often do.[13] Many ordinary nuns in Yachen are in fact far from literate; many began learning the Tibetan alphabet after they arrived in Yachen. They have neither the aspirations nor the resources to make themselves known to the world like the male lamas (and some monks) often do through (auto)biographical writings or by utilizing online platforms to advertise their stories, teachings, and personal lives. Furthermore, the nuns are not particularly political—if we define "being political" narrowly, for example, as being about aims and actions such as standing up for one's opinions and rights in the form of street protests; joining political organizations; or distributing media aimed at criticizing authority figures, institutions, and policies. Even during the time when the Tibetan plateau was undergoing daily self-immolation protests in the early 2010s, the nuns in Yachen chose to preserve a peaceful Buddhist ethos, praying quietly for the lost souls instead.[14]

Yet the fact that the nuns with whom I worked in Yachen have little enthusiasm for self-promotion and are not overtly political does not mean that they are passive and submissive. In keeping with their somewhat utopian quest, they quite rigorously embrace something else, something that is not usually recognized within narrowly defined ideas of self-fulfillment and political subjectivities: what they embrace is a set of rules and values that are *indifferent* to the rules and values set by the society in which they live. Although the nuns with whom I worked in Yachen are subject to the conventional gender norms of Tibetan society, they do not succumb to them completely; at times, they choose to prioritize their own interests over the existing values and to tenaciously push through their own agendas. As they do so, they take on new roles and situate themselves in new places; and in the course of this, they upset the normative sense of the seen, the said, and the counted. The notion of indifference allows me to focus on how the nuns *act* rather than how they *react*. Yet the nuns' indifference is not the indifference of the renunciant or the hermit; the nuns in Yachen, as I will show in this book, are too active and too engaged to fall into either of those categories.

In addition, the nuns' indifference should not be confused with acts of resistance that aim to subvert dominant norms, rules, or expectations. Indifference is not a strategy or one of the "arts" of resistance that marginalized people adopt to secure their survival (Scott 2009). Although the concept of resistance has been defined and applied in a wide variety of ways in a range of studies,[15] here I refer to "resistance" in the narrow sense as acts undertaken by the oppressed with the clear aim or motivation to disturb, challenge, or even overthrow the power of dominant groups and authorities. The Tibetan nuns with whom I worked in Yachen do not exhibit such intentions. They do not exist in a state of conflict with the authorities who control them; and therefore, they do not engage in "resisting" domination in the narrowly defined, binary sense given above. Similarly, studies of Tibetan resistance under Chinese rule have been done largely within the dichotomous framework of the Chinese state as oppressor and Tibetans as victims who "resist."[16] Yet the Tibetan nuns with whom I worked in Yachen neither see themselves always and only as victims, nor do they single-mindedly demonize the Chinese state and Chinese people. They exhibited an authentic sense of pride about Buddhism when they spoke of the endless flood of Chinese disciples from large cities who undertook arduous journeys to see the Tibetan lamas and to learn Tibetan Buddhism in Yachen. The nuns are in the position of being generous givers in this context, and they receive homage from Chinese disciples for being Tibetan monastics.

Indifference should also be distinguished from the notion of refusal. Although "refusal" can be a useful term for explaining some of the decisions the nuns make about their lives in Yachen (such as refusing marriage), it cannot be used as a general description of the nuns' actions because "refusal" still connotes a sense of being aware of a target, of something that the refusal is against. In many cases, the nuns with whom I worked in Yachen were acting simply because they set out to do things for themselves and not because they were acting to refuse something. They are not drawn into agendas that are preset for them by the authorities or by conventional norms but instead remain attentive to their own goals, and they do so with remarkable simplicity, tenacity, and calmness. To an extent, they live in and with a profound sense of "otherness"; in other words, they are profoundly sovereign to themselves and their own desires, seeking out a purpose in life that does not meet the conventional roles expected of nuns, women, or minority subjects in contemporary Chinese society. The concept of indifference in this sense means that the nuns honor the very difference they embody. Far from being a pejorative, indifference thus enables a mode of living that situates these nuns outside a conventionally distributed framework of actions and reactions.

This does not mean that the nuns in Yachen exercise a utopian freedom; they are, after all, Tibetan female practitioners and ethnic minority subjects under a patriarchal monastic system and Chinese rule. In reality, the nuns are in a precarious position both as Buddhist practitioners and as minority subjects. The nuns with whom I worked in Yachen still provide various services for the monks at the expense of time for their own practice, and most of them take this role for granted. While they are subject to a precarious status as ethnic minorities and as women, what is important is that the nuns persist in their continuous engagement with and expansion of their own agendas: they attend more classes; seek out new subjects, such as learning computer skills, speaking English, and playing musical instruments for their annual exams; and visit different lamas individually to receive advanced teachings. If their huts are demolished by the state authorities, they begin building new ones at a new location in the following days. Yachen is an outcome of the nuns' continual attempts at getting by as nuns, within a politically restrictive context, as they put forward their own interests and purposes indifferently to the world.

The Politics of Tranquility

The politics of tranquility emerges from the nonresistant, contingent, material, and mundane practices of disempowered people who, through their unassuming and minor daily activities, generate political outcomes and changes. Such a politics is therefore not confrontational but creative. It is not concerned with macropolitics per se but nonetheless affects it. It is not drawn from conceptual inputs and political theorizing but arises from material and mundane actions. And it does not function as an intentional political apparatus for the weak and the marginal but simply arises out of what they do. The politics of tranquility also allows us to see the generative, material, and mundane interworking of the underrepresented (the uncounted) while never forgetting their inherent sociopolitical precariousness in the real world. Yachen is the immanent material outcome of such a politics. And it is also a radical embodiment of unacknowledged potentialities in the relationships between form and content, bodies and tasks, and the seen (the said) and the unseen (the unsaid).

I use the term "tranquility" to emphasize a form of Buddhist embodiment that describes the peaceful motivation of the Tibetan nuns who join Yachen. "Tranquility" emphasizes the quiet yet resolute choices the nuns make for themselves that reflect their indifference to their expected roles in society, to bustling urban lifestyles, and to the pursuit of material prosperity and comfort. "Tranquility" is also the embodiment of the mundane life of the nuns—moving, building, meditating, making do, dwelling, and so on—that makes possible and maintains their peaceful mode of life. Nonetheless, this unassuming way of doing and living produces unexpected political effects, despite the restrictive context in which the nuns live. Through the politics of tranquility, the uncanny moments and movements within this tranquil, indifferent, and improvising mode of life result in fresh political possibilities and new subjects, both in the lives of ordinary Tibetan nuns in Yachen, and more broadly in the gendered Buddhist sphere and in Sino-Tibetan politics at large.

Yachen is neither the hard-earned outcome of serious resistance struggles by the Tibetan people nor is it the fulfillment of a supernatural revelation by a long, spiritual lineage of male lamas. Above all, it is not a "gift" from the Chinese government (Yeh 2013). I argue that Yachen *has evolved* to become one of the largest Tibetan Buddhist encampments in the People's Republic of China, first and foremost, because of thousands of ordinary Tibetan nuns and their inexhaustive acts of getting by. Even after the Chinese government reduced Yachen's size by more than half in 2017—by literally bulldozing half of the nuns' residential area—the number of nuns in Yachen is still a few thousand or more, and it remains one of the largest concentrations of Buddhist nuns in

China and beyond. As an encampment that is ad hoc and unfixed, Yachen remains an event par excellence. Its beginning, development, and demise are subject to contingent and unexpected circumstances beyond anyone's or anything's control or plans. The nuns' way of living and their politics of tranquility embrace precisely such a mode of existence for Yachen and the revival. What the Tibetan nuns in Yachen show and reassure us about are the ways in which ordinary people participate in the redistribution of their assigned roles in different places and times.

A Brief Overview of This Book

The book is based on fieldwork from 2010 to 2016 as well as a brief visit to Yachen in 2019.[17] To show what the nuns do in Yachen and their ways of living, each chapter examines a mundane form of acting: traveling, building, decorating, learning, practicing, cooking, and eating. Most of these are not the kind of activities that usually draw attention or are considered worthy of examination in discussions of the religious revival in Tibet. But in Yachen, these are the material sites in which the essential processes and changes in the evolution of the encampment occur and in which the lives of the Tibetan nuns are shown most prominently.

Chapter 1 discusses how the nuns move and travel across the plateau. I focus on the particularities of three Tibetan women—a nun-to-be, a nun, and a half-nun—and their mobilities in relation to the different social milieus they embody: border-crossing, escaping, and standing by. In this chapter, I use the individual nuns' stories to illustrate the struggles, affects, and negotiations that make up the very everydayness of their lives in, or as they look toward, Yachen. By focusing on individual stories and particularities, I hope to illuminate the significance of everyday life for people in general, without risking the production of sweeping generalizations in the name of culture (Abu-Lughod 1993). In particular, this chapter focuses on why mobility—a fundamental, mundane activity for human beings—is pivotal for the nuns in initiating and maintaining their nunship in Yachen.

Chapter 2 addresses the nuns' building practices that lie at the heart of the emergence of Yachen. The nuns in Yachen build their individual residential quarters themselves. They construct basic living structures with their limited skills and time, using whatever construction materials they can procure. Building huts in Yachen does not mean simply obtaining a space for one's dwelling; in their encounters with state power, the nuns engage in improvisational responses to the political forces they face and, in the process, they obtain the skills and sensitivities required to achieve their daily goals. The chapter shows the politics of tranquility prominently at work through the improvisation of the nuns as they create wholly new modes of dwelling despite the immensely restrictive and shifting political conditions they face. By contrasting the nuns' hut building with the mainstream discussion of the treasure movement—the male lama–focused account of how Yachen emerged—I analyze the gendered nature of the Buddhist monastic establishment in the revival.

Chapter 3 shifts from the exterior perspective of Yachen in chapter 2 and moves indoors to the nuns' intimate spaces to show how daily concerns and mundane dynamics also make up a significant aspect of the lives of the young nuns in Yachen. I discuss the nuns' seemingly transgressive deeds—platonic love stories with monks, secret diaries, and voluntary confessions—which allow us to understand that, to the nuns, nunship is not a static title and position but something to be revalued and reasserted through constant reworking. In this chapter, I also pay attention to the indoor decorations of the nuns in Yachen to show how political meanings can be expressed through overtly trivial and private activities—such as choosing curtain fabrics, putting up photos of lamas, family members, celebrities, and so on—that allow the nuns to create and embody their own spaces despite the spatial restrictions placed on them.

I take a different approach in chapter 4 to discuss another aspect of the creative politics taking place in Yachen through self-improvement opportunities for the nuns. In Yachen, the nuns participate in creating curricula, sometimes even proposing subjects they wish to study, and they present their new knowledge publicly during a yearly oral exam in front of the head lama. Some nuns are also selected to attend medical training in cooperation with medical institutions outside Yachen, including hospitals in metropolitan Chinese cities. The various forms and intensity of the learning opportunities offered to nuns in Yachen are unprecedented in the history of Tibetan Buddhism. This chapter attests to one of the most promising and unlikely outcomes of the opportunities available to the nuns in Yachen against the gendered strictures of Tibetan monasticism in general. In doing so, it shows vividly how the nuns reassign themselves to different tasks, roles, and places.

Chapter 5 looks at food and eating as a mundane and material activity that reflects personal values, social class, and cultural distinctiveness across different ethnicities. I examine various and minute interactions between Tibetan nuns and Chinese nuns in Yachen over food and its treatment, as well as beliefs about diet.[18] While the growing influence of Chinese lay devotees in Tibetan Buddhism and the active relationships between Tibetan lamas and Chinese disciples have been discussed elsewhere,[19] I look at this issue from the perspective of food consumption and show how food is not just about nutritional values and food-related hygiene issues. In Yachen, it also involves economic power, cultural superiority, and concerns with morality. In this chapter, I discuss the recent ban on meat consumption implemented by Yachen's head office and its perplexing effects and impacts on the Tibetan nuns. I consider the possible connection between this meat ban in Yachen and other Tibetan monasteries and the growing presence and influence of Chinese disciples. I speculate about how, in this case, it may be the Chinese practitioners who are succeeding at practicing a politics of tranquility.

BECOMING A BUDDHIST NUN IN POST-MAO TIBET

For many young, rural women in post-Mao China, leaving home—not through marriage but through participation in the labor market—has been a popular way to reclaim a new social identity. Numerous ethnographic studies have given us stories of young female workers (*dagongmei*) who take part in the most menial and labor-intensive sectors in China's burgeoning economy.[1] These young women and girls, largely ethnic Han, envision a financially stable future as their compensation for migrating to urban regions and enduring prolonged hardship and often unfair treatment. While this kind of capitalistic upward mobility in China's reform era has become the objective for many peasant women who leave home, a very different and largely dismissed migratory movement of women has been quietly taking place at one of the far ethnic margins of the country. A growing number of young Tibetan women in rural regions have left their homes and moved to even more remote and isolated regions in order to practice Buddhism. Although their total numbers are much smaller than the massive influx of young Chinese women into factories, these Tibetan girls and women are nonetheless involved in creating something new and significant in Sino-Tibetan politics and in the history of Tibetan Buddhism: on the far side of Sichuan province in China, they are building the largest Buddhist encampment of Tibetan nuns in existence. This encampment, Yachen Gar, is unprecedented in the history of Tibetan Buddhism in terms of both its scale and the speed of its development, and it has been an epicenter of the Tibetan Buddhist revival in China for the past four decades.

From the outset, the purpose of the migration of Tibetan girls and young women (the majority are girls in their teens) and their insistence on dwelling in such a physically and politically challenging environment is puzzling from a capitalistic perspective. Most of the Tibetan nuns I met in Yachen had left home—or more precisely, escaped from home—to make a lifetime commitment to nunship. From an economic perspective, joining a monastic community in Tibet often means both an explicit and an implicit demand for a lifetime of financial support from their families, and thus the women's decisions to join Yachen often signal a considerable drawing down of resources from their families, who are often poverty-stricken, and from their own futures.[2] But instead of attempting to resolve their financial precarity as many Chinese peasant women have done, these Tibetan women and girls seek out spiritual and psychological fulfillment, willfully moving from bad to worse economic circumstances. Yet it is reductive and even unfair to look at these Tibetan women from a capitalistic perspective and to treat their "inverse" migration as quixotic or irrational in comparison to the mainstream migratory trend in China. As I will discuss, the sociopolitically, historically, and psychologically complex and specific Tibetan context cannot simply be subsumed into a logic of economic rationality; this context must be taken fully into account when assessing Tibetan women's decisions to leave home.

In Yachen, when I asked the nuns why they left home, their immediate answers were about how much they wanted to pursue spiritual attainment and how they felt genuinely grateful to have such an opportunity in Yachen. Yet as time went by, I also heard another set of reasons that reflected their perception of the harshness of life in Tibet, especially for women; they left home to elude immersion in worldly concerns, including marriage, childbearing, childrearing, and endless daily household labor. In other words, they also left home to escape the default roles of wives and mothers. The Tibetan nuns with whom I worked are critically aware of women's *samsara* (suffering) in Tibetan society; to them, it is a blessing if one can circumvent this suffering. In another, much subtler sense, joining Yachen is also their preferred choice because they can avoid the unmotivating path of life that awaits them as ethnic minorities under current Chinese rule: receiving a limited education, obtaining menial and unsteady jobs if they are lucky, and remaining as submissive (thus proper) minority subjects framed by the Chinese state.

The Tibetan nuns with whom I worked exercised active mobilities as an essential part of initiating and maintaining their nunships. I treat the mobility of the nuns as a site where their very everydayness and physical engagements unfold as they face embedded political and gender restrictions. Yet more crucially, our understanding of their mobility should not be limited to recognizing how they overcome obstacles on their way to becoming nuns; we should also see how they themselves perceive what it means to be nuns in their own sociopolitical context. I will elaborate further below but state it briefly here: to the nuns in Yachen, the acts of moving to a new location and occupying a space of their own crucially define how they become who they are. This may sound unusual to some readers, especially compared to other Buddhist contexts where monastics are recognized foremost and formally when they achieve their full ordination status. In fact, neither ordination nor its lack in the lineage of nuns in Tibetan Buddhism surfaced as an active concern among the Tibetan women and nuns I encountered as they pursued their life path as nuns. In other words, the absence of full ordination for nuns in Tibetan Buddhism—which, by default, means that Tibetan nuns have a lower status than monks and are thus restricted from accessing certain religious teachings and opportunities—has rarely been an issue in how they define their own nunships. For them, the more urgent concerns related to their nunship status have been whether they could leave (or escape) home and safely arrive in a monastic community and whether or when they could secure stable living quarters of their own so that they could practice Buddhism for the rest of their lives in those communities. To the Tibetan nuns and women with whom I worked, mobility (along with spatiality) takes priority in how they perceive and recognize proper nunships.

Yet discussions about the mobilities of the nuns and of the women who are nuns-to-be are largely dismissed, if they are even recognized, in the current conversation about Yachen and the Buddhist revival in Kham.[3] In that conversation, the nuns in Yachen are quickly treated as a human backdrop or as the anonymous bodies of practitioners who are useful only as evidence for how "large" the community is. Worse than this, a group of women exists who are even more invisible than the nuns; these are the "half-nuns," as I call them, who attempted to join monasteries but failed and have since remained at home while maintaining celibacy and taking the renunciate vows. I treat the mobility, or in this case precisely the immobility, of these half-nuns as equally important as the nuns' mobility, and I will show that this immobility is an indispensable yet hidden enabler of the successful mobilities of many other women who join monastic communities.

In what follows, through the stories of Deshi, Jubei, and Puthi,[4] a nun-to-be, a nun, and a half-nun, respectively, I present three distinctive mobilities frequently exercised by Tibetan women and nuns. I emphasize again that mobility is a prime factor in whether Tibetan women perceive themselves as nuns, and these acts of mobility by these women initiated and sustain the very existence of Yachen as it has evolved.

Deshi: Forging a New Path

Deshi was born into a Tibetan peasant family in a small village in the Tibet Autonomous Region (TAR). Her family members made their living mainly by growing barley and raising domestic animals, and were devoted Buddhists, as are most ethnic Tibetans in the region. As the youngest child in her family, Deshi was able to go to primary school and delighted in studying. In her final year there, however, her mother suddenly became ill and had difficulty moving. Deshi had to drop out of her classes to stay home and care for her mother and do the household chores. Her other siblings were either married and had their own households in nearby villages or were busy laboring in the fields and grasslands all day. She was the only one left who could help her mother at home. After her mother got a little better around half a year later, Deshi managed to return to school during the final exam period. Despite the serious study gap, she worked very hard, caught up with the class quickly, and made it through all her final exams.

Seeing her potential, her teacher strongly advised her not to drop out of school and encouraged her to move on to secondary school. Many Tibetan children in rural areas begin school but discontinue their education after primary school for various reasons: finances, availability of educational institutions, family obligations, and so on. Girls have a much higher dropout rate.[5] Deshi never intended to give up her education and, in fact, she was full of hope about moving on to the secondary school in the township. But her plan did not go as she wished. Not long after she began middle school, her mother's condition suddenly became worse. Deshi was again pulled back home to take care of her mother and do the household chores. On the next school-day morning, when her friend in the village called out to her from outside to walk to school together as usual, Deshi shed tears inside as she listened to her father shouting out to her friend that Deshi would no longer go to school. She was fifteen. From then on, she stayed at home to help with chores. About a year later, when her mother's condition improved, Deshi felt that it was too late to reenter school.

Time passed quickly, and she soon turned eighteen years old. Her father had already begun searching for a husband for her since, in her village, weddings are still largely arranged by parents. It is thus not unusual for young people to marry someone whom they have never met before the wedding. The wedding process for Deshi was quickly settled and the wedding date was set. Her future husband was nineteen years old and lived in a nearby village. He was known as sincere, filial, and good-looking. People told her that her father had found a good one and she would be happy with him. But Deshi had a different concern. Some while ago, while she was circumambulating the village stupa, she had secretly taken a vow to the Buddha to devote her life to Buddhism (as a nun). Even though this had been an informal, private, and rather spontaneous vow, her commitment was serious. Deshi confronted the dilemma of either going against her father and her family obligations by refusing marriage or going against the Buddha by breaking her sacred vow.

Deshi decided to keep her vow. To do so, she had to act quickly because the wedding date was rapidly approaching. First, she needed assistance since no one in her village had ever left to become a nun before. She explained her run-away plan to her elder brother and sister who lived nearby. At first, they tried to persuade Deshi to give up her plan, but after long conversations, they eventually accepted her firm determination and gave her their support. They planned Deshi's escape together. To avoid her father's suspicion, Deshi told him that, before the wedding, she was going to visit a relative who lived deep in the mountains. This way, her father would be fine with her being absent from home for a few days. During this time, Deshi had to make it to the other side of the county, which was extremely far to reach on foot.

She left home early that day and hid at her sister's until it was dark. Her destination was Yachen. She had heard of Yachen before, that it was a special place to practice Buddhism with eminent teachers and many other fellow nuns. But it was in the far eastern corner of the plateau, where Deshi, and most of her family and relatives as well, had never been. In fact, she had never been beyond her village and the nearby township. She also knew that there were other nunneries in much closer places, including Lhasa, the holy Tibetan capital. But due to strict governmental control policies, monasteries and nunneries in Lhasa were under heavy state surveillance, and she was certain that she could not practice Buddhism well in such an environment. Thus, Deshi chose Yachen.

On the departure day, Deshi's brother was so worried about her that he insisted on escorting her for part of the journey. It was January, the coldest month of the year, on a jet-black night. Packing a bit of *tsampa* (barley flour)[6] and bread in a bag, Deshi and her brother set out from the village. At first, they could not even turn on their flashlights for fear of getting caught by the villagers. The town had a severe lack of modern infrastructure—no paved roads, no public transportation, no reliable electricity, and so on. Soon they were walking in the deep, dark mountains. Deshi's brother walked ahead to clear away bushes and twigs, making space for Deshi. She kept asking him to go back, but he would not listen. Her brother probably could not bear to leave his younger sister alone on a dangerous mountain in the middle of the night. But sooner or later he had to turn back. Otherwise, he would not be able to return to the village by morning. Parting with her brother a little later, Deshi was left alone with nothing else to do but continue. Although she was extremely tired and her body felt almost frozen, she never stopped walking during the night. At one moment, she came upon an empty, abandoned house. "Do you know how scary it is to see an abandoned house in the mountains during a dark night?" Deshi asked me and paused for a bit, as if she felt the horror of that night again.

She prayed silently and repeatedly called the lamas' names she knew while passing the deserted house as quickly as possible. Continuing to walk for a few more hours, she saw a village. It was already dawn, but Deshi was not sure where she was or what time it was. She simply moved her feet forward in the direction her brother had pointed out to her the night before. She was famished, and her legs were no longer able to carry her farther. She decided to knock on someone's gate as she passed through the village. A fierce dog barked as an aged woman opened the door. Like a beggar, Deshi asked her for food. The woman led her into the kitchen and offered her a cup of hot tea and bread. Deshi lied and said that she was going to a relative's house but had gotten lost on the way. The woman was kind and generous to Deshi, but did not seem to believe her. Deshi noticed this. Even though she had walked all night—it felt like a hundred kilometers—maybe she was not that far from her home. This woman might know her father or one of her relatives. Because Deshi feared that the woman would call someone to ask about her or inform others about her sudden appearance, she quickly left the house and walked away from the village, passing a stream, fields, and a few more villages by the late afternoon. She could not remember exactly where she was when she met a group of minivans and drivers gathered to recruit passengers. It turned out that most of the minivans were heading to Chamdo (Changdu in Chinese),[7] a traffic hub in the eastern Tibetan region. Deshi got a ride in one of the minivans and arrived the next morning in Chamdo, the largest city she had ever been in.

Deshi stayed in the same cheap inn where other passengers had chosen to stay and began asking how to get to Yachen. It seemed that, although many people had heard of Yachen, no direct transportation was available from Chamdo. Based on information she gathered from various people on the streets, the next morning she hopped on another minivan heading to Pelyül (Baiyu in Chinese), which was a township in Sichuan closer to Yachen (approximately 120 kilometers away). On the way, Deshi bought a cheap phone and a SIM card to call her brother and sister, who were extremely worried about her by then. Deshi's brother told her that her father was becoming suspicious because more time had passed than was needed for a short visit to her relative. But there was nothing Deshi could do about this. For now, the important thing was to keep moving and to reach Yachen as quickly as possible. Deshi looked for another vehicle heading to Yachen, which was much easier to do in Pelyül. By the time she found a minivan heading to her final destination, she was almost out of money.

The minivan driver immediately noticed her, an exhausted-looking young girl heading to Yachen by herself—another escapee from her hometown—and learned that Deshi had no contacts in Yachen who would come to meet her. Feeling sympathy for her, he introduced her to a senior nun he knew who might give her help.

After a harsh four-day journey, Deshi finally arrived in Yachen. She called her brother and sister and discussed how to break the news to her father. Her brother suggested that they wait for a few more days because her father was now extremely angry at Deshi. But within a few days, his wrath would turn to anxiety, and that would be the right time to break the news to him. Her brother was right. A few days later, her father began worrying about Deshi and feared something bad had happened to her; the mountain roads to their relative's house were snowy and slippery, so he thought that Deshi might have fallen on the way and died there. Her parents had gathered people to search for her—or for her body. Deshi called her father and told him that she had arrived in Yachen to be a nun and that she felt so sorry for lying to him and letting him down. Her father said to her, "Deshi, you foolish one, why didn't you talk to me first? I would have let you go. How could you travel to such a remote place by yourself? You could have died on the road, you foolish girl!" And the next thing her father said made Deshi feel surprised as well as grateful: "Now you are in Yachen to be a nun. I am proud of you; be a good nun."

I met Deshi for the first time soon after she arrived in Yachen. She was dressed in worn-out jeans and a jacket and had long, dark hair that reached her waist. But in the next few days she was robed and tonsured. Deshi's father brought her a large load of *tsampa* and butter from home the following summer. I heard that Deshi's relatives and several villagers were also planning to visit her in Yachen. Deshi had become a pioneer figure in her village as the first to join Yachen. Her sincere practice and the growing reputation of Yachen allowed Deshi to become a role model for girls back home; she was an example of someone who had successfully realized an alternative path. A few years later, when I met Deshi again, there were already two nuns from her hometown who had followed her path. Thanks to Deshi, these two nuns did not need to make a dramatic moonlit flight; their parents heard about Deshi's life in Yachen and did not hesitate to agree to their daughters' wishes to be nuns.

Deshi's experience is both unique and not so unique, both personal and not so personal. Her family background—poverty, educational deprivation, and her mother's sickness—had all along been interwoven into her decision to become a nun. Her secret vow to the Buddha and the abrupt wedding setup were the final events that motivated her escape. The theme of running away from marriage repeatedly appears in the life stories of Tibetan Buddhist nuns.

In Yachen, I was assured many times that Deshi's story, with some variation, is one of the common narratives about "how to become a nun." Poverty and the lack of educational opportunities are not unusual in rural Tibet, and girls tend to be especially affected when family situations become difficult. In addition, as an ethnic minority, Deshi's social ambit is in many ways even more limited than that of Han peasant women, who are also underprivileged. Cultural and linguistic hurdles and various forms of discrimination against ethnic minorities in Chinese society diminish, if not block, opportunities that might have otherwise been pursued by Tibetan women. Given the sociopolitical context of rural Tibet, nunship seems, after all, to be the most likely alternative path for rural Tibetan women who are not interested in spending the rest of their lives being mothers and wives. However, it is important to note that, for these women, nunship is not just a last resort they settle upon when they run out of other options. In Tibetan cosmology, taking monastic vows is one of the most rewarding actions one can take in this life. The Tibetan women passionately, and with full agency, choose this blessed opportunity for themselves.

To achieve their goal, the first essential step is physical relocation. For much of her journey, Deshi traveled on foot across deep mountains, valleys, and streams on the Tibetan plateau. She was neither equipped with information and basic tools (maps or a navigator) nor in possession of enough money for her journey. The regions through which Deshi traveled had few developed routes or established forms of transportation that could guide her on her way. She literally forged a new path for herself across completely undeveloped terrain. Even though the physical paths Deshi traveled might instantly disappear once she passed through, her journey has left another kind of indelible trace. Travel stories like Deshi's inspire many other girls in villages searching for an alternative path in life. While it is easy to dismiss such stories, the beginning, as well as the maintenance, of a Tibetan nunship in this context cannot be fully grasped without considering the robust and resilient mobility of individual Tibetan women like Deshi.

Jubei: To Live Time Itself

The nuns in Yachen continue to move and travel even after they settle in Yachen, largely because they maintain ongoing relationships with their natal homes after becoming nuns. For most of the nuns I met in Yachen, joining a monastic community does not mean total detachment from their familial associations; even though they are physically distanced from their pre-nun living environments, while they live in Yachen, they continue their familial ties in psychological, economic, and any other ways that ensure their ongoing nunships in the monasteries. For example, when nuns in Yachen are sick, especially if they suffer a chronic illness that requires long-term care, they are advised to return home for proper treatment and come back once they recover. In addition, those nuns who are frail also return home during the winter season to avoid Yachen's harsh weather. Their home visits often fulfill a more utilitarian purpose as well: the nuns' living costs in Yachen are partially supplemented by their family members (and partially by participating in monastic activities), and this money is usually given to the nuns during their visits home. Even after the recent installation of ATMs in Yachen, many nuns still rely on receiving money through this conventional method. While their escape stories focus on their personal determination to initiate a nunship, a nun's continuing travels after joining Yachen are necessary for properly maintaining her nunship.

The following story is a travel account of when I accompanied a nun named Jubei on one of her trips back to her home. Jubei and I left Yachen in late February 2013, near the end of Yachen's winter retreat as the Tibetan New Year, Losar [lo gsar], was approaching. Jubei had suffered hemorrhoids for some time and required surgery and proper recuperation, which were supposed to be taken care of by her intimate kin. In addition to her medical treatments, for this trip, she was also anticipating a family reunion at the New Year's festival, an event that she had missed for the past three years.[8] Jubei's innocuous return trip home had become politicized, however, because of the much-tightened governmental surveillance on the plateau. Within the heightened and complex political context at the time, Jubei's nun-identity alone—to be precise, her appearance in robes and with a shaved head—would be sufficient reason for the Chinese police to stop and interrogate her.

Since the protests in Lhasa in March 2008 and the spread of self-immolations that followed,[9] the mobility of Tibetans has been strictly controlled, especially for those traveling toward the TAR. The governmental surveillance of monastics has become even stricter because the state has ascertained that monastics were at the center of the recent antigovernment protests. In those few years when the self-immolation protests continued, any Tibetan who entered the TAR was required to submit a government permit paper at border checkpoints, but obtaining such a permit was extremely laborious, if not impossible. By implementing such a rigid measure, the state sought to prevent antigovernment movements from spreading to other Tibetan areas. Numerous checkpoints were set up in villages, towns, and cities across all Tibetan-populated regions. Surveillance cameras were also installed in monasteries, on main streets, in schools, and any place where a large number of Tibetans might gather. In major monasteries, to affirm their loyalty to the Chinese state, practitioners are forced to undergo patriotic education, which includes denying the four-teenth Dalai Lama as a Tibetan spiritual and political leader (see Powers 2017).

During the year, as Jubei and I were preparing to travel, horrible stories were circulating about how brutally the Chinese police were treating Tibetan monks and nuns when they caught them at the ethnic borders (the provincial bor-ders between Sichuan and the TAR). Yet some nuns in Yachen, despite all the rumors and concerns, continued traveling and taking the risk of being con-fronted or caught. At first, Jubei wasn't entirely sure if she should travel, and she carefully examined her plan as she collected information about the most up-to-date border situation. I had already decided to follow Jubei no matter what deci-sion she made, but my own judgment was that it was not a good time to travel because we—a nun and a foreigner—were both primary targets of governmen-tal surveillance, and I believed that Jubei shared my concern. Therefore, I could not help but pause for a moment when Jubei told me, "I think the situation is slowly getting better since self-immolations haven't been reported for months, and *now is the time to move*. There is a way. Are you still coming with me?"

It was still dark around six in the morning in Yachen and the cold, chilly winds pierced us on the day of our departure. The walk from Jubei's hut to the entrance area where we could find transportation took us half an hour or so. We each carried a small lantern and a piece of luggage as we made our way into the dark narrow alleys in the nuns' residential area. Jubei walked ahead, chas-ing the fiercely barking dogs away. I followed her, constantly checking behind to see if any dogs were tailing us. (Dogs in Yachen often attacked people from behind.) We stood in the freezing weather for about an hour before we could find a minivan that was leaving that day, and it took another hour before the van started its engine. Jubei and I held each other's hands tightly to keep warm while we waited for all the empty seats to fill with passengers, and by the time the vehicle finally began to move, our feet had become completely numb.

After a bumpy, five-hour road trip, we arrived in the town of Ganzi. As soon as we unloaded our luggage, which was already covered in dirt from the trip, we checked into a cheap inn near the area where people usually look for vehicles and for fellow passengers who are traveling in the same direction. Because of the lack of public transportation on the plateau, travel arrangements are usu-ally made between individual drivers and passengers; they find each other and negotiate the price for their trip. Many shops and stores on the main street in Ganzi were already closed because of the Chinese and Tibetan New Year's festivals.[10] Lively, seasonal street-market stalls had transformed the original commercial area. People had set up temporary stands on the streets with vari-ous festival foods such as candies, cookies, nuts, meats, and fruits. The goods displayed on the racks were so colorful and variegated that they created a festive spirit. Jubei and I momentarily forgot the risky trip we were on and indulged ourselves in the joyful mood on the streets.

In normal circumstances, Jubei can find a minivan in Ganzi that is heading directly to her hometown in the TAR. This makes the entire trip possible in about two days. Because of the border restrictions in recent months, however, a nun and a foreigner could not take regular routes of travel. We already knew that the checkpoints were activated throughout; what we didn't know was *how strict* a checkpoint would be at the particular time we were about to pass through it. For Tibetan residents, ever since the checkpoints have been set up in Tibetan dominated towns, the degree of strictness in the daily operation of checkpoints has often mattered more than the existence of the checkpoints themselves. The checkpoints are usually small, one-story structures with barricades and with room for two or three police officers inside. They are set up at the main gateways of each Tibetan village, town, and city throughout the plateau so that they can effectively control the daily flow of Tibetans. From a management point of view, however, keeping so many checkpoints active at all times is a resource-consuming endeavor. The checkpoints thus seem to be managed rather flexibly in response to the urgency of the political situation at any given time. En route to Yachen, I saw checkpoints that were at times full of officers checking the IDs of every passerby, at other times they were rather loosely operated, and sometimes they were completely closed. To local Tibetans who have been living under prolonged, daily surveillance, being able to sense and judge the precise degree of strictness at the checkpoints, rather than the mere existence of checkpoint structures in and of themselves, and the subtle changes in the actual mode of control, rather than the existence of such policies, is much more crucial to their businesses and livelihoods.

Jubei clearly acknowledged the situation of the checkpoints before our departure. Since the self-immolations had been at a lull for some time in the winter of 2013, Jubei believed that the checkpoints would be relatively inactive along some of the borderlines of the TAR and that she could pass through without being asked for a permit. She had collected information about the least strict checkpoints from other nuns who had recently traveled, and we decided to travel through one of these. But this required a long detour from the usual path. We anticipated several small stops on the way because the small border town we were heading toward was too remote, and no driver was willing to take us directly there. By changing minivans a couple of times and passing through a few desolate nomadic towns, we finally arrived two days later at the border town that we had heard was the least strict checkpoint.

The border town was quiet and dark, as if it were abandoned. Several dirty street dogs wandered around like starving beasts. From this town, our van crossed over the border bridge on the river. As we had been informed, or perhaps because it was too late in the day, the checkpoint office was closed and no one stopped us. From that checkpoint on, we were traveling inside the TAR. We stayed in a nearby monastery rather than a hotel and took a route farther away from townships and villages to avoid active checkpoints as much as possible. After two more days of detours, we were able to reach Jubei's hometown. Looking back, the unlikely success of our trip to and within the TAR that winter was perhaps a combination of many components: Jubei's judgment about the subtle changes in political tension; our recklessness and bravery; the holiday season; and our luck, or in Jubei's terms, our karma. I am not sharing this story as a travel adventure across the frozen plateau in Tibet. The aim of sharing this story is to highlight the kind of challenges ordinary Tibetans (including the nuns) face and live with constantly to exercise their mundane mobilities under Chinese rule.

The Permit

Spatial control over the members of its society is by no means new in China. Through the *hukou* (household registration system), the mobility of Chinese citizens—where people are permitted to live and work—has been highly regulated and restricted.[11] By using place of origin as a semipermanent marker for individual citizens, hukou has become a systemic means of controlling the influx of rural populations into cities and managing citizens' mobility between regions. Hukou has been a coercive system that limits citizens' mobility; but at the same time, as recent migration studies have pointed out,[12] it also makes possible a much needed and easily exploitable low-cost labor source for the country's miraculous economic development. The extreme exploitation of Chinese peasant workers as a source of cheap labor in cities is largely the result of workers' lack of city hukou, which would provide them with some measure of legal access to residency, minimum wages, and other benefits in the city. Since its implementation, the hukou system has politicized the mobility of people in China so that individual intentions to move or live in places have been understood and interrogated as a political matter.

The politicization of hukou has had an especially severe impact on China's ethnic minority regions. The strictness of ethnic border control around the TAR and other Tibetan regions has intensified in the past few decades and has also become more and more unpredictable. Tibetans living outside the TAR, such as in neighboring provinces like Sichuan and Qinghai, cannot freely visit the TAR, especially the capital city of Lhasa. For Tibetans, Lhasa is more than just a mere administrative center; it holds a unique position as one of the holiest places in Tibetan civilization, and it has also been the center of Tibetan political movements against Chinese rule. The city bears the bitter history of rigorous Tibetan resistance.[13] In the context of Sino-Tibetan politics in the People's Republic of China (PRC), therefore, Lhasa has become contested as both a genuine repository of Tibetan cultural and religious heritage and, simultaneously, a geopolitically acute site of Tibetan national politics against China. For these reasons, it is even more essential for the Chinese state to maintain a tight grip on Lhasa, and controlling the inflows of Tibetans from other regions is often a crucial part of this process. In the years since the Lhasa protest in 2008, Tibetans traveling to Lhasa, whether for worship, visiting relatives, sightseeing, or business, have frequently been treated by the Chinese authorities as harboring the potential for rebellious political action, that is, the potential for disturbing the Chinese order of things.

The policy of the Chinese Communist Party (CCP) on Tibet is straightforward: there is no tolerance for any social movements that promote Tibetan autonomy or for any activities that threaten the CCP's project of promoting a unified, harmonious Chinese society. Nonetheless, when this coherent line of policy is executed by towns, villages, or individual officers, its degree and intensity are flexibly and specifically applied to meet distinctive local situations. From a Tibetan perspective, while it is always important to be aware of the set of old and new policies implemented in their regions, there are in fact few policies that Tibetans haven't previously experienced or that catch them by surprise. Therefore, it is more useful to pay attention to the locally specific political atmosphere and its shifting modes as well as how the state's policies are actually implemented on a daily basis.

For an example of how Tibetan mobility is controlled on the plateau, I offer an account of one permit system to which Tibetans living outside the TAR have been subjected since the 2010s when they travel to Lhasa. The following information was obtained through conversations and observations during my travels with Jubei in the winter of 2013 and on various occasions thereafter. Thus, it contains elements that are locally contingent and specific to a given political situation within the general circumstances of the state's sweeping controlling policies toward Tibet.

If a Tibetan without a Lhasa hukou tries to visit Lhasa for a personal reason, they must obtain two government-authorized documents in advance. One is a police statement from the person's original town attesting to their legal residential status and showing that the person has no record of violating Chinese laws and rules. The second is also a police statement from Lhasa, but this one is much more complicated. Once the traveler successfully secures the first document, they must contact a Lhasa-hukou holder who is able and willing to guarantee the traveler's political conformity; willing to confirm that the person has no intention of agitating against social security and stability in Lhasa; and has no plans for participating in any type of religious activities, including paying homage at Buddhist temples or stupas, or associating with lamas. If the person obtains all the needed documents, they are now eligible to apply for a temporary residence permit (*zanzhuzheng* in Chinese) in Lhasa. Until this temporary residence permit is obtained, however, their personal ID card will be taken and held by the Lhasa police and returned when they leave the city. Even for those who carry all these documents, they are asked to stop, leave their vehicle, and fill out forms each time they pass a checkpoint at the provincial borders and any towns inside the TAR. Once a person has gone through this process numerous times on the road, they will finally get to see a glimpse of Lhasa.

In fact, Jubei was born and raised in the TAR and therefore holds a TAR hukou. Her personal identification card indicates this clearly. But even though she was simply heading back to her hometown, the place that she is legally and solely bound to by her hukou, she has a problem because she is a Buddhist nun. I heard this confounding story from Jubei on our way to her hometown. At the beginning, I couldn't process the logic of it; the TAR is the only place that grants her legitimate residency, but at the same time, her identity as a nun makes passing through the TAR border a challenge. She could disguise her appearance by wearing a wig and dressing in regular clothing, but the problem wouldn't end there. Although she possesses a legal TAR ID card, in her ID photo, she has a shaved head and is wearing maroon robes. She had become a nun at sixteen, before registering for her ID. By showing her ID, she is placed in a difficult situation: she will either be accused of trying to disguise her identity as a nun or she must deny her nunship by saying that she has already disrobed. Despite her fully legitimate ID, which is her legal proof of citizenship provided by the government, Jubei would be stopped at the entrance of her hometown by a Chinese police officer and might not receive a permit to get through the checkpoint because in both her self-presentation and the picture on her ID she is clearly a nun. Given this preposterous situation, I was wondering, what made Jubei think the journey was possible?

Living through Rhythm

Jubei had gained an insight from observing the repeated protests that had recently occurred on the plateau and the specific government restrictions that followed. During the years when small-scale protests (such as self-immolations) occurred frequently across Tibet, Jubei and other nuns noticed that the government responses to these incidents had become almost automated and followed predictable steps: the existing checkpoints were reactivated immediately if they were previously dormant or lax, travel bans for Tibetans were reinstated if they had been loosened, internet access was blocked, and armed police (*wujing* in Chinese) were deployed in and around the town where the protest occurred. Because of the observable patterns in these repeated government reactions, local Tibetans can often evaluate the seriousness of the situation by assessing what kinds of measures are taken and how seriously they are implemented, for example, the number of police deployed and how fully they are armed, and the severity of the travel and communication restrictions being implemented.

Even in the most agitated political contexts, the number of Tibetans, including nuns like Jubei, who did not participate in the protests themselves was always larger than the number who did. Many of those who did not participate held a deep respect for their fellow Tibetans who sacrificed themselves for Tibetan causes. But while they sympathized with and, on their own terms, tried to assist the protestors, many Tibetans were also struggling to get by and make a living during the repeated cycles of political turmoil. Since the institution of semi-martial law on the plateau, the issue for Tibetans is no longer simply about the presence of an armed force or the installment of certain restrictions. When the state of exception is no longer an exception, the real concern for Tibetans is to assess and to anticipate the degree, intensity, and length of the restrictive measures so that they can manage their livelihoods accordingly. Closely sensing the subtle infinitesimal changes—for example, the shifting arrangements of armed police and the ways in which travel bans were executed—and thereby assessing the level of suppression at a particular time became increasingly necessary as the politics on the plateau became more and more volatile. Such an assessment was often not based on palpable, objective evidence but on a series of subjective cues—personal experiences, word of mouth, gut feelings, and the overall evaluation of the political ambience at the time. Nonetheless, these appraisals, based on murky criteria, played a crucial role in determining the right time for individual Tibetans to move, do business, and take pilgrimage trips.

The nuns and lay Tibetans I met during my field research were keenly aware how the government restrictions would evolve over time: from an intensive initial period to reinforcement and continuation, and finally to a gradual remission. When another Tibetan protest occurs, this cycle is initiated again. Sometimes during a time of intensive suppression, more protests occur in response to that suppression, and this leads to an increase in the level of control before the stages of reinforcement and remission. But the overall pattern remains largely intact. Aware of this, Jubei listened carefully to other nuns' border-crossing stories before our departure from Yachen. By analyzing these stories, Jubei concluded that the situation had passed a critical point, and things were gradually moving in a calmer direction because no protests of any sort had been reported on the routes to her hometown. She inferred that "now" was a state of lull, a fissure between incidents and serious restrictions, and therefore the right time to move before another protest occurred; otherwise (once the next protest occurred and the cycle resumed), she might miss her chance to go home anytime soon. Jubei had concluded that this segment of time, like an aperture, was a relatively safe interval period between previous events and possible future incidents.

The most precarious time to move, according to her, would be the time right after a political incident, for example, after a self-immolation or other protest had just occurred and various government restrictions had been reinstated and tightened. But if time passed for a while without further incidents—meaning that, from the Chinese perspective, the unrest was successfully suppressed and under control—then restrictions would likely diminish. This could provide a little breathing room for Tibetans to resume their business activities, travels, and pilgrimages. Jubei grasped that this was such a moment, an in-between time that was relatively far from previous incidents but hopefully not too close to the next possible incident and thus a good time for us to depart.

To locate this in-between time properly and exercise her mobility amid unpredictable political incidents and the ensuing restrictions, Jubei had to determine "the now" (of our departure) by considering *simultaneously* the past and future. Yet "the now" is not a discreet fixed spot that Jubei identified within a linear timeline. "The now" is the result of a subjective understanding of the present; it is what Jessica Wiskus (2013, 111) might call a "dimensional present" in which past and future events coexist and are actively brought into contact by the subject. Similarly, Maurice Merleau-Ponty (2002, 321) states that "the lived present holds a past and a future within its thickness." The kind of temporality that Jubei and other nuns perceive is not based on steady, homogenous, and rational repetitions of events; the cyclical patterns in the government responses do not repeat themselves with the same duration, interval, and intensity each time they occur. The patterns they discern are instead uneven, irrational, and embodied, and they are based on the nuns' intuitive, subjective understandings about how an event is intertwined with the past and future simultaneously. Through this intertwined thickness, "the now" is momentarily crystalized and becomes the "lived present."

Jubei focuses on perceiving a sense of rhythm across the events and restrictions that come and go in the mingled past and future rather than focusing on each event as a separate individual moment. Jubei's perception of rhythm in the political tension around her, in fact, allows us to see more clearly her way of being and living as a Tibetan nun in post-Mao Tibet. As a Tibetan nun in China, Jubei doesn't just live through time; she lives the very time itself by grasping the simultaneity of past and future. Her focus is, in other words, never on singular incidents existing separately as unrelated points spread across a unilateral flow of time, but on the crevices, silences, and viscous relations between singular events that pull and push each other in "rhythmicized time" (Wiskus 2013, 111).

Puthi: Living as a Half-Nun

While the stories of Deshi and Jubei show how essential mobility and the exercise of the right timing are to the Tibetan nuns, here I would like to share a story of immobility that also plays a crucial role in the making of Tibetan nunship. This is the story of a rural Tibetan woman whom I call Puthi, whose failed escape made it possible for her sister to become and remain a nun. As studies in mobilities show and as also alluded to in Deshi's case above, the flip side of mobilities is stable, fixed, and unmoving "systems"—infrastructural, social, cultural, and otherwise.[14] While these "moorings" sometimes become obstacles to the exercise of mobilities, they are also essential for facilitating mobilities. Puthi's story shows that the price of one sister's mobility is the other sister's immobility, through which the necessary "moorings" for a society are maintained. The entanglement of mobility and immobility revealed through Puthi's failed mobility allows us to see a broader structural immobility assigned to women through the social and gender structures that individual Tibetan women face in general. I treat Puthi's situation as an indispensable structural component that makes possible Tibetan nuns' migration into Yachen in the current context of Tibet. She is also a potential joiner who will travel to Yachen later. This is because Puthi does not see her situation as completely irredeemable; she has not given up but has chosen to wait while being a nun in her own way at home. I call her a half-nun precisely for this reason.

I met Puthi for the first time when I visited the natal home of Lochik, a Tibetan nun with whom I was acquainted from my first field trip to Yachen in the summer of 2010. Because the location of Puthi's hometown was convenient to my itinerary, I often visited her home on my way to and from Yachen, staying there for a few days to a week each time. I was struck by Puthi's appearance, her shaved head, when she removed her scarf for the first time in front of me. I had observed a few times that some Tibetan widows keep their hair short as a signal that they are not looking for a new husband. But Puthi, in her late twenties, had never been married. Why then did she look like a nun?

Puthi's family—at that time only her mother and herself resided in the house—lived in a traditional two-story Tibetan house made of mud and wood that was built by Puthi's grandfather. In this large but humble house, the first floor was used for keeping livestock and food staples; people lived on the second floor. Puthi's family kept five cows, one horse, two dogs, and one cat under their roof. The structure of the living space was simple. It included one large versatile room that served interchangeably as both living room and family bedroom, an adjacent kitchen, and a house shrine. The shrine was the cleanest, brightest, and most decorated room in the house and was filled with butter lamps, scriptures, offering cups, incense, and numerous photos of renowned lamas. Through their hospitality, I was always offered the family shrine for my use while I was visiting. The remaining part of the second floor was an open space that was also connected to a neighbor's house through a ladder on the flat roof. Since its initial construction, the house hadn't undergone much improvement because of the family's straitened circumstances. For example, it was not equipped with an indoor toilet. While this made my stay in her home each time a highly challenging experience despite her heartfelt welcome, it nonetheless allowed me to have a special bonding moment with Puthi: every night, Puthi, carrying a flashlight in her hand, would gesticulate at me to go pee outside before going to bed. We often went out together and kept an eye out for each other in the dark while we were squatting in the field.

While my visit at her house was mostly spent in idle time, Puthi's days were very hectic. She would leave home to go herding even before the sun rose because she needed to walk a few hours to find rich pasturelands for the animals. In addition, for quick cash, Puthi occasionally participated in menial construction work around the village as a day worker. And in early summer, she sometimes joined a group that traveled in the mountains for months to gather caterpillar fungus. Except for her time doing these extra activities, Puthi usually spent more than twelve hours each day herding and farming from sunrise to sunset. Upon returning home, there was no time for her to rest. She immediately began milking because this had to be done before the animals were put out to rest in the evening. Puthi's mother made butter with this fresh milk every morning for their usual breakfast with *tsampa*. She also stored some for other family members who visited occasionally. After milking the cows, Puthi would go out to the water tap outside the house to draw water for cooking and cleaning. Her mother then prepared dinner, usually a bowl of simple hot noodles. The TV was on when electricity was available; dinner was simple and quick but chatting over tea often extended late into the night. Puthi would finally take off the scarf that covered her head all day and beat it in the air. Puthi's long day was nearly over.

Puthi has two brothers and three sisters, all of whom had left home and settled in other towns and cities. Her eldest brother was settled with his own family in Lhasa in the TAR. Her second eldest brother, a Buddhist monk, was about to finish his Khenpo degree in a monastery in another town and was expected to become a teacher there soon. Her eldest sister, who was single, ran a small restaurant by herself in a nearby town and gave financial help to her mother and Puthi and to her two robed siblings. Her second eldest sister, Lochik, left home to be a nun nine years ago. Her younger sister, also the youngest child in her family, was far away in college. She would be the first college graduate in her family. Puthi, on the other hand, has never left home and has never gone to school. Each time her siblings left home, one by one, to pursue their own livelihoods or religious careers, Puthi was left with more and more work inside and outside the house.

On the surface, it may seem that there is nothing distinctive about Puthi's life as a lay Tibetan woman living in a rural village, except that she keeps her hair short. Yet I came to know that Puthi has also made a lifetime commitment to remain celibate because she has wanted to be a nun since she was a child. I wondered why she didn't join a monastery as her sister Lochik had already done. But it didn't take long to learn how naïve my query was. Puthi had in fact attempted to join Yachen, but she missed her chance by one night. When Puthi was a teenager, many girls in her village began to leave home to become nuns. Around the time when I was often visiting her house, fourteen of the girls from this village had already become nuns in Yachen. Puthi had planned to be among them. About nine years earlier, when Puthi, Lochik, and their mother lived together, Puthi had set the date for her nighttime getaway. For her escape, she had saved up money, carefully checked the local bus schedule, and even bought a hat and a muffler in case she might need to disguise herself from acquaintances. She did not tell anyone of her plans, not even Lochik, the sister she felt closest to, for fear of word getting out. Everything was ready. However, something unexpected happened on the night before Puthi's escape: Lochik ran away. The next morning, family members and villagers went out to look for her. The villagers guessed that she had fled together with another nun from the village who was visiting home at that time. People went out to the township bus station to look for Lochik, but it was too late. She had made it to Yachen and shaved her head. Puthi was more shocked and devastated than anybody else. She could do nothing but give up her carefully drawn-up plan and her life-long dream of a monastic life because Lochik's escape meant that Puthi and her aged mother were alone at home.

After Lochik left for Yachen, Puthi, as the only grown-up child remaining at home, became bound by her endless household labor and her obligations to her mother. At first, I thought that Puthi's situation was an individual case of bad luck, but I soon discovered that there was another woman in the same village who also shaved her head and refused marriage just as Puthi did. Later, many other Tibetans I met in rural regions told me that they have a female member like Puthi in their family, among their relatives, or in their village. These women wear robe-like clothes, often take the renunciate vows (*rabjung*)[15] at home, and practice Buddhism on their own when they can.

Female lay renunciants exist, albeit not in large numbers, across the Tibetan regions.[16] (To my knowledge, no similar group of males has been reported.) But the local terms for these women are different, and in fact, there is often no term at all. Because no particular name has been set for lay renunciants, the general terms used for Buddhist nuns, such as *ani* and *jomo*, are used interchangeably for lay renunciants as well.[17] Interchanging the names used for monastic and lay figures reflects not only the ambiguous social position of female lay renunciants but may also insinuate the lack of security and authority of nunship in general in Tibetan Buddhism. Overall, there is insufficient social awareness of or willingness to recognize female lay renunciants as a social group in Tibet. Despite their crucial role in maintaining the household economy and thereby providing hidden support that allows their sisters to leave home to be nuns, the existence and the stories of female lay renunciants have been almost completely downplayed. I have come to see that Puthi's situation cannot be simply understood as a personal matter; her socially ambiguous position is partially the result of an entrenched, gendered structure that is imposed on women in Tibet and is subsequently responsible for the lack of titles, spaces, and acknowledgment of their work and contributions both at home and in monasteries.

Suspended Mobility and Enabling Nunship

Puthi's entrapment and Lochik's successful escape are not isolated events. They provide once again an important insight into what matters most in Tibet about becoming a nun and maintaining that nunship. Both sisters had hoped since childhood to become nuns, and there was nothing crucially different in how they had implemented their plans for achieving this aim. A set of actions taken by Lochik—packing a bag and leaving home to join Yachen—was planned and nearly executed by Puthi as well. The difference between Lochik and Puthi is only that Lochik departed one night before Puthi could implement her own plan. If Puthi had not been at home taking care of her mother and the house,

Lochik would not even have tried to leave for Yachen. Lochik's nunship in Yachen is assured and successfully maintained at the cost of Puthi's suspended mobility back home. Puthi's housework and family obligations allow Lochik to focus fully on being a nun in Yachen.

My emphasis on mobility in the lives of Tibetan nuns draws from a broader consideration of how nuns are treated in general in Tibetan society. It would be a mistake to assume that monks and nuns share a similar experience at home and in society when they join monastic communities. For the nuns with whom I worked in Yachen, mobility was often the crucial factor, and one of the biggest challenges, in their path toward becoming nuns; for the monks, their own or their families' determination matters the most, and their mobility is executed accordingly. Among the nuns, I encountered various versions of "escape stories" about joining Yachen, while this was hardly ever the case for the monks. As I have shown, however, the nuns' successful mobilities also likely account for the failed mobilities of their female siblings at home.

In Tibetan Buddhism, full ordination for nuns has never existed. Although recently it has become a heated issue in places like the Tibetan exile community in India, ordination has not generally been as serious an issue among the Tibetan nuns practicing and living in Tibet.[18] The nuns I met over the years of fieldwork in Tibet also did not treat the full ordination issue as urgent and crucial for their nunships, as it has seemed to be outside Tibet. The nuns with whom I worked in Yachen rarely talked about their status as being lower than the monks because of the lack of a full ordination tradition. They said that, in Yachen, they were treated equally with monks in terms of access to teachings, lectures, and monastic rituals.[19] As long as they stay and practice in Yachen, they feel that they are treated almost as if they were fully ordained nuns; whether they formally receive *gelongma* (full ordination) or not doesn't seem to matter significantly.

To have one's nunship recognized by oneself and by others, and to be able to maintain it, performative effort is more crucial than gaining a title (see Makley 2005). For the nuns in Yachen, physically joining and remaining in a monastic community is the most effective way to be acknowledged and to function as a full monastic. In other words, for the girls and women I met in Tibet, what makes them fully nuns is not determined by what kind of vows they have taken (their monastic status) but by where they reside and what they do every day. I do not mean to dismiss the lack of full ordination of Tibetan nunship as trivial; the lack of full ordination for the nuns has perpetuated systematic discrimination in Tibetan nuns' practices and has produced gendered monastic treatment overall. These issues should be addressed rigorously for the benefit of the nuns and women in Tibetan Buddhism. Yet my emphasis here is that what it means to be a nun in contemporary Tibet does not come from titles (or lack thereof) but from more down-to-earth considerations: the kind of mobilities the women can or cannot exercise, the places they can claim as their new home, and the activities they do there every day. Both Lochik's successful mobility and Puthi's suspended mobility attest to the limited path open to Tibetan women who wish to become nuns; at the same time, their experiences emphasize how crucial "acting" and "moving" are in obtaining and maintaining nunship in Tibet.

Another aspect that should not be forgotten is that Puthi's entrapment is only temporary—or at least this is how Puthi envisions her life. In Puthi's view, she simply has not been able to execute her lifetime wish *yet*. She is *waiting*. She has kept her renunciate vows (*rabjung*) and maintains tonsure and celibacy as if she is halfway to being a nun. Many such half-nuns ultimately lose their chance, and sometimes their will, to join a monastery because of the general lack of resources for women and nuns in Tibet. But their initial determination and extended hope are enough to set them on a path toward nunship, even if it is a path that may be filled with unexpected delays. One night, when Lochik visited home, the two sisters laughingly reminisced about Lochik's escape night and how that single night changed their lives so dramatically. Lochik said that if Puthi had run away earlier, she would now be doing the exact same work that Puthi does at home. *When the time comes*, Puthi will follow Lochik's path, and they both acknowledge that that time will arrive when their mother dies. In the meantime, Puthi's celibacy and shaved head confirm that her life is unfolding as an active "waiting." Puthi is spatially tethered to her house and to ceaseless labor and obligations, but it is only temporary; she has taken up a nun's way of living already, not only to cope with her current situation but also as a way of escaping it altogether in the near future. For Puthi and many other half-nuns like her, waiting is an active mode of living in the present and holding onto the promising future. Despite their invisibility, these half-nuns are, partially yet crucially, shaping and supporting Tibetan nunhood through their structural limits, sacrifices, and hopes.

Coda

The Tibetan women's leaving home and their mobilities in general are executed out of personal determination, necessity, and hope (or waiting) in their pursuit of spiritual attainment. Their mobilities enable the actions that end their status quo—whether that status quo is staying at home and getting married (Deshi) or staying in Yachen and suffering from illness (Jubei)—and they initiate a new path in life (even if only potentially in Puthi's case). The nuns' mobilities are the thresholds for their acts of geographical relocation, their acts of flight, which allow them to depart the predetermined social, political, and gendered expectations and roles for them, and begin to embody a new status, values, and roles. Indeed, mobility is a defining feature of becoming a Buddhist nun in post-Mao Tibet, one through which the gender and political norms on the plateau are produced, exercised, and also challenged.

BUILDING AN ENCAMPMENT

If not for its devoted practitioners and the nuns' tenacious building practices, Yachen would still be a typical nomadic region on the plateau, a place where occasional herds of yaks come and go and the pace of life is slow and uneventful. Even after Tibetan disciples began clustering together, Yachen remained a small, isolated Buddhist retreat shelter amid the wild and endless pasturelands. In the early 1980s, Achuk lama settled in this nomadic valley, locally called Yachen, with a small number of disciples who had dedicated their lives to practicing Buddhism under his tutelage. Life in Yachen in those early days, when almost no modern facilities were available, was much harsher than it is now. Winters are long and cruel at this altitude (four thousand meters above sea level), and while the rich pasture can be bountiful for animals during the summer season, it is still barren for humans. The disciples sometimes consumed twigs and mud when no other food was available. As an ad hoc type of encampment (gar), Yachen has evolved to require its practitioners to support themselves during their stays; this includes not only food and clothing but, above all, creating dwelling spaces for themselves. The early practitioners thus set up the simplest cave-like residential structures to avoid rain, wind, and snow throughout the seasons.

Either because of the nondiscriminatory nature of the encampment, which doesn't strictly impose an institutional threshold for living and practicing in Yachen (e.g., age minimums, parental permission, etc.) or, as many say, because of Achuk lama's incredible compassion, equal access to Yachen has been given to Tibetan women from the beginning. Such inclusiveness has made Yachen one of the most diversified Buddhist communities, one that embraces Tibetan nuns, monks, lay practitioners, and non-Tibetans seeking short- and long-term pilgrimages, lifetime refuges, and short excursions. Even the occasional tourist is welcomed. Precisely for this reason, Yachen has grown to be more like a Buddhist town than a traditional monastery. Despite its unusual openness and liberal attitude, however, Yachen is still run like a formal monastery. Its openness at times confuses outsiders who see only a monastic system in Yachen and expect strict monastic operations.

Because Achuk lama himself was an ordained monk, many monastic rules, celibacy in particular,[1] have been strictly upheld in Yachen. Therefore, anyone who newly joins Yachen as a nun or monk is required to take monastic vows if they have not done so elsewhere.[2] For most of the nuns, Yachen is the first place they take their (novice) vows. The fact that most nuns take vows for the first time in Yachen has particular significance; unlike monks, who usually have home monasteries near their birthplaces, the nuns are likely to treat Yachen as their semipermanent home. Building activities for the nuns, therefore, are not aimed at creating temporary shelters for short-term stays but at securing spaces for living and practicing for a lifetime. It is thus not surprising to see that hut building is deeply and urgently embedded in the nuns' daily lives.

Once they arrive, the nuns build their living quarters on the other side of the river that divides their living area from the monks' and the original residence of Achuk lama, now the residence of Tulku Asong, the current head lama. The nuns live and practice in this separate zone and cross the river to visit the head lama when they receive teachings from him. The flow of Tibetan women arriving in Yachen has rapidly and steadily increased over the past few decades. Until 2017, over ten thousand nuns built their living quarters and practiced in this zone, which had become a large shantytown island of huts (figure 2). The ceaseless influx of Tibetan women indicates the central position and popularity of Yachen as the liveliest center of Buddhism among Tibetan nuns in contemporary Tibet. Another important but overlooked fact about the nuns' inexhaustible building activities is that the boundaries of the nuns' residential zone—and thereby the very scale and the shape of Yachen itself—are constantly being redrawn and remade by the nuns themselves.

Yachen is no longer a small, unknown retreat shelter in a remote corner of the plateau. Its rapid expansion and increasing influence have caught the Chinese state's attention, and the state's response has focused primarily on controlling the growing size of the encampment. But state officials soon recognized that the usual methods for controlling the number of admissions in monasteries, by assigning a fixed quota, for example, would not work effectively in Yachen. Given the openness of the encampment, both physically and administratively, it is difficult to control the daily inflow and outflow of people. Rather than focusing on people's movements per se, the Chinese government instead began controlling the building activities of individual members of Yachen as a way to curb the ongoing growth of the community. As a result, the Tibetan nuns' building practices in Yachen stand against the state's effort to maintain spatial control. On any of the small hut-building sites in Yachen, the nuns' most mundane and material struggles to get by and to settle into their spiritual lives clash firmly with state power. A close look at the nuns' building practices is thus crucial, not only for what they can tell us about the nature of the Chinese state's control in Tibet but also as a means for seeing how the nuns' way of doing and living is able to ruffle the constant stream of government restrictions placed on Tibetan Buddhism at large.

The nuns' hut building, and thereby their building of the encampment, goes against a conventional trope in the grand narratives of the Buddhist revival, namely, that charismatic male lamas found monasteries—which, in the case of Yachen, becomes the story of Achuk lama. The nuns' daily building practices in Yachen, which require their endless physical labor, in fact complicate such grand narratives. But the nuns' contributions are not recognized, much less appreciated, even among the nuns themselves. In the following sections, I focus on the nuns' hut- and tent-building activities and the material, political, and gendered conditions of these activities, which crucially define the nature of the encampment as an ongoing, bottom-up, contingent, and material process. In doing so, I examine how their building activities can elicit consistent outcomes for the nuns in the face of the Chinese state's usual approach to controlling Tibetan monasteries and how their role is nonetheless discounted in the gendered monastic system in Tibetan society and religion. I will conclude this chapter by moving beyond the gendered condition of encampment building to discuss the gendered nature of sacredness in Tibetan Buddhism.

The Conditions of Hut Building

What can we say about the huts, the residential structures that the nuns build and rebuild constantly in Yachen? What does it take (i.e., what construction materials, skills, and networks) to build a hut from scratch in a place like Yachen? From a materialist perspective, the huts that the nuns are building have the simplest floor plans possible (mentally drawn in the builder's head, not on paper), and even such modest plans are often created and revised on the spot as the building process is taking place. Although the huts have evolved over the

FIGURE 3.   The nuns' residential huts in Yachen. Photo by the author, 2013.

years with the introduction into Yachen of various new construction materials, their basic concept hasn't changed much: a minimal space, with walls and a roof, in which a nun can sleep, eat, and meditate. In fact, in recent years, as the nuns' building activities have become more tightly monitored by the state, the size of the living space available for a single nun has grown even smaller, and many nuns are now forced to reside together in tiny huts that were meant for one person at most (figure 3).

Among the various construction materials required to build a hut, lumber pieces are considered the most essential. However small and poorly built, every hut must have enough pieces of lumber to construct the walls and a roof, and at least one strong piece that can be used as a beam to support the roof. The nuns usually will not start the building process until they are equipped with the minimal amount of lumber they need. Precisely for this reason, one of the state's policies for controlling the nuns' hut building has often been to ban lumber importation. When lumber shortages peak, the time needed to obtain the proper amount of lumber may be months to over a year. The nuns therefore recycle as much secondhand lumber as they can from huts that have been torn down, and they buy pieces one by one whenever possible from secret Tibetan vendors. On one occasion, some bold Tibetan merchants foresaw a lucrative business opportunity in the imbalance between lumber supply and demand in Yachen and contrived to bring in lumber from outside to sell to the nuns at an exorbitant price. Due to the limited quantity, each nun was allowed to buy only one plank of lumber at a time. Nonetheless, the nuns made a long queue for this rare purchasing opportunity. Because this was a covert business activity for both the nuns and the vendors, the transactions occurred at an odd hour, around 4 a.m., when the Chinese authorities weren't likely to be patrolling. For many weeks and months, the nuns lined up, waiting for hours in the dark and cold until the merchant's minitruck quietly slipped into Yachen, carrying stacks of lumber to sell.

When the nuns begin building a hut, they never do so alone; other nuns, who are mostly from the same village, are quickly mobilized to help. Since the nuns share a common understanding of the urgent nature of hut building in the specific context of Yachen, they willingly forgo their daily practices and gather to hurriedly complete their fellow nun's hut. There are no fancy tools to use; construction must be done with shovels, saws, hammers, and bare hands.[3] The most important part of hut building is to make the ground flat and even, and to set up a firm beam at a central position on the floor to support the roof. To this end, the nuns first go to the riverside and pick up rocks and gravel for leveling the floor. They mix these rocks together with mud and spread them evenly on the ground to make the floor flat. Bricks are used when they are available. While the floor is being made, in another corner, a couple of nuns will be cutting lumber pieces into equal lengths and will begin nailing them together to make the walls. If lumber or any other materials are lacking at this point, some of the nuns will run back to their huts to look for materials to bring to the worksite. Any construction materials left over are collected and stored to build another hut (figure 4).

On the day of Jubei's (see chapter 1) hut building, about ten nuns showed up and smoothly took part in different building tasks, something that they have done many times. Jubei, while busy at different tasks herself, did not forget to make milk tea for her fellow nuns who were sharing their expertise to build her hut. When she joined Yachen as a sixteen-year-old girl, Jubei knew little about handling tools or construction materials, much less building a hut. But after years of living in Yachen and helping other nuns in their frequent hut building and hut repairing, she has become quite adept at using heavy tools and completing a hut. Among the nuns, skills and practical knowledge about building naturally develop and are shared and passed down through their participation in the numerous building activities that occur during their time in Yachen. For Jubei's hut, each nun seemed to know without being told what she

FIGURE 4. The nuns are constructing a hut. Photo by the author, 2013.

should do and what step followed after each task. They functioned like a well-organized orchestra but without a conductor. Their years of accumulated experience; their improvisational skills; the collegial work environment; and, most of all, the urgency of the work they shared coalesced at each and every step of Jubei's hut building.

After several hours of hammering, sawing, and shoveling throughout the morning, Jubei's hut had already begun taking shape by late afternoon: the walls were standing, and the roof was in place. (And the work team wasn't patrolling that day around Jubei's construction site.) The nuns skillfully installed a small window and a door as well. As a final step, the roof of a hut must be blanketed with a few layers of thick vinyl cloth to prevent water damage. To make sure the plastic covers are firmly attached to the roof, the nuns place several large stones on the roof's surface. But Yachen's vigorous winds and the wild dogs who run across the roofs can easily dislodge the stones. To solve this problem, the nuns usually spread a layer of mud on top of the plastic and let the grass grow from it; having their own vitality and energy, the grass and mud hold tightly onto the roof. After applying mud to her roof, Jubei's hut was nearly done, and all that was left were the tasks of arranging the indoor space: setting up a bed, a shrine, and a tiny kitchen. At this point, the process is no longer rushed because the most nerve-racking part of hut construction, the erection of the structure, has been completed safely without alerting the Chinese authorities. A nun will take her time in arranging and decorating the indoor space of her hut as a way to express her individuality.

However, the nuns' hut building activities in Yachen are not always as successful as they were in Jubei's case. If the nuns are not fast enough in building or if they choose the wrong location—too close to the main street, for example—then the hut can easily be discovered by the Chinese authorities (the work team) and will likely be demolished. With exceptions for high-ranking lamas' quarters and public construction projects such as stupas and assembly halls, ordinary hut building by the nuns is never technically "permitted" in Yachen. The thousands of huts that have been built exist because the nuns rush to complete the building of a hut within a day in the hopes of evading the work team's surveillance, which can be looser or tighter at different times. The state institution called the work team (*gongzuozu*) that operates in Yachen is separate from the uniformed Chinese police force. The members of the work team do not wear uniforms or any other distinguishable marker that signals their political authority. They coordinate with the police yet are also independent. Above all, they exercise supreme power when it comes to monitoring the daily activities of both ordinary practitioners and key figures in Yachen.[4] The high-ranking lamas receive direct supervision from the work team (more so than from the police), and the nuns recognize the work team as the state's ultimate controlling body in Yachen. Even those nuns who do not speak any Chinese understand the Chinese term "Gongzuozu" as a proper noun and use it not only for the work team but to indicate more broadly all "hostile Chinese forces" operating in Yachen.

The work team is committed to ensuring that the nuns' residential area remains legible as newcomers continue to settle into any available nooks and crannies in the already crowded residential area. The work team once attempted to register all the huts by attaching to each one a sign with a unique number (figure 5). These markers were supposed to be placed on the visible surfaces of individual huts, but they keep disappearing because of the ongoing transformation of the huts by the nuns. In addition to hut construction, small-scale hut repairing and remodeling projects are frequently executed as well. During these processes, the registration numbers and signs are often covered, disfigured, or discarded. Because of their unusual capability and flexibility when it comes to transforming and adapting to their residential environment, the nuns have been able to elude the work team's efforts to exercise total control. The nuns

FIGURE 5. Numbers on the nuns' huts as marked by the work team. Photo by the author, 2013.

both utilize and reinforce the fluid nature of the encampment with their distinctive, everyday material practices, and, in doing so, they quietly perturb the Chinese attempts to order Tibetan affairs in Yachen.

The work team's goal is straightforward: to monitor all the activities of the practitioners in Yachen and to catch any suspicious movements that have the potential to disrupt the social harmony the Chinese Communist Party (CCP) has rigorously propagated. Yet from the work team's perspective, Yachen is in fact unusually incident-free for a Tibetan Buddhist community of its size and influence. Because the primary goal of the practitioners in Yachen is to advance their practices, there have been almost no political protests within its boundaries. Yachen's head office and its members both share this interest very keenly. Yachen therefore maintained its usual peaceful attitude and activities even when intense Tibetan protests swept through the plateau in the early 2010s. Yet no matter how "exemplary" Yachen is viewed to be by the state's authorities, its unrelenting growth and increasing influence cannot be dismissed by the authorities.[5] And as the work team knows well, at the core of Yachen's physical growth are the nuns' ongoing migration flows and hut-building activities that constantly push Yachen's outer rim toward the vast, open grasslands.

The Materiality of Tents

The nuns' residential area is half-encircled by the river and half-encircled by a cement ring road (figure 2). The ring road demarcates the nuns' residential area from the rest of the grassland, which stretches endlessly to the horizon. To prevent the nuns from building more huts ceaselessly on the grassland, the work team put up the ring road to mark the line across which hut building was absolutely banned. Strictly speaking, hut building is banned everywhere in Yachen, but the nuns continue to build inside the ring to accommodate new arrivals. The road has facilitated the work team's patrolling tasks and has also served more crucially as a practical borderline for partitioning Yachen into the zone (outside the ring) where hut building is absolutely banned and the zone (inside the ring) where hut building is routinely monitored and deterred but not completely prohibited. Over the years, the nuns have had to improvise their building practices and their living conditions constantly—for example, building smaller huts or sharing space with another nun—to make sure that their huts are located inside the ring zone. Yet as the continual flow of new arrivals adds to the intense crowding inside the ring, the need for land for new huts has soared. Some nuns, out of desperation and urgent need, attempted to build huts outside the ring, but these huts were immediately spotted by the work team and torn down. Until around 2014, only a few public structures, such as shops and toilets, were allowed in the outer ring zone; the nuns were not permitted to venture into this forbidden land for the purpose of engaging in their usual hut-building practices.

But the situation changed in 2014: a complex of nomadic tents began to appear outside the ring. In fact, it was not unusual to see tents set up there occasionally for short periods by lay Tibetan pilgrims during their stays in Yachen. But this time, the number of tents was unusually large and growing fast as well, forming itself into a small tent city (figure 6). The emergence of such a tent complex, not to mention its growth and continuation, was atypical for Yachen in many ways. First, the tents were not set up by short-term visitors but by residents (the nuns) of Yachen who were seeking alternative living spaces in the prohibited area. In addition, the change was not a gradual one that spanned decades; the tent city sprang up in a few weeks. This is partially because it takes much less time to set up a tent than to build a new hut from scratch; furthermore, there is no need to obtain lumber, a task that often requires an extended period devoted to collecting materials beforehand. Above all, the most unusual feature about the tent city was the fact that the work team did not immediately restrict it, thereby allowing this pirate residential complex to exist and grow.

FIGURE 6. The tent city. Photo by the author, 2014.

The tents the nuns set up consisted of factory-manufactured materials with a standardized size and shape, so there was little variation from one to the next. These tents are widely used on the plateau as portable houses by nomads. They have high ceilings and rectangular indoor spaces that provided a better spatial environment for the nuns than their wooden huts did. The nuns living in tents enjoyed almost quadruple the amount of space available in the regular huts inside the ring, and their personal shrines, kitchens, and bed areas were more appropriately sized and arranged. The only thing missing in the tents, I was told, was electricity because electrical wire could not be extended outside the ring at that time. While there were pros and cons to using a tent as a semi-permanent residential structure, living in it remained more challenging than living in a hut because the tents had an ambiguous status as permitted residential structures for the nuns.

It has been difficult in Yachen to distinguish in advance what is permitted and what is not. It is considered unwise to seek answers about this from the Chinese authorities because doing so only presents the work team with a chance to give a negative answer. Living with uncertainty is better than living with illegality. The nuns learn to know what activities are not permitted by first doing and observing the outcome of their actions—for example, they know clearly that building a hut outside the ring is not permitted when the hut is bulldozed. The amassed information and experiences can provide the nuns with good judgment about many similar situations, but outcomes remain uncertain until something is actually done. Sometimes, even seemingly permitted actions lose their permitted status, with no sound reason offered for the change, while prohibited actions can suddenly become fine to pursue. Although the Chinese state's policy directives for Tibetan affairs are clear and straightforward, the detailed rules, regulations, and measures that are executed at the micro level are often determined and implemented flexibly by local authorities. In Yachen, uncertainty has thus become a norm that the nuns must learn to live with; for this reason, they must constantly seek out and test other possibilities. Even when the tent city was growing and persisting, its status was nonetheless unstable and doubtful because it was not clear whether having a tent was permitted. The nuns thus continued to seek more stable residential arrangements for themselves, even as they were settling into the tent city.

In any case, the existence of the tent city in Yachen is puzzling. Why were the tents left alone while the huts were immediately bulldozed? Why did the work team acquiesce to the explosive growth of the nuns' new residential complex while they maintained a strict control policy over the nuns' hut building? I find one possible explanation to this baffling situation in the distinctive materialities of the tents and the huts. The tents are made of a fabric that is thick yet pliable. The materiality of the tents seemed to produce a pause, a rift, in the work team's ongoing controlling policy for hut building. To be more specific, the tents created confusion about the object targeted by the control policy. To the work team, no matter how poorly they were built, the huts were considered solid dwelling structures that were to be placed under strict control, while the status of the tents was unclear. Tents can be erected within a few hours and dismantled just as quickly, and their purpose and usage lie precisely in their temporality and malleability. The pliability of tents signals transience, ephemerality, and impermanence. What is there to control if the object is already movable and temporary? What is there to bulldoze if it is already less than a shack or a hut? By the summer of 2014, when the work team was still uncertain about the tents, the tents were already firmly entrenched as an alternative residential option for nuns who did not yet have quarters of their own. The division between the permitted and nonpermitted zones had turned into a division between different types of residential structures for the nuns. When the nuns improvised on the concept of a dwelling structure in the unauthorized zone, the work team could not determine how to respond to such improvisation. By forming a tent city, the nuns redrew the physical boundary of Yachen and augmented its material possibilities once again. The flexibility of the tents made the tent city a solid structural fact in Yachen.

The tent city lasted for a year or so and was then transformed into a new residential configuration in Yachen. Since 2015, the tent city has slowly been replaced by a large complex consisting of prefabricated (prefab) metal housing

FIGURE 7. The prefab metal housing structures in Yachen. Photo by the author, 2015.

structures (figure 7). Each prefab unit consists of a bedroom, kitchen, and spacious yard. The unit itself is not spacious, although it is certainly larger than most of the existing huts inside the ring, and it provides a separate, independent space for each resident, which is an advantage that many nuns value greatly. Those nuns who used to live in the tent city were assigned to this new complex first, and some nuns who had huts inside the ring were also allowed to move in if they wished and if there was availability.[6] The nuns in general welcomed the arrival of the prefab complex because it immediately relieved the longstanding problem of hut shortages in Yachen, was sanctioned by the work team, and provided a more stable residential arrangement than the tents. Yet the state had, so it seemed, its own logic in allowing the prefab units outside the ring. The metal complex was made of identically manufactured housing units that were brought in from outside. They were placed in rows where the tents in the tent city had once sprung up like mushrooms. Each unit has a sign with a uniquely assigned number so that the work team can easily keep track of each one. There are no longer maze-like, meandering pathways to confuse outsiders. For the first time, a part of the nuns' residential area in Yachen has now been set into an overt geometrical grid by and for the state, and the work team has continued to reshape the rest of Yachen in similar ways that are spatially controllable and legible.

Another prominent example of this new legibility is the construction, completed in 2015, of several roads in the nuns' residential area. The newly paved

FIGURE 8. The newly paved road crisscrossing the nuns' residential area. Photo by the author, 2015.

roads, which are straight and broad enough to function as two-lane thoroughfares, crisscross the nuns' residential area, replacing the curved, mud-filled pathways that were inconvenient not only for the nuns' daily lives but also, more crucially, for the work team's surveillance tasks (figure 8). Such infrastructure projects are frequently happening in Yachen in recent years under the pretext of improving the quality of life for the residents. It is true that, with the new paved roads, electricity, and proper public toilets,[7] the nuns' lives have indeed been improved, and Yachen has become a more livable place year-round. These infrastructural transformations are also making Yachen a more suitable place for short-term visitors, both pilgrims and tourists. Although it is too soon to assess the actual impact of this series of physical transformations imposed by the state, one thing has been assured: because of the infrastructural enhancements, there is less and less space left for the nuns to navigate and manage independently without being monitored by the work team.

The material dimension of the nuns' daily lives—for example, building huts, setting up tents, or adjusting to the prefab complex—shows how some aspects of Sino-Tibetan political tensions are unfolding in Yachen. For now, the state's overall policies in Yachen are not directed toward complete prohibition or total destruction (even after the government bulldozed half of the original huts in

2017 and half remained just as they were) but toward making Yachen more visible and legible so that it is more susceptible to government control. The nuns
continue to build huts despite government restrictions, and in doing so, they
make changes every day to the physical place in which they live and practice as
nuns. The nuns' building activities, in other words, affirm the nature of Yachen
as an encampment that is under constant making and remaking. The emergence of the tent city and its transformation into a prefab complex attest once
again to the transformative character of Yachen and reflect how Yachen comes
into being through the micro and material—as opposed to the grand and
ideological—struggles and daily efforts of the nuns on matters of living and
practicing as Buddhist nuns in a politically volatile space and time.

Gendered Material Conditions of Hut Building

One detail behind the nuns' indomitable building practices that should not be
overlooked is the hidden and deeply entrenched, gendered material conditions of
Tibetan society. Having a monastic member in one's family was traditionally considered both desirable and honorable, and the most promising son was often sent
by his parents to a monastery for a quality education. It was much rarer for daughters to be sent to a nunnery in the same way. Although the zeal for and meaning-
fulness of joining monasteries seem to have withered in contemporary Tibet, the
gendered conditions under which girls and boys are sent to monasteries have not
changed much. Many nuns with whom I worked in Yachen told me that, at the
beginning, their parents strongly objected to their decisions to be nuns. One parent told me why she so strongly opposed her daughter's decision: "My biggest concern was that she might quit the nunship after a couple of years of trying. It is
really, really bad to break the vows. Once you take the vows, you must keep them
until death. Otherwise, it's better not to take the vows in the first place." I heard a
similar version of this answer several times, both from the parents and the nuns
themselves. Daughters are made constantly to doubt themselves, overthink, and
double-check their resolution and qualifications to carry out a nunship, as if being
female is somehow essentially unsuitable for a monastic life. Sons usually do not
experience such objections at home; when they voluntarily join or are sent by
their parents to monasteries, they will likely have full familial trust as well as
financial support. When a boy joins a monastery, he is seldom required to question his qualifications or the seriousness of his commitment to be a monk.

This is true in Yachen as well: nuns and monks receive different kinds of
social and individual support. Although both groups receive the same financial

subsidies from Yachen, their familial and social webs of support often diverge. Unlike the nuns, many monks in Yachen remain connected to monasteries in their hometowns where they were initially sent, ordained, and trained. These monks are dispatched to Yachen from their own monasteries for temporary periods of further education and solitary retreat. Because they have home institutions that support them financially and otherwise, what they acquire in Yachen are additional opportunities for receiving sets of high-quality teachings and thereby further enriching their lives as practitioners. More important, when Yachen is under tight surveillance, these monks can return to their original monasteries to avoid immediate trouble and return to Yachen when things are calmer. This is why there are many empty, available huts in the monks' residential area in Yachen and why the same intense sense of struggle to secure a living space does not arise among the monks as it does for the nuns.

With no home nunneries and thus no firm network of institutional support and accompanying material and nonmaterial resources to draw from, the uncertainty and urgency the nuns face in acquiring living space in Yachen is much more dire. The ad hoc nature of the nuns' hut building results precisely from this gendered material inequality in Tibetan society. The disorderly residential area that is continually created and re-created by the nuns' hurried building activities is partially the outcome of this inequality. After decades of migration and hut building, the nuns' residential area has become a giant maze connected by narrow and meandering passages that lead nowhere and anywhere. This is still true even after the recent road constructions in Yachen because a maze of small passages still connects thousands of huts. The huts are nestled in every possible location, point in every possible direction, and come in every size and shape.

The gendered material conditions of hut building not only reflect a facet of gendered Tibetan society but they also speak more broadly and deeply, directly and indirectly, to the construction of gendered sacredness in Tibetan Buddhism and the revival overall. Next, I would like to discuss a communal construction project done by the nuns in Yachen that illustrates the deeply embedded and taken-for-granted maleness of Tibetan society, the automated spiritual authority assigned to male bodies, and the nuns' self-perception of gender issues in Buddhism.

Material and Gendered Sacredness

Yachen's continual metamorphosis has been neglected or taken for granted in the dominant narratives of the Buddhist revival in Tibet. These narratives emphasize the spiritual role of a handful of charismatic male lamas who have, without doubt, been a consistent spiritual source for Tibetan Buddhism in general and certainly in the current revival occurring in Tibet as well. Yet an excessive focus on these towering figures funnels our attention to the discursive aspect of the revival: the ancient prophecies (treasure movement), the spiritual lineages, and the words and mystical power of the lamas. This results in a fundamental denial of the active role of the nuns, who have rarely been part of the discursive formation of Tibetan Buddhism. As Charlene Makley (2007) aptly notes, the Tibetan Buddhist revival and the dominant understanding of it is a gendered process in and of itself. This has proved valid once again in Yachen because, as I have shown, Yachen's existence relies heavily on the active participation of female practitioners, but their physical labor and presence are magically stripped from the dominant understanding of Yachen and the revival in Tibet in general.

While the nuns build huts and tents to fulfill their residential needs in Yachen, they are also frequently mobilized to toil on large construction projects such as stupas, assembly halls, and lamas' housing structures. In a sense, the nuns are a free, standby labor source, available at any time and for any occasion, expected to perform various small and large communal building assignments alongside their regular Buddhist practices. To carry out these extra physical duties, some nuns may forgo their daily religious practices for months at a time. In Yachen, it has been exclusively the Tibetan nuns (not monks, lay practitioners, or Chinese practitioners) who have been assigned such labor obligations. Even those young monks who have just taken their novice vows in Yachen (thus having the same monastic status as the nuns) are never asked to provide labor for communal projects. In Yachen, labor mobilization seems to occur largely based on gender.[8] In the summer of 2010, I spotted one such construction scene on the hilltop near the nuns' residential area. Roughly forty to fifty nuns were busy working on the site, transporting construction materials— bricks, mud, and bags of cement—on their backs to the hilltop (figure 9). A few male carpenters seemed to be directing the construction. As usual, no monks were present.

As the years went by, the structure being built on the hilltop slowly began taking shape: it was a statue of the Indian saint and tantric master Padmasambhava (Guru Rinpoche), who is believed to have planted Buddhism in Tibetan soil around the eighth century by taming the local demons.[9] The final form of the gold-plated statue is over thirty meters tall. Because of its hypervisibility— its colossal size and elevated location as well as its gleaming surface—the giant Padmasambhava statue has quickly come to serve as an impeccable identifier of Yachen as a monastic community. Since the completion of the statue in 2012, the hilltop has become a must-visit site for both monastics and visitors alike for

FIGURE 9.   The nuns working on the hilltop. Photo by the author, 2010.

various activities such as circumambulating, meditating, taking photos, and simply spending time and relaxing. Yet the statue is used not only for religious or leisurely purposes; more important, it transmits a symbolic message about the sacred legitimacy of the encampment, namely, that Yachen belongs to the direct lineage of the great Padmasambhava and his highest teachings such as Dzokchen (the Great Perfection).[10]

Padmasambhava is important for understanding the Tibetan Buddhist revival in Kham not only because he was a legendary figure in the history of Tibetan Buddhism but also because he is the source of what might be called the treasure movement from which the current revival in Kham seeks its legitimacy. The Tibetan Buddhist revival has often been characterized as the resurrection of monasticism, along with the restoration of monastic architectures, from the ruins of a despairing Maoist past. Indeed, across the plateau, many monasteries were reconstructed, monastic educational systems were recovered, and old members welcomed back after Mao.[11] However, on the other side of the plateau (in the Kham region in particular), where the largest encampments have emerged, a different set of circumstances is unfolding. Under the heavy influence of the Nyingma school in the area, Buddhism has been widely practiced outside strict monastic rules and elements. Borrowing from Geoffrey Samuel's (1993) distinction, it might be said that this region of Kham tends to have a more "shamanic" bent.

Different historical trajectories led to different forms of resurrection in the revival. The leading factors of the revival in Kham are less about bringing back bricks, mortar, monks, and lamas to "previous ruins" or rebuilding tumbledown monastic architectures and educational systems. The Tibetan Buddhist revival in Kham has taken place in a fairly radical way: through producing *new* spaces and attracting a *new* group of people to its core. The newness that characterizes the revival in Kham has added a sense of mystery and purity to its temporality and geography. It enables the revival to develop its own narratives as something envisioned and sacredly predicted from an untraceable beginning. The Nyingma sense of time, or its "ontological conception of the past," as Holly Gayley (2007a, 213) puts it, offers repeated and direct access to a timeless and flawless past. The leading Buddhist encampments in Kham such as Yachen Gar and Larung Gar began in remote, unspoiled locations—isolated pasturelands or deep nomadic valleys—that were seldom linked to regular transportation or provincial infrastructural grids. In these geographical contexts, the flows and movements among places, people, materials, and ideas have taken place in unexpected and often dramatic ways, linked along unfamiliar paths and moving in unfamiliar directions. A new, sacred geography is being (re)written along these alternative routes.

Because of the lack of traditional monastic systems in the revival in Kham (of which Yachen is a part), religious authority and legitimacy must be drawn from less conventional and sometimes mystical sources, such as the treasure movement. According to treasure narratives, Padmasambhava (and other great lamas) buried treasures in the earth and prophesized that the treasures would be revealed at *the right time by the right figure* for the purpose of reigniting Dharma teaching in Tibet.[12] The "treasures," the objects and the texts that are found, are called *terma* and the discoverers are called *tertön*. Selected masters reveal sacred texts, images, and ritual implements based on their visions, or they unearth sacred objects such as relics, jewels, and medicinal substances from the ground. These visualized and exhumed materials have become the main sources for teaching and practicing in newly emergent encampments such as Yachen. The late Achuk lama of Yachen was recognized as a renowned *tertön* in the region. According to his biography, he discovered numerous sacred objects and texts in the uncharted earth, mountains, and rocks. The physical actions of "digging up" from the earth and "visualizing" in the mind emphasize the directness of an object's connection to its sacred origin and provide a material basis for unaltered transmission from the ancient Buddhist kingdom of Tibet. A text unearthed from the ground contains the purest teachings and words, with no intervention by human or demonic forces. This "borrowed authority" from the ancient saint is realized in the treasure movement as well as in the current revival in Kham (Gyatso 1993).

The treasure movement is a savvy and sophisticated—and, in my assessment, ultimately gendered—apparatus. The movement is ingenious because it holds the potential to create instantly omnipotent authority and charisma. It spins powerfully through all obstacles, unfortunate events, and harmful thoughts and energies and flattens them into a reductive master narrative in which all events and forces in this current moment of the Buddhist revival have already been plotted out. The treasure movement works through and beyond the limitations of time and space; the dark era and other profane moments in Tibetan history are vindicated retroactively, once and for all, by and within the selected sacred lineages of extraordinary masters; the future will be protected or rescued by the same sacred force. In this regard, the treasure movement seems to be extremely hierarchical and exclusive, but it also simultaneously bears a grand equalizing message: it is a genuine attempt to make the teachings accessible to all, especially to those who have lacked proper opportunities to practice and to those without monastic affiliations. Sacred geography can be found in many places in Tibet, and revealers and their spiritual power can spread widely without discrimination. In a uniquely Tibetan manner, the treasure narrative and its operation can absorb all walks of life in Tibet and beyond.

This is in part associated with what David Germano (1998), among others, has argued: that the treasure movement signals a distinctive Tibetan way of responding to the encroachment of Chinese capitalism into Tibet since the 1980s. Tibetans have reclaimed the land as a sacred, pure space where moral superiority, self-confidence, and Tibetan civilization are reinvigorated as antithetical to the Chinese form of modernity. Similarly, Antonio Terrone (2010) argues that the treasure movement reflects Tibetans' own struggles for reidentification with Tibetan-ness in the wake of the massive destruction of Tibetan culture, religion, and language throughout the dark era of Maoist China. Despite the powerful insights and influence of these arguments and interpretations, however, I see a systematic and mutual exclusion, both in the treasure movement itself and in analyses of the treasure movement, of female participants and their significant role in the revival in Kham. Male lama–focused succession and lineage-driven narratives have been central to the dominant approach in understanding Tibetan Buddhism, and the treasure movement is another familiar narrative in this tradition. In it, the omission of the experiences of ordinary practitioners, especially those of women, has been accepted without question. It is more alarming that there has been no recognition that such omitted experiences in fact crucially support and make possible the gleaming accomplishments of the many lamas to which the treasure movement owes its influence.

I find the issue of gender hierarchy in Buddhism quite tricky to address in an adequate manner. This is not because gender issues are difficult to locate, define, or articulate. In fact, gender bias in Buddhism in general is often all too clearly observable in typical monastic settings—in the different roles, powers, and rules for nuns and monks, for example. Monastic gender bias is even more confounding when considering the radically egalitarian messages that Buddhism advocates. From early Buddhism, a story about the Buddha's obdurate initial refusal to allow women to join a *sangha* (Buddhist community) remains controversial to many. A tenet such as "nuns serve monks" is still widely accepted, albeit not spoken of directly, as a norm even in a relatively progressive monastic community like Yachen. Some scholarly efforts have been made to give alternative interpretations of the entrenched gendered rules, practices, and codes of conduct in Buddhism.[13] Yet the issue of gender in Buddhism remains largely unclear and unsettled. This is partially because of the insufficient attention given in the existing scholarship to the actual lives and situations of ordinary nuns.

In general, scholarship about the people who participate in Tibetan Buddhism has largely focused on extraordinary figures and relies on and is restricted by the availability of written records about these figures. The Tibetan literary genre *namtar* [*rnam thar*], about the life stories of enlightened figures, offers accounts of those who have superb spiritual achievements. For various reasons, women are rare in these archives. Although ethnographic works on Tibetan Buddhism certainly address the experiences of ordinary monastics, few of these exist, and studies about nuns are even scarcer.[14] Yet even if one were to converse with the nuns, they would be unlikely to express critical opinions about the gendered monastic system of which they are part because, in their community, having even a slightly doubtful attitude about the monastic rules could be associated with devaluing the teachings and the teachers, who are often treated as proxies for the monastery and the sacred teaching itself. In Tibetan Buddhism in general, a solid teacher-disciple relationship is fundamental to advancing one's practice; in Yachen, this relationship is exceptionally significant because of the specificities of Dzokchen practice. In Dzokchen, as practiced in Yachen, learning and teaching are less likely to occur through reasoning and debating than through the unilateral transmission and submission that occurs only through absolute trust and caring between teachers and disciples.

In this spiritually hierarchical context, criticism of and even the possibility of criticizing one's own institution must be fundamentally avoided. In Tibetan monastic settings in general, and in Yachen in particular, the gender hierarchy has been systematically buried through this orchestrated indifference, acquiescence, and acceptance of the status quo by the members themselves. It would be misguided, however, to judge the nuns as simply passive and inert in all matters of gender. The Tibetan nuns with whom I worked in Yachen recognize, and some even speak straightforwardly, about the ill treatment of women in domestic realms. They have a critical assessment of women's lives in the villages—the shackles of marital life, endless childbirth and child-rearing, tedious housework, and frequent domestic violence. Over the course of my fieldwork, I was advised directly and indirectly, in both joking and serious tones, by the young nuns not to get married because men would freeze my mobility and freedom. I was then given numerous vivid examples based on the nuns' families and relatives about how mothers and wives are mistreated and abused at home.[15] Without using a political vocabulary of "rights" or "status," the nuns are unequivocally aware of how women should and should not be treated at home. Marriage, considered as the epitome of female subjugation, is one of the few non-Buddhist-related topics about which they have firm opinions. In some sense, for the nuns, escaping from home itself can thus be a radical feminist declaration. In a Buddhist sense as well, avoiding all the *samsaric* sufferings experienced at home and joining Yachen are part of a great fortune and blessings that are given only to select people, those who have accumulated good karma in their previous lives.

Yet it is still puzzling that the nuns have such keen awareness and strong opinions about women's rights and statuses in the domestic realm but appear quite oblivious to the discriminatory gender treatment occurring in Yachen. During my time in Yachen, I avoided invoking or steering conversations with the nuns to any specific gender questions that might presume or impose onto our discussion the narrow spectrum of liberal Western feminist politics. I usually waited until such a topic arose naturally, but on some occasions, I couldn't help bringing up practical gender questions—for example, why are only nuns mobilized in communal construction projects? Why do nuns prepare the tea and food for the monks' practices and rituals? Why are nuns not allowed to have cellphones while monks can use them freely? I received an almost identical answer every time, which went like this: "This is the way it is. It has always been like this." The nuns treated my inquiries as self-evident, as something unquestionable or not worth questioning.

What causes them to hold such divergent perspectives on the issues of gender bias? The nuns in Yachen recognize and accept gender hierarchy when it can be aligned with the rightful Buddhist path. Critiques of the marriage system and the ill treatment of women in lay contexts can be recognized by the nuns so clearly because these critiques echo the Buddhist *samsaric* circle of life. And the realization of this gives them a path to reconcile it by seeking a higher aim in life; that is, they join a monastic community to surpass the suffering-stricken circle of life all together. It also allows the nuns to have a certain moral or karmic superiority because not all people can pursue monastic life in Tibet. At the same time, various gender-discriminatory practices in Yachen are *not* recognizable to the nuns because such a negative thing simply does not happen under the umbrella of Padmasambhava's and Achuk lama's blessings. Within their sacred presence and power, nothing inauspicious or negative can possibly occur.[16]

It is not clear whether the far-reaching power of the lamas in Tibetan Buddhism makes the treasure movement possible, or the treasure movement itself enhances the already strong authority of the lamas. Equally, it is not clear whether the leading treasure revealers in the revival simply happen to be male lamas, or if it is precisely because of their male bodies that they can become renowned revealers. The great masters in Tibetan Buddhism are usually reincarnated as male-bodied lamas; female bodies are acceptable but uncommon. As Makley (2007, 37) rightly puts it in her analysis on *tulku* (reincarnate lama) worship: "Maleness was largely an unconscious given." Without exception, in the current revival in Kham as well, Padmasambhava's maleness and the maleness of those in leading roles within the movement are legitimized and unconsciously accepted as the norm, while female bodies and female presences in supreme positions have become atypical. With its distinctive material associations, the treasure movement grants its central (male) figures magical capacities that supplement their spiritual authority. The objects excavated directly from the earth and the words visualized in the revealer's mind (and then written down) are themselves sacred. Without being associated with mediations or interpretations, these sacred things become, in their own materiality, the sacred teachings themselves. From the outset, this collapse of the division between things and meanings in the treasure movement confers enduring charisma and spiritual power on the selected male figures who retrieve materialized sacredness.

The two largest encampments in Kham (Yachen Gar and Larung Gar) find their spiritual legacy in these sacred "treasures" that were revealed. While the materiality of the treasure movement (including the lamas' physical activities of excavation) so easily validates the masters' spirituality and the sanctity of the tradition overall, the nuns' material engagements do not seem to provide a similar benefit to them. In other words, while the treasure movement celebrates the value of the material practices (finding *terma*) of a handful of male masters, it ignores the nuns' material activities that have contributed to the building of Yachen, which conditions and constitutes the male lamas' spiritual feats. The nuns' inexhaustible physical labor, in both private and public realms, has been absorbed into the premise of the dominant narrative: that the male lamas and the sacred teachings they offer are the exclusive reasons for the success of Yachen. In the end, the treasure movement is a gendered device that avails itself of sacred authority, history, and morality to create knowledge, power, and sacred spaces in Tibetan Buddhism and to further enhance the power of the male lamas as it subsumes all the material struggles endured by the nuns in their efforts to maintain Yachen.

Padmasambhava's sparkling golden body, erected on the high hill in Yachen, looks down into the valley with his wholesome compassion (figure 10). This giant statue gazes directly at Achuk lama's bedroom and the monks' quarters. It is as if Padmasambhava has forgotten those who actually molded his body by laboriously carrying mortar and bricks to the hilltop for years, as if his

FIGURE 10.   The statue of Padmasambhava. Photo by the author, 2012.

blessings pour onto Yachen's monks who are largely temporary residents but not onto the nuns who are Yachen's permanent residents as well as its builders. The compassionate body of this ancient master on the hilltop, a sacred phallus soaring up to the heights, is unable to find his way back to the majority of his disciples living and building in the valley below who have yearned for his blessings for so long.

INTIMATE THINGS

While the huts the Tibetan nuns build in Yachen look squalid and unkempt from the outside, their indoor spaces are neat, effulgent, and cozy. Wangmo, a Tibetan nun in her early twenties, lived in one of these squalid-looking-but-snug-inside huts deep in the nuns' residential area in Yachen. Yet the coziness in her room did not come easily. Due to its location, her rickety hut was dim and damp, more so than other huts. To improve the luminosity and the sense of warmth in her room, she planned to replace the darker color of fabric that originally draped her tiny window with a translucent piece of fabric. She thought that if more light came in during the day, her room would be brighter and less dank. Wangmo tried several different shops but failed to find material that she liked. It took her almost three months to acquire the right fabric for her window, although she didn't mind repeatedly visiting different shops during this time.

The Tibetan nuns in Yachen with whom I worked decorate their rooms with aesthetic care. In addition to fabric, they adorn their rooms with various pictures, including lamas' photos (this includes photos of the fourteenth Dalai Lama, which is officially forbidden across Tibet), tangka [thang ka] paintings, and family photos. In some young nuns' rooms, one or two photos of Chinese celebrities can be found as well. Books, scriptures, offering cups, incense, and other personal items such as radios, albums, and stuffed animals are neatly arranged, adding a colorful, intimate, and inviting atmosphere to their rooms (figure 11).

FIGURE 11.   The room of a Tibetan nun in Yachen. Photo by the author, 2013.

Unlike hut building—a politically hazardous task that must be done as quickly as possible at all costs—arranging indoor space is treated as a meticulous and time-intensive process by the nuns. Once a hut has been hastily erected through the collaborative labor of fellow nuns, the decoration of the indoor space is left to the nun who will stay in the hut. She then takes her time to modify, rearrange, and adorn her living space with various but modest objects such as different kinds and colors of fabrics, wallpaper, small pieces of wood, rugs, and varied personal items. Talking about the personal aesthetic pursuits of Tibetan Buddhist nuns living in a remote encampment may seem trivial, insignificant, or irrelevant in the context of the volatile Sino-Tibetan politics on the plateau or the Tibetan Buddhist revival in China on which this book is centered. However, my experience of sharing intimate spaces with the nuns for a long time—literally sleeping, cooking, and eating in the same rooms—has convinced me to see that so-called trivial things are in no way insignificant.

In other words, the small items and practices that make one's own space more comfortable and livable can take on significance and value in a community in which severe and entrenched political suppression has been the norm. In a situation where the individual pursuit of religious practices is monitored by the state, adorning her hut according to her own taste can be seen as a nun's modest claim to the ownership of a tiny intimate space filled with objects of her own. I will explain this point further from ethnographic vantage points throughout the chapter, but here I'd like to borrow a powerful insight from Krisztina Fehérváry's (2013, 1) study on the politics that inhere to the aesthetic quality of materials in socialist contexts: "In Hungary, gray is far more than a color. It is an aesthetic quality that powerfully links material environments with political affects." Following her insight, this chapter attempts to trace the aesthetic and affective engagements of the nuns in their mundane and material lives, especially in their intimate spaces, and to examine the transformative effects of these engagements in relation to the ongoing political restrictions they face.

By intimate spaces, I refer not only to the nuns' private spaces such as their rooms and kitchens; more crucially, these intimate spaces include "state-free" and "(monastic or male) authority-free" spaces, in which the nuns can escape, if only briefly and partially, the panoptic surveillance of the government as well as the patriarchal monastic gaze. By intimate things, I include intimate objects, spaces, affairs, and feelings that underpin the constant formations and reformations of the nuns' moral and political selves as Tibetan Buddhist nuns living in contemporary China. For a fuller discussion of these intimate things, I divide the chapter into two sections: the first addresses the room decorations of the nuns and their efforts toward making a home in Yachen; the second part looks at the nuns' communal journal writing and their self-reconfirmation of their nunship.

Sharing the same living spaces with the nuns for an extensive period allowed me not only to observe their room decoration practices but also made possible encounters and exchanges about somewhat secretive, sensitive, or even controversial topics that I would never have known about otherwise—the communal journal writing taken up by a group of nuns, for example. In these journals, the nuns wrote about intimate feelings they had about monks they were acquainted with and their internal moral battles over such feelings. As Buddhist nuns, pursuing romantic feelings toward a monk, or toward any man, transgresses the vows they have taken. Given the clandestine nature of this issue for monastics, I was not able to follow up on this topic actively and openly. Regardless of my inattention to the issue, however, over the course of my fieldwork, I was constantly exposed to occasions where some nuns shared their intimate feelings in their intimate spaces. As a layperson and an outsider, I maintained a sense of empathy about this issue. Even before I noticed the existence of such journals, it had crossed my mind that "love affairs" of some kind, whose existence couldn't be openly or widely circulated, might exist in Yachen. (I felt it would be too naïve or blinkered on my part to completely dismiss such possibilities in a community filled with thousands of young people.) Yet even after concrete evidence of such events was revealed one by one, they simmered for years in my mind until I was finally able to connect them to a wider Tibetan sociopolitical and monastic context and assess their affective impacts and meanings for the nuns' lives in Yachen. My discussion about intimate affairs among the nuns is not intended to reveal the moral shortcomings of Buddhist monastics. Instead, I focus on uncovering how a sense of sociality and selfhood is continuously forged, checked, and reconfirmed among the nuns themselves in a politically challenging space and time.

A Home of One's Own

All shops in Yachen are either run directly by Yachen's head office or strictly monitored by it to ensure fair prices and fair transactions. The shops used to be run very simply, as a means to address the most basic and immediate needs of practitioners. Yet as more visitors and practitioners have come to Yachen in recent years, the number of shops has increased dramatically, and the items sold have been greatly diversified (figure 12). The choices of fabric available to

FIGURE 12.   A shop in the nuns' area in Yachen. Photo by the author, 2013.

Wangmo were in fact much greater than in previous years, but she still couldn't find what she wanted for her room. In Yachen, purchasing an item that one desires often requires not only money but also perseverance and perhaps luck. Because most products consumed in Yachen arrive infrequently as part of large shipments, and because transportation to Yachen is a laborious, time-consuming task, if Wangmo missed an opportunity to buy a particular item, she might have to wait for a long time until the next shipment arrived.

One day, after visiting all the shops in the nuns' residential area and failing to find the fabric she wanted, Wangmo asked whether I could go across the river and check the shops in the monks' residential area. These shops are usually larger and often have a greater quantity and selection of items. Wangmo thought that one of these shops might have the right kind of fabric. In addition to nicer shops, the monks' area contains all the other essential buildings that the nuns utilize, including the lamas' houses, the clinic, and the transportation hub. But Yachen has a strict curfew for nuns who enter the monks' area (the curfew is not imposed on laypeople like me). The nuns are allowed to enter only every other day for a limited period. Around six o'clock in the evening, a group of monitor nuns sits at the edge of the bridge on the nuns' side to prevent nuns from crossing.[1] I went to the monks' side and looked for Wangmo's fabric, but I couldn't find it. While I disliked the idea of disappointing Wangmo, who was waiting for me on the other side of the river, I also wondered why she cared so much about a piece of fabric. Among the many things that a nun might wish to purchase in Yachen, a curtain is, after all, neither as important as lumber nor as sacred as scriptures or photos of lamas.

Yet Wangmo is not the only one who is exceptionally particular about decorating her hut. Most of the Tibetan nuns with whom I worked in Yachen are similarly meticulous, if not more so, about adorning their indoor spaces. In their huts, their beds, bookshelves, and small shrines are covered with clean pieces of fabric and placed tightly against the walls to save space. Objects such as books, scriptures, offering cups, photos, and personal belongings are neatly arranged and dusted regularly to keep them clean at all times. All the surfaces inside the huts are covered with carefully chosen colorful fabric, and no bare wood is exposed. Some nuns also arrange strings of lights around their small shrine to light up the photos of the lamas and create a festive mood. The items sold in Yachen are usually of low quality, but the nuns do their best to decorate their rooms as delightfully and colorfully as possible. Of all the decorative elements used by the nuns, fabric seems to play a critical role in affecting the overall atmosphere of their indoor spaces; the type of fabric determines the level of lighting and the main color of the rooms. If a red translucent fabric (similar to the one that Wangmo wished for) is attached to the window, it creates a soft, pinkish ambience in the room when the sun shines directly through it. While most nuns prefer this, some also choose a darker, thicker fabric that prevents too much sunlight from coming through, and in this way, they enjoy a calmer mood. Creative combinations of different colors and textures of the fabrics often communicate the distinctive character and tastes of the owner of the hut.

Chinese Nuns in Yachen

To better understand the Tibetan nuns' decorating practices, I would like to take a small detour into the daily lives of some of the Chinese nuns who lived side by side with the Tibetan nuns but who usually cared little about decorations. This detour will give us a clue to the underpinning logic behind the adornment of indoor spaces by the Tibetan nuns. But this comparison by no means suggests that the Tibetan nuns are more aesthetic by nature or that they uniquely possess skills necessary for decorating their indoor spaces. And it does not follow that because the Tibetan nuns care about indoor decoration, they are less serious about their practices than the Chinese nuns. The purpose of this particular comparison is to examine how a certain practice is adopted or not by different groups who reside in the same place, follow the same teachings, and share the same monastic rules and norms. This prevents us from jumping hastily to the conclusion that the decoration practices of the Tibetan nuns are childlike, girlish, or the result of immature behaviors, all of which are common ways for many Tibetans and Chinese to characterize young nuns in Tibet.

The nights in Yachen are long. Before electricity arrived in the nuns' quarters in the spring of 2013, the nuns relied on dusky solar bulbs when they cooked or read at night.[2] The unreliable supply of electricity in Yachen's early years meant that the nuns kept solar energy panels on their roofs for backup. But if it was rainy or cloudy all day, a solar generator could not sustain even a small bulb at night. The Tibetan nuns in Yachen often went to bed at an early hour simply because of the darkness. The Tibetan nun who was my hut-mate at the time often stayed up a little longer than I did because of her daily prayers and meditation, but it was common for us both to go to bed no later than nine o'clock when we had no lights.

One evening, when we were about to finish dinner, I heard a vague mumbling sound from outside; it turned out to be the chanting sound of a nun. The nuns recite scriptures regularly on their own schedules—normally at dawn or at night—so it was not at all odd to hear the faint sound of chanting when it was dark. What was unusual this time was that the recitation was in Chinese. There were a few hundred Chinese nuns practicing in Yachen who lived in the same residential area as the Tibetan nuns. Perhaps because of their small number or their preference for silent meditation, it was rare to hear chanting in Chinese in the nuns' quarters. I went out to the yard and looked around the neighborhood where I was staying at that time, trying to find the source of the sound. It was Jamyang, a young Chinese nun who had recently moved into the neighborhood. She had shaved her head about a year before, and since then she had practiced rigorously with her lama. Every day she left her hut early in the morning to practice in the lama's hall and came back late at night. When it was too late and too risky—because of dog attacks—to come all the way back by herself, she would stay the night in the hall and return the next morning. Because of her hectic schedule, Jamyang could not even find the time to set up a solar panel on her roof. Without a solar bulb, her hut and yard were in complete darkness once the sun went down. Yet she did not seem to care about this. Relying on dim moonlight, she would stand outside and recite the scriptures. She read them in the fastest manner possible, as if she had something urgent to do immediately afterward. Later, she told me that she had a target number for her daily recitations, and she wanted to complete what she planned for each day. Her hut, a short-term rental from another nun, was also in poor shape. Even the most basic things, bedding and a kitchen, much less decorations, were not properly prepared and organized in her room. She simply had no time to take care of anything but her practices and her daily tasks in assisting her lama.

In Yachen, the nuns' practices are largely divided into three parts: one part is receiving teachings from lamas (meetings with the lamas); another is attending lamas' lectures, rituals, and prayer sessions (communal activities); and the last is individual practices. While meetings with lamas and communal activities are part of inflexible routines for all nuns, personal practices can vary widely depending on an individual nun's attitude, situation, and style. The Tibetan nuns with whom I worked had flexible schedules for their individual daily practices. They followed their own daily plans as assiduously and sincerely as possible, but not in an exhausting and laborious way. For example, when there were no lights at night, the Tibetan nuns with whom I stayed went to bed early and resumed their practices the next day, when practice was easier to do and more effective. For them, practice was something that continued beyond this life cycle, and there was little sense in rushing to meet an artificial goal as if this were the only and last life they would have.[3] In sharp contrast, the Chinese nuns with whom I worked in Yachen appeared to have a different attitude toward their practices. Jamyang forced herself to recite scriptures in the darkness so that she could finish her goal for the day. What was the source of such pressure and urgency in her practices? Perhaps it was because she was a novice nun who maintained the working habits she had during her days in the city before she became a nun. Jamyang summarized her life this way:

> I am the only child in my family and grew up in a middle-class family in a city. I studied quite well and went to the best college in the province and pursed a master's degree after college graduation. I was well prepared for a comfortable life once I finished my degree. But since college I had also been deeply interested in Buddhism. Whenever possible, I found a way to visit temples and to study Buddhist teachings throughout my college years. During summer vacations, I even packed a bag and visited temples for long-term stays. Karma eventually led me to meet my current lama at a lecture in the temple of a southern city where I was living a few years ago. (The Tibetan lama from Yachen had just begun traveling to Chinese cities and giving lectures to Chinese disciples at that time.) I was deeply moved by his lecture and spoke to him after the talk. After graduation, I followed him and came to Yachen. A year later, I shaved my head.

Jamyang's experience reflects the important moment of the first encounter between Chinese disciples and their Tibetan lama, which is a moment that is frequently retold among the Chinese disciples. Almost all Tibetans are born into Buddhist families and grow up in heavily Buddhist environments where a pre-Buddhist life is virtually unimaginable. But unlike Tibetans, most Chinese disciples have an unforgettable moment when Buddhism fatefully arrives in their lives. The destined encounter with their teachers is often followed by the more formal step, called *guiyi*, of becoming a Buddhist. Guiyi in this context means to take refuge in a particular teacher (*shangshi* in Chinese). It is not necessarily a prelude for joining a monastery but is instead the mutual acknowledgment of a spiritual bonding between a disciple and a teacher under the basic precepts of Buddhism. Guiyi sometimes occurs instantly, right after the first encounter, but a disciple may also take some time to think about who they want to choose as their lifetime spiritual guide. Some disciples first try different shangshis (teachers) to ascertain the so-called best karmic match. While the encounter may be predetermined through a fateful or karmic force, guiyi seems to involve greater consciousness and determination by the disciples. When Chinese lay disciples first meet, an important question they ask each other is whether they have taken guiyi already and, if so, to whom. Guiyi is a sign of membership in a Buddhist family; once guiyi is mutually confirmed, they call each other *shixiong* ("dharma brother"). Guiyi can be done either as part of a large communal ceremony or in an individual meeting. In either case, the process is not usually complicated. Consisting of a reminder of the basic set of precepts and lama's mantras, the entire guiyi process can be done in less than five minutes. Once guiyi is performed, the Tibetan teacher becomes the root teacher (*genben shangshi* in Chinese) of the disciple and guides the disciple's spiritual progress by offering personalized teachings and advice, while the disciples wholeheartedly support the teacher by making donations and paying their deepest respect and gratitude.

Since most Chinese nuns were not raised as Buddhists or in Buddhism-friendly environments, converting to Buddhism marks a crucial moment of transition in their lives. In Jamyang's case, she was attracted to Buddhism almost instinctively when she was a college student (she called the attraction her karma). But meeting her Tibetan lama in the city a few years ago was the critical watershed moment that marked the transition from being interested in Buddhism to becoming a serious practitioner and later pursuing her nunship in Yachen. For Jamyang, the encounter with her teacher was a life-changing event. Since joining Yachen, she had focused all her energy and passion on her lama, his teaching, and his extended missionary work—she helped with his outreach activities, made websites and visual materials, edited his words and turned them into books, and made recordings of rituals and lectures. It seems that her knowledge and education from her pre-nun days, such as her computer skills and her experience writing official documents, were of great use to her teacher's mission. For Jamyang, helping with the lama's various tasks was as important as conducting her practices—the two activities were indistinguishable for her. Given such a straightforward goal for her life in Yachen, for Jamyang, activities that did not directly serve this goal, such as having leisure time, socializing with Tibetan nuns, and taking care of her room arrangements and decorations, were simply unnecessary if not wasteful. She set up a tight schedule for herself each day and drove herself to complete all her goals.

Jamyang, in other words, did not view Yachen as a place where she could nurture a full life that included daily living and sharing with fellow nuns. She saw Yachen strictly as a place to practice Buddhism. Her hut did not function as a typical nun's residential space in Yachen: solar panels were missing, the bedding was not washed and organized, and the kitchen had not been used for a long time. After joining Yachen, Jamyang sought to rent a hut rather than to build one for herself. She simply could not spare any time to deal with issues other than her practices and her lama's missionary work. She treated her body equally poorly (later, her frequent fasting and lack of sufficient sleep eventually forced her to leave Yachen for a period of recuperation). By relinquishing a promising life in a Chinese city and deliberately turning to the life of a nun in remote Tibet, Jamyang also abandoned her parents' expectations and the social norms and networks she had grown up with. Her parents refused to talk to her

for years after she became a nun. Because they have little support or understanding from their own families, many Chinese nuns in Yachen experience a
much more challenging life both financially and psychologically. This is what
caused Jamyang to be driven even more strongly toward her goal of obtaining
ultimate teachings and truths. She was obliged to prove to herself, as well as to
her family back home, that her second life, which she chose by going against all
family expectations and social norms, was the right and worthwhile choice.

In addition to the powerful moment of the first encounter with their lama,
many Chinese nuns have also experienced tragic or traumatic experiences that
have led them to renounce the worldly life they once had and join Yachen. To
them, Yachen is an alternative when they decide to shun a life that is no longer
viable or meaningful. Yeshi shared the tragic story of her life before she became
a nun in Yachen:

> I started off my career in a pharmaceutical company in a city in south-
> ern China. I was married and had a son. I had a financially stable life
> and a loving family. However, my happiness was shattered in a single
> day when my husband and my eight-year-old son died in a car acci-
> dent. I attempted suicide a few times. All I wanted to do was to leave
> the world that had left me alone and miserable, and to get completely
> away from the place of my excruciating memories. I found the farthest
> place possible from my former life and my tragic situation. I came to
> Yachen and became a nun.

Unlike Jamyang, Yeshi wouldn't have found Yachen, much less joined it, if this
horrible incident in her life had not occurred. For her, at the beginning, Yachen
was not a place where she hoped to obtain ultimate teachings and enlightenment but a place where she could simply be physically far away from the places,
memories, and people that constantly reminded her of the worst torment of her
life. The geographical remoteness of Yachen served this goal well. The early
years of her life in Yachen were therefore a time for subduing the pain of her
ordeal; it was a period of gradual healing rather than a time for learning and
embracing a new life. During this process, Yeshi met her teacher and slowly
learned to sense the depth of Buddhist teachings. She began to understand her
personal tragedy from the perspective of Buddhist cosmology; she was able to
find a new—or, from her perspective, the real—purpose of her life, one that was
perhaps determined by an unknowable force emanating from intricate webs of
karma set in an aeonian time frame.

Although her beginning was quite different from Jamyang's, Yeshi had also
become driven by a focus on obtaining ultimate teachings and truths under the
tutelage of her current lama. It had been nearly twenty years since she joined

Yachen, and Buddhism and her lama's teachings in particular had given her the motivation to live and a purpose in life once again. Yeshi visited her lama a few times per week, not only to seek out teachings but also to serve him by doing things such as giving him a foot massage as her gesture of gratitude and respect toward her lama. Whenever she visited her teacher, the first thing she did was to change into a clean robe and wash her face and hands. (If taking a bath had been a manageable option in Yachen, there is no doubt that she would have done this as well.) To be in the same room with her lama, not to mention touching his feet, was an extraordinary experience for her; everything about him—his body, his clothes, the objects he had used or touched, and even the food or water he had eaten or drunk—was considered sacred. She wanted to make sure that she showed the highest respect to her lama each time, and it was a great blessing for her if her teacher felt comfortable and relaxed because of her service. For hours, every other day or so, this elderly Chinese nun happily and gratefully gave a foot massage to her middle-aged male Tibetan teacher. When she returned home, she was usually too tired to tidy her room.

Unlike Tibetan nuns, most Chinese nuns plan to leave Yachen at some point and go back to their hometowns to continue practicing and teaching until they die. As the Chinese nuns age and their health deteriorates, it becomes more and more difficult to sustain themselves in Yachen, especially during the long and harsh winters. Yachen's lack of medical facilities adds a sense of urgency to this matter. Among the Chinese nuns, returning home is also considered a way to give back to society by spreading the Buddhist teachings they have learned to a wider Chinese audience. Even someone like Yeshi, who had lived in Yachen for nearly two decades, planned to leave Yachen eventually (she eventually left in 2017). She just wanted to be certain that her level of practice was good enough that she could be an independent practitioner for the rest of her life without her teacher's guidance. To most Chinese nuns, therefore, Yachen is not a place where they nurture friendships, build a new life, or create a home; it is a utilitarian space where they are provided with resources for their practice and given an opportunity to serve their teachers. They want to maximize this hard-won opportunity before they leave. For most of the Chinese nuns, decorating their rooms would thus likely be a waste of this precious opportunity.

A State-Free Space

From a religious vantage point, focusing on decorating one's room with colorful fabric and secular items is not particularly encouraged for monastics; and in many cases, it is probably prohibited. Yet the Tibetan nuns in Yachen (including the monitor nuns) are quite liberal on this matter, and decoration

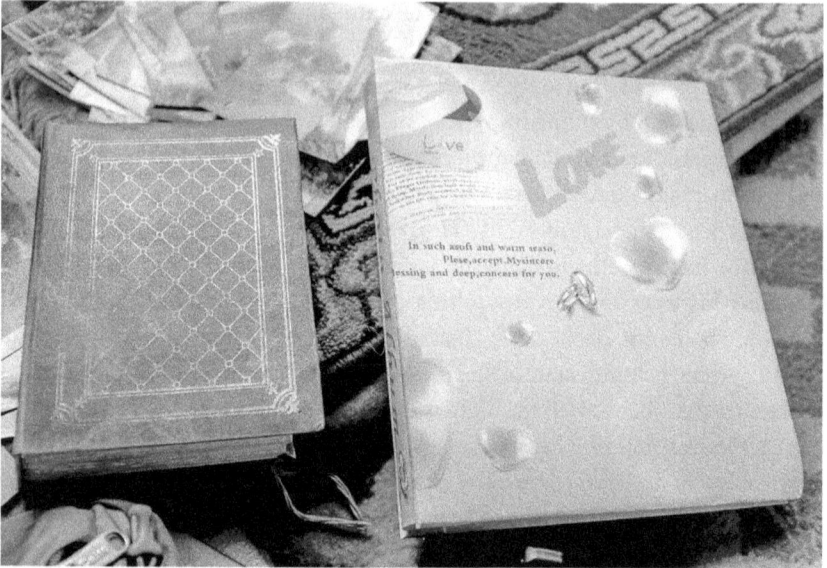

FIGURE 13.   The photo albums the Tibetan nuns keep in Yachen. Photo by the author, 2015.

seems to enrich their lives as nuns. For them, decoration is not only about arranging objects and placing floral curtains in their rooms but about claiming their personal spaces and shrines neat, clean, and pleasant. In addition, decorating creates relationships and specific forms of bonding among the nuns. Unlike hut building, room decoration is a slow process, requiring meticulousness and attentiveness, that takes place over several months and reflects individual sensibilities, preferences, and tastes. The nuns ask their closest fellow nuns to accompany them when they shop for materials for their rooms. Frequent trips to the shops for a trivial item rely on mutual understanding and close relationships.

Apart from the large photos they put on the walls, the Tibetan nuns also keep several photo albums in their rooms (figure 13). In these albums, they collect various lamas' photos that they have acquired in Yachen and family photos they've brought from hometowns, including photos featuring their own pre-nun appearance. Each nun has at least a few photo albums, and the number of volumes increases as she continues to collect photos after joining Yachen. The albums are not meant to embellish the rooms per se, but they constitute a reservoir of personal recollection that is ready for sharing with others at any time. When I visited a nun, she would likely take out all her photo albums and show me every photograph inside, one by one. Through these photos, I would get to meet nearly all the members of her family and receive a brief introduction to each figure in the photos. In return, I was often asked to show my photos—in my case, the photos saved on my cell phone. The Tibetan nuns with whom I worked are not only willing to share their lives but they are also very curious about the lives of others. Seeing and sharing photos in albums and cell phones is an excellent way to satisfy both impulses.

Once her hut is built, a nun finally has a space of her own for her solitary practices and her daily life in this remote corner of the plateau. No matter how unstable and fragile the exterior of her hut may appear, the inside is considered a secure and solid space where she can create a world of her own with little interference from either the Chinese state or the monastic authorities. Even though the work team can officially inspect any place in Yachen, they rarely look into the nuns' rooms. Also, Yachen's lamas and senior nuns are usually generous about the young nuns' decorating practices, allowing or at least acquiescing to the nuns' displays of various non-Buddhist items. While the exterior surfaces of the hut are the primary target for the work team's surveillance, on the other side of that surface a sense of autonomy and individuality is secretly blooming. In their interior spaces, the nuns can freely display photos of the current Dalai Lama and other respected lamas from the exile community in India that are prohibited in Tibet. Through photo albums, the nuns share stories about their parents, married cousins, a big brother who works in the city and sends money, the pilgrimage trips they took to Lhasa a few years ago, and so on. The nuns' rooms become spaces not only for sleeping, eating, and practicing but also for sharing life and developing companionship.

For the Tibetan nuns with whom I worked, Yachen is a home rather than a straightforward Buddhist practice center. They leave their natal homes and make a new home in Yachen where they mature, become wiser, and grow old. They share lives with companions, forge relationships, help and educate other nuns; and finally, they face their last day in this life with the blessings and prayers of their fellow nuns and teachers. The phrase Tibetan nuns use to describe their plans for living in Yachen is: "until I die." Although a nun sometimes leaves Yachen or ceases her nunship altogether for unexpected reasons, the number who do so is very small, and most nuns plan to live in Yachen until their final day in this world. Fabrics along with photos and other decorative items, therefore, matter to them; ugly fabrics cannot be tolerated because their rooms perform the function of home that their natal homes once did—their rooms are the most private, liberating, and intimate life-sharing and life-nurturing spaces possible within a hostile environment.

As I explained earlier, this is quite different from most Chinese nuns who plan to live in Yachen temporarily. Although the Tibetan nuns and the Chinese nuns receive the same teachings and are guided by the same teachers, they have radically different sociocultural experiences and personal backgrounds before joining Yachen. These differences have led to different attitudes and senses of urgency about their practices and their ways of living in Yachen. In their own unique ways, both Tibetan and Chinese nuns find a way to survive and continue to practice and live in Yachen as nuns. Under the ongoing repressive power of the state, the Tibetan nuns with whom I worked treasure any slight chance to have a state-free space of their own in Yachen. A Tibetan nun's neatly decorated room is part of a creative effort to secure such an autonomous space, however slightly and momentarily, for herself. Decorating one's hut is, in other words, a rigorous yet quiet process of securing a space that constitutes home. In Yachen, choosing a piece of fabric can be a political act after all.

Buddhist Love and Shame

I am so sad. My heart was broken.

I broke up with my boyfriend. . . .

Let's forget everything.

Practicing Buddhism is the most important thing.

I have a great, great teacher.

Why shouldn't I be happy?

I am happy.

[A passage written in the communal journal by a nun]

Don't be so hard on yourself, it is the work of karma.

We have our great Tulku Asong.

He is always with us.

[A response to the above from another
nun in the communal journal]

I was reading one of the Tibetan nuns' communal journals. These journals, fashioned out of inexpensive, medium-sized notebooks with cheap vinyl covers, are filled with mixed messages, including words about recent breakups with "boyfriends,"[4] words of solace from other nuns, and religious devotions. (The term "boyfriends" was meant platonically at the time when the journal was written and circulated.) The messages are written in both Tibetan and Chinese, with occasional doodles and drawings. I noticed later that Chinese is sometimes deliberately used as a limited method of encryption for sharing a secret since many nuns, especially the senior ones, do not read Chinese. This partially encrypted, communal notebook was shared and circulated within an exclusive circle of young Tibetan nuns with whom I grew close during my stay in Yachen. This secret journal came to me somewhat by accident. One evening, I found Samchul, my hut-mate at that time, occupied in reading something at the foot of her bed. In a small space like our hut, which was tiny even for one person, two adults are bound to become involved in each other's private affairs. In addition, my role as an ethnographer often led me to be more invasive and bolder in meddling in other people's lives. I had an instant and casual curiosity about the notebook she was reading because it did not seem to be one of the scriptures or other printed materials that I had often seen in Yachen.

Samchul hesitated for a moment before responding and then, instead of offering an explanation, chose to hand the notebook over to me. I began turning the pages, little prepared for what I was about to read: *nanpengyou* (boyfriend), *fenshou* (breakup), and *tongku* (grief), which are words not usually heard in a Buddhist monastic community. At the beginning, these words passed before my eyes like floating signifiers for which I could not locate meanings in the real world. My brain was simply not fast enough to process this unexpected semiotic disturbance—Samchul had a boyfriend; a Buddhist nun was in a romantic relationship with a man. In contrast to my perplexed reaction, Samchul, sitting next to me, was quite nonchalant. She made no particular comments other than simply to ask me to be discreet about the journal, especially with the monitor nuns and the senior nuns. If the monitor nuns were to find out about the journal, Samchul would not be able to avoid a serious (mostly verbal) punishment.[5] The topic of the boyfriend came up briefly a few times later, when Samchul and I were alone at night in our quarters, but on that evening when she allowed me to read the journal for the first time, I remained mute for the rest of the night.

When the nuns' secret "love" stories—their (platonic) relationships with monks—were *revealed* to me, I did not know how to begin to understand these accidental findings.[6] The only thing that seemed appropriate at that time was to make notes for myself and to remain silent about the issue. To my surprise, however, despite the clandestine nature of the subject and my own discreet attitude toward it, such secrets continued to be "leaked," "disclosed," and "materialized" over the course of my fieldwork in Yachen. These secret affairs, through some unnamable force, kept unfolding before the outsider. What was this "unnamable force"?

The existence of such a journal in a community like Yachen could itself be seen as a sensational event, given the higher standard of morality that is so strongly associated with the Buddhist ethos, including strict celibacy and the prioritization of taming bodily and emotional desires. The journal, or, more precisely, what was written in it, is antithetical to the norms that Yachen and the nuns themselves produce and value. Violating such norms will usually subject a nun to severe moral condemnation. In Buddhist monasteries in Tibet and in many other Buddhist communities as well, such a transgression is often a direct cause for disrobing. For the nuns with whom I worked in Yachen, however, this seemingly simple rule is more complex than it appears. Its complexities arise from the nuns' full self-awareness of their moral violations and their revelations of their wrongdoings in a semipublic way in order to "fix" these problems themselves. In this way, they ultimately emerge with a stronger moral affirmation of themselves as Buddhist nuns.

Why do these nuns create written evidence of their shameful experiences, at the risk of, in the worst case, losing their nunships? Why do they deliberately form a communal space for confession about their secret, immoral actions? In other words, why do they need to *reveal* their disgrace at all?

The Technique of Confession

It is difficult to inquire about issues that are meant to be hidden and secret and that would cause disgrace to my informants if they were revealed. I could not "ask around" about the nature of the relationships, who the monks were, how they met, how long a relationship had lasted, and whether there were other cases. So many questions inundated my thoughts, but there was no easy or justifiable way that I could seek answers. That first evening, while I was puzzling over the whole situation and still remained outwardly passive about it, I also felt slightly flattered because I interpreted Samchul's willingness to allow me to read the journal as evidence of her trust in me. For some time following this incident, I thought that, to the nuns, I might be trusted enough to be included in their secret conversations. Yet soon after, during the following summer, I encountered another similar event that led me to abandon my premature interpretation.

That event occurred one afternoon when, out of the blue, Dekyi, a nun whom I wasn't close to yet, told me a story about her several inappropriate encounters with a monk in Yachen. This incident opened a new way of looking at the secret-sharing activities among some of the nuns in Yachen. I tentatively concluded that the secrets had reached me not because I was especially reliable and sincere but because the secrets were somehow meant to be revealed, not to me in particular but to "others." It seemed to me that the nuns had perhaps found a way to express their transgressive behaviors to gain something more important: a sense of atonement or a sense of truth about themselves. This following is Dekyi's narration:

> I tried to ignore the uncomfortable feeling that a young monk behind me was staring at me all morning. It had been weeks since I felt that the monk sitting across from me was sending easy smiles my way during Tulku Asong's lecture. He gave me the warmest smile whenever our eyes met. It made me feel baffled and anxious. One day, the monk passed close by me during the commotion after the lecture was dismissed. I didn't know how to respond when I found a slip of paper in my hand that he had just secretly handed to me. My heart began pounding and my face blushed, and I looked around to see if anyone was watching me. I cautiously opened the note. It said in Chinese, "*wo ai ni* (I love you)."

The daily morning lecture that Dekyi attended was part of a yearlong program that Tulku Asong, Yachen's current head lama, had recently embarked upon to spread the accomplishments of the late Achuk lama and his teachings. The lectures began in March 2013 and continued through November of that same year, except for a few weeks during the summer that were reserved for official rituals and ceremonies. Because the lectures were meant for both nuns and monks, both groups were expected to attend. For about three hours every morning for nine consecutive months, the nuns and monks gathered in the square outside the monks' assembly hall and listened to their head lama's teachings. Yachen's head office is very cautious about unnecessary encounters between monks and nuns, so the lectures were rare occasions for interaction between the two groups. Dekyi was assigned to sit at the end of the nuns' line, adjacent to the monks' seats and about a meter apart from them. Once the seats were assigned, each attendee brought a handmade wooden seat of their own and left it in their designated spot to mark their seat during the yearlong lecture series (figure 14). Although this lecture series was initiated for the benefit of the practitioners so that the great lama's teachings could be passed on in an intensive way, it had also produced an unintended side effect among the young members of the audience. The combination of the long time and

FIGURE 14.   The wooden seats after the morning lecture. Photo by the author, 2013.

the fixed seating policy provided the attendees with a mandatory space and time for indirect yet steady interaction, just as in Dekyi's case. Dekyi's narration continued:

> My feelings were stirred when I read the note, and I could not or did not want to tell anyone about it. From then on, the monk became bolder and passed notes to me every day, asking to meet me and giving me his phone number. I acknowledged that what he was doing was morally wrong, but I also felt curious about him. I decided to call him one day. [Since the Tibetan nuns in Yachen, unlike monks, are not allowed to have cell phones, the only way that this relationship could actually be initiated was through a phone call made by Dekyi from one of the public phones at the shops.] We met briefly a couple of times in a carefully chosen spot where we could avoid the monitor nuns' scrutiny.[7] Every time we met, the monk offered gifts, snacks, and even small amounts of money in order to ingratiate himself with me. He seemed to be very capable of providing anything I might want. I refused all the gifts at first. One day, he lent me a DVD player with a

film about Milarepa [a legendary tantric yogi of Tibet], and I accepted it. Watching the movie about the ancient Tibetan saint was a good thing; having a relationship might not be a totally bad idea. The monk tried to convince me and make me feel easy by saying that no one would know about us and that he wanted to continue the relationship. All he wanted from me, according to him, was to continue to see me once in a while. But I sensed it was wrong. I stopped calling him and ended the relationship.

Dekyi's confession was unexpected and surprising. What astonished me more, however, was that she shared this confidential story about herself with a near stranger. We had met briefly once before and exchanged names. Her confession made me wonder if such stories might be shared not solely because of a listener's credibility built through long-term rapport but for some other reason. I realized that what the journal entries and Dekyi's confessions had in common was their endings, which showed a clear turning toward and reclaiming of moral righteousness. The writers in the journal almost always concluded their stories with grateful acknowledgments of the privilege they are given because they practice Buddhism under the tutelage of such a great master in Yachen. They reaffirm and reassert their position as nuns in this blessed environment and advise each other not to waste this rare opportunity. Samchul perhaps allowed me to read the journal because she knew that each entry contained a firm reaffirmation of the value of the eminent teachings and the blessings they have as nuns in Yachen. Dekyi also ultimately determined that she should terminate her relationship with the flirtatious monk, and she emphasized her action several times to me as if the whole story was narrated to declare its rightful ending.

The significance of these confessions lies in the reassurance they give of having a firm moral grounding, an affirmation of the righteous agentive choices the nuns make, and ultimately the confirmation of a specifically Buddhist notion of the moral self along the way. In other words, the fact that the nuns expose their shame to an outsider is a way to practice their agentive morality, not a morality that is given and must be followed because it is the norm but morality as an achievement that must be earned and reclaimed through and within constant struggle, effort, and restraint. For some nuns, morality is something that grows and is achieved on this transgressive terrain. By straddling the terrain between what is morally right and wrong—by way of satisfying personal curiosity, temptation, and worldly desire—and then choosing to reveal their stories, the nuns reaffirmed their moral triumph at the end of their struggle.

Yet questions still linger: Why must this moral claim be spelled out in front of others, especially outsiders? How can the nuns act so boldly about such sensational matters? Why did Samchul and other nuns decide to leave written records of their inappropriate deeds and casually handle and circulate their shared journal in such a way that it ended up in an outsider's hands? Why on earth did they create the possibility in the first place that their secrets would leak out? Why did Dekyi, in only our second meeting, share her scandalous experience? During my stay in Yachen, in addition to the journal and Dekyi's sudden confession, similar secrets were divulged several times by the nuns. Why do they see themselves through the lens of confession; in other words, why do they process and interpret their private stories in a semi-open way?

In *Confessions of the Flesh*, his then-unpublished fourth volume of *The History of Sexuality*, Michel Foucault (1993) discusses the early Christian invention of confession as a means of developing sexual ethics through the technique of self-disclosure. Foucault focuses not only on how Christian sexuality was created by people through the act of confession but how, by verbalizing certain private details about themselves to others, people began thinking about themselves and began focusing on discovering the truth about themselves as reflected within the sociocultural context in which they lived. What interests me in this Foucauldian framework of confession in relation to the nuns I am studying is the way in which the pursuit of the truth of oneself is integrated into structuring and being structured by social norms. Judith Butler (2005, 23) described Foucauldian subjects as follows: "If we conclude that Foucault's failure to think the other is decisive, we have perhaps overlooked the fact that the very being of the self is dependent, not just on the existence of the other in its singularity (as Levinas would have it), but also on the social dimension of normativity that governs the scene of recognition." An act of confession, enunciating a certain shameful truth about oneself to others, is a way, albeit one that is perhaps a bit risky, to maneuver oneself into a position of recognizability within a given context and scheme of normativity. Rather than concealing themselves from norms and blaming themselves for doing something inappropriate, the nuns, by revealing the most sinful parts about themselves, create a liminal space for negotiation in which they can confirm themselves as recognizable members of a community, as able to acknowledge right and wrong, and as possessing the ability and the will to turn things around when needed. By doing so, they reaffirm their social position as nuns and exercise power over themselves in interpreting their own actions within the scene of recognition.

The Karmic Self

In the passages above that I cited from the secret journal, a nun comforts her fellow nun by using the notion of karma. Karma (*lé* [*las*]) in Buddhism is generally understood as an interdependent logic of cause (*gyu* [*rgyu*]) and effect (*dré* [*'bras*]) that applies widely across all human history, lives, and cosmologies.[8] The working of karma is often mysterious because it does not necessarily link actions and results within the scope of a single event, and it frequently links multiple lives over one's past, present, and future in a non-straightforward way. Therefore, people living their present life often miss the connection between the real cause from a past life and its much-delayed result in this or a future life. One cannot easily remember or trace the exact cause and effect between events; therefore, the most plausible thing one can do is to rely on wild speculation and subjective interpretation. In the Buddhist worldview I learned about in Yachen, all forms of human encounter are considered a result of or a reflection on people's intricate karmic networks. Whether a meeting culminates in sharing friendship or resentment depends on its own logical threads of karma from multiple previous lives. My presence in Yachen, for instance, was often interpreted in terms of the work of karmic force. Samchul once mentioned to me the mystical nature of karma regarding my arrival in Yachen. She often marveled at how I ended up visiting Yachen and how, among the over ten thousand nuns there, I ended up staying with her as a hut-mate. This is karma, according to Samchul.

Karma theory can indeed suggest certain answers for inexplicable events, although sometimes such answers are not quite satisfactory or clear, especially if one does not fully reside in this system of karma. Interpretations remain subjective and circumstantial after all. To the nuns with whom I worked in Yachen, however, karma serves as a powerful explanatory mechanism. The nuns understand their love affairs as the working of karma; certain actions they performed in their previous lives eventually lead to the things that happen to them in this life. To some, karma can be treated as a convenient justification that one can apply to give oneself an easy alibi for whatever mistakes one makes. Indeed, if one thinks about everything only retrospectively, karma can be understood as a panacea that lifts away severe moral condemnation for every negative action or behavior. Karma has a flip side, however; it is also very much a forward-looking theory because the actions that one performs in the current moment will affect and result in future events, including in one's future lives. What karma offers to the nuns is a term with which they can recognize themselves and with which they can understand their antinormative behavior within the realm of normativity in monastic settings. But karma also compels the nuns to work toward their many lives ahead by actively and voluntarily correcting their wrong deeds in the present life. The self makes an inexcusable mistake and transgresses norms and regulations, yet the self is aware of its fault and feels shame, enunciates the problem, eventually fixes it, and thereby actively steers the work of karma in future lives. In doing so, the self can situate itself in a rightful, recognizable position within the consecutive flows of karmic networks. Through the technique of verbalizing and writing about their shame—that is, through the technique of confession in the presence of others and the approbation they receive for acknowledging their transgressions—the nuns constantly declare and reaffirm their "karmic selves."

As long as one actively reflects on one's own transgressions and tries to fix them, no matter how abnormal those actions may be, they can be incorporated into the dominant norms and morality, and they can be seen as having their own karmic trajectories within the existing framework. A conversation that I had with an older nun in Yachen about the love affairs of the young nuns resonates here. Neither of us explicitly mentioned the phrase "love affairs" or any other words that directly referenced this issue, but the topic of our conversation was clear to both of us. The middle-aged nun lived near Samchul and me at that time, and she also knew some of the nuns' secrets that I had discovered. That afternoon, she told me that transgression is part of life and Buddhists cannot avoid it; in fact, Buddhism fully recognizes its existence. To my many follow-up questions, her only answer was, "This is a part of the process, of life, and we all know it, and if you just fix it and turn it around, then things will be okay. It's all part of life." Although my ignorance prevented me from fully perceiving how exactly Buddhism recognizes transgression, what I understood from this Zen riddle-like conversation that afternoon was that, for the people who make mistakes, even those who live under strict monastic vows, there should be a space or a chance to turn those mistakes around, to correct things in the right way.

At the very least, it seems Yachen allows its members such a chance. Unlike other religious traditions that focus on transcendent, supernatural figures who set nonnegotiable rules, the rules and precepts in Buddhism are created by humans (including the Buddha) rather than by a divine force, and these rules are constantly reapplied and renewed by the people who create them and participate in them. I do not intend to generalize about Buddhist attitudes toward rules and regulations here, but from my observations and experiences in Yachen, I view Buddhism as more likely something "practiced" rather than "believed." For the same reason, perhaps the nuns should be called "practitioners" or "path seekers" rather than "believers." The nuns in Yachen, by making mistakes and amending them, are "practicing" Buddhism on their own terms, and they are creating an alternative possibility and means for continually remaining within the renewed sacred. Buddhism in Yachen is not an inaccessible lofty monument; rather, it is something the nuns "practice" through their actions and through making do every day.

Coda

It is difficult to know what percentage of nuns in Yachen engage in such bold transgressions. We also do not know how strictly and clearly transgressions are defined and recognized among the monastic authorities and the nuns. But in part because of their youth and general curiosity about the world outside, it is likely that a not-so-small number of nuns cross, to varying degrees, the line of "Buddhist morality" once or twice, perhaps more, in their lifetimes. On these momentary transgressive occasions, some of them make an alternative space for themselves that is not defined or recognized by the monastic rules or their vows. Through this, they breathe alternative air for a moment, which eventually leads them to reanchor themselves on firmer moral ground. To them, practicing Buddhism is not simply about accepting precepts, regularly performing rituals, or meditating daily. For many nuns in Yachen, practicing Buddhism is a constant process of renewing moral boundaries, creating the self, and sharing life in intimate spaces. The nuns' room decorations show how the nuns actually live in Yachen and how they treat the mundane objects and surroundings in their lives. Their decorations are not merely a reflection of their aesthetic moods in daily lives; they are also a reflection of their determination and the actions they take to pursue their own life paths firmly and quietly.

4

NEW GESTURES

The thousands of flickering lights of the Tibetan butter lamps (*karmé* [*dkar me*]) in Yachen's main assembly hall exude a calm, meditative atmosphere. The lights are warm yet also imposing, allowing the disciples who walk into the hall to feel a sort of solemn devotion. With their distinctive smell and luminosity, the butter lamps capture an experience specific to Tibetan monastic halls. Although butter lamps can be found everywhere in Yachen, from the lamas' residences to gathering halls, to individual nuns' huts, one particular hall in the monks' area is dedicated to keeping thousands of butter lamps lit daily all year round. There, the lamps sit in rows on the long tables that encircle the inner hall, inviting a quiet attentiveness from visitors. Yet the lamps are not just a mood enhancer; they also signal the spiritual liveliness of Yachen, where great teachings are actively sought and continuously transmitted. Among the numerous and endless visitors in the hall, however, few people know, or feel the need to know, how such a large number of lamps remain lit every single day. In fact, managing thousands of butter lamps requires an enormous amount of physical labor; the individual lamps must be cleaned thoroughly before they are refilled once the old wax has burned away. Lighting, cleaning, and refilling the lamps are tasks that must be repeated thousands of times a day to make possible this special meditative space in Yachen (figure 15).

Dawa, a Tibetan nun from Kham, was one of the nuns who took care of the butter lamps in this assembly hall in Yachen. As of summer 2016, she had been commuting between her hut and the hall to light the lamps every day for about seven years. Upon arrival, she began her job each day by using pieces of fabric

FIGURE 15. The nuns lighting the butter lamps in the hall. Photo by the author, 2016.

to clean thousands of individual lamps, a laborious task that took several hours because the remaining wax in the bottom of the lamps was often difficult to remove. Once the cleaning was done, Dawa poured the hot liquified wax into individual lamps in which other nuns had already placed wicks. By late afternoon, when all the butter lamps were lit and arranged neatly on the tables in the hall, Dawa and the other nuns in her group would be covered in soot and sweat, often with burn marks on their hands. This was also around the time that the monks began entering the hall to recite scriptures or take afternoon classes. Dawa and the nuns would rush to finish their remaining tasks before all the monks arrived. The scene of monks flooding into the butter lamp–lit hall, fully ready to receive teachings and recite scriptures, created a striking contrast with the remaining nuns in the hall, who were soaked in sweat and dirt from the lamps, and who must have been hurriedly withdrawing from the hall.

In Yachen, the nuns take turns at various communal labor assignments, but because of the specific skills and experience required for dealing with wax and fire, the task of attending to the butter lamps is usually assigned to a single group of nuns for an extensive period. Since Dawa was assigned to this task, in service of making sure that the lamps are always lit, she had relinquished attending all classes, small-group studies, and daily chanting sessions as well as any rituals in Yachen that conflicted with her lamp-cleaning tasks. The proper management of the lamps took priority over her other practices and studies. Judging from her attitude toward the lamp work, however, Dawa did not consider it a sacrifice that she had missed all the opportunities that she and other nuns initially sought when they came to Yachen. She did not think that she had been discriminated against or mistreated by the head office for having to do this task. In fact, it was quite the opposite; she believed that she was assisting in something important that had to be done by someone, and she had been honorably chosen to do the endlessly repeated physical labor of caring for the lamps as part of the sacred affairs of Yachen. While I fully respect Dawa's perspective about the lamp task and her long-term assignment to it, what remains unclear is why only the nuns are mobilized to do such physically demanding work for such a prolonged period in a hall that is located in the monks' quarters and is used exclusively by the monks.

In Yachen, to speak about gender issues as they are broadly understood in Western scholarly discussions—in terms of gendered inequalities, discrimination, and norms—is to attempt walking a tightrope. The employment of Western feminist liberal politics—which often emphasizes entitlements, rights, and the status of women in society at large—to measure and discuss gender (in)equality in Yachen relies on an outside point of view; simplifies the issues involved; and results in ignoring the voices of the Tibetan nuns, who say that they feel almost no gender discrimination in Yachen. On the other hand, following a more contextually grounded approach—which is attentive to the local and historical specificities in which the women are situated and which emphasizes the voices of women within such contexts to explore and redefine the agency of women—may not be immediately or fully applicable to the nuns in Yachen either. This is partially because the nuns in Yachen are not participating, or mobilizing themselves, in any socially and religiously recognizable "movements" or actively "voicing out," as women are doing in other contexts such as the Islamic revival (e.g., Mahmood 2005). In Yachen, gender issues as they are understood in the Western sense have little currency in themselves; if they are ever evoked in such a sense, it is likely in temporary circumstances, such as when an outsider like myself poses a question about gender and demands an answer. In these unusual situations, such questions are unlikely to change the nuns' firm belief that no gender bias exists in Yachen.

The Tibetan nuns in Yachen rarely advocate for or engage in political agendas of their own or for any other group, nor do they develop or articulate a communal perspective in this regard. They rarely offer explanations for or assign to their actions any special meanings that would indicate a collective feminist consciousness. Topics such as equal entitlements, rights, and status—for example, the issue of full ordination for nuns that has been raised and discussed in other Buddhist contexts across Asia—rarely appear as part of their conversations or concerns.[1] Despite their lower monastic status (as not fully ordained), the Tibetan nuns with whom I talked simply disregard the existence or the possibility of any gender discrimination occurring in Yachen, and it is simply unthinkable for them to imagine a scenario in which they are discriminated against, especially when everything in Yachen is guided by Achuk lama (and now Tulku Asong). Apparently, the gender agendas that are widely upheld in Western feminist studies have neither the same potency nor the same suitability for identifying and analyzing gender issues in Yachen.

Is it then possible or reasonable to discuss the nuns' agency or the existence of gender discrimination when the nuns themselves are not seeking to challenge their status, the existing system, or the norms that treat them as lesser subjects than monks? Can raising an issue that does not currently register among the group of people involved result in *creating* an issue that has not organically emerged from within? Even if these questions are not appropriate to pursue, a trickier question nonetheless remains about whether it is fine to exempt from scrutiny the gender discriminatory arrangements, as in Dawa's case, that apparently do exist in Tibetan monasteries and Tibetan Buddhism at large. Does the nuns' seeming "nonaction" toward such arrangements automatically and instantly offer them intellectual immunity from examining and engaging in such matters at all? Do we (researchers, outsiders, and those who are interested in Yachen and Tibetan Buddhism generally) have any choice other than to accept this immunity?

While the nuns in Yachen do not perform the kind of organized actions that can be easily identified by outsiders, they are not socially paralyzed and do not limit themselves to traditionally subordinate roles either. As I stayed in Yachen over the years, I found that the nuns were fully participating in activities that used to be off-limits for them—although they were doing so in a less organized and less vocalized way than we might expect from self-conscious agents of change or resistance. For example, they take the initiative to learn new subjects (foreign languages, computers, medicine, etc.) that are far beyond traditional monastic educational criteria. They do all this without self-consciously formulated and expressed agendas, statements, or goals. In other words, the nuns innovate not because they are deeply critical of the misogynistic practices of Tibetan monastic systems and imagine themselves as reforming these practices but simply because they see opportunities for doing new activities that are possibly useful and good for them, and they straightforwardly and individually pursue these opportunities whenever they can. We therefore need an alternative approach for understanding

gender politics in a place like Yachen. Such an approach must begin with the recognition of a realm, perhaps much larger than the existing scope of gender politics, where the subjects do not always clearly articulate and enunciate particular
actions as part of an organized effort. The meanings, motivations, and expectations for particular actions may be unspoken and unorganized, even as the
actions nonetheless continue to take place and expand and alter circumstances.
At the very least, we should not take for granted the existence of linguistic registers, verbal reasoning, and a level of organization behind every action; a group's
actions can still produce significant effects without prior planning and without
clear articulations or awareness by the members of the group.

As a result, rather than searching for the reasoning behind and descriptions
of an action, I focus on nonlinguistic, material, and mundane aspects of the
lives of the nuns, including their bodily postures and bodily attitudes, in their
ongoing interactions with monks, lamas, and traditional monastic norms. In
these material and mundane realms, one can see how the nuns take actions to
embrace new learning opportunities that are not usually open to them while
simultaneously the most rooted and habituated gender norms continue to be
applied and performed. Actual and concrete changes to existing gender norms
in Yachen are not occurring because of changes to the nuns' entitlements,
rights, and status or because of a raised feminist consciousness or articulations
of that consciousness by the nuns. Change occurs instead in the thoroughly
material and painstakingly mundane realms of practice. Marcel Mauss (2006
[1935], 78) noted the "masses of facts," or the "miscellaneous" in our lives, that
are not yet reduced to concepts yet are themselves social phenomena. He
observed that individual bodily techniques, even the most subtle and mundane,
are not cultivated without a set of socially sanctioned assemblages (for him, the
most important of these were education and imitation). Buddhist nuns are a
special group of people whose bodily presentations offer a certain visible coher-
ence because of both the institutionalized codes of conduct and the culturally
embedded expectations that define who they are in the most fundamental and
corporeal sense. Their miscellaneous bodily arrangements, such as walking,
speaking, and posturing, and their relations to surrounding objects, spaces,
and other people (especially males) more or less follow a strict set of techniques
that make them properly nuns. I would like first to discuss these minute bodily
and mundane engagements that make them properly nuns in order to juxtapose them with how they have sometimes defied expectations.

Perhaps even as this book goes to press, Dawa and the other nuns, and if not
them then some other group of nuns, have gone to the hall to clean, refill, and
light the butter lamps and have then retreated from the hall before the monks
arrive. Yachen's thousands of lamps that are lit daily in this hall are inviting

monks, visitors, and pilgrims to the hall, but not the nuns who tend to them. Few pay attention to this fact, including the nuns themselves, because what matters is the presence of the sacred assembly hall with thousands of neatly arranged flickering lamps. Who did the work and who is simultaneously excluded from enjoying the hall is no one's concern as long as the lamps are lit. This serves as a reminder once again that talking about the nuns' lives and position in Yachen first requires one to go behind the clean and spiritual façade of flickering candles and into the grimy, physical world of the sites of labor.

In these dirty and sweaty sites, along with their silent and endless labor, the nuns are quietly and unassumingly beginning initiatives that have never or only rarely been attempted before in Tibetan monasteries. In their bodily gestures and specific code of conduct, the Tibetan nuns in Yachen are subject to the traditional roles and images of Buddhist nuns in Tibetan Buddhism; however, they have also played unfamiliar roles and presented unfamiliar images of themselves as they participate in activities that are not typical of nuns, including the exam taking and medical training that I will elaborate upon later in this chapter. What the nuns do and show with their new engagements is a redistribution of bodies and tasks; they disturb, albeit only momentarily, the customary expectations about the tasks considered proper for nuns' bodies.

I do not want to convey the idea that the nuns' overall status has improved significantly. With few exceptions, their position, both in Tibetan Buddhism in general and in Yachen in particular, remains largely the same. Therefore, it is important to begin by addressing what it has meant to be a proper nun in the Tibetan context. By focusing on bodily gestures and attitudes in particular, I want to show how profoundly embedded traditional expectations are and how unchanging the lives of the nuns have been in their daily settings in Tibet, and thus, how striking it is to see nuns who study and practice medicine and who manifest and debate their expertise in front of high-ranking lamas, to see how, in this regard, they are treated as serious practitioners equal to the monks.

Being a "Proper" Nun

Speaking about what makes nuns properly nuns may bear the risk of essentializing them in preconceived ways and thereby inadvertently reaffirming conventional norms about what it means to be a nun in Tibet. Because of this potential issue, I would like to show what the nuns' habitual attitudes and gestures toward their lamas and monks look like rather than attempt to define what a proper nun is in Tibetan Buddhism. Their attitudes, despite the specific context from which they are drawn, speak largely to how Tibetan nuns act, talk,

and behave in front of male monastic figures in Tibet. I believe such phenome-
nological observations will effectively show what makes them so-called proper
nuns at the deep bodily and unconscious levels operating in traditional as well
as contemporary Tibetan Buddhist contexts.

A Sense of Awe toward Lamas

One afternoon, the Tibetan nuns were reciting scriptures in the hall, a daily
chanting session in which the nuns communally prayed for donors on the
prayer lists.[2] Several thousand nuns, sitting closely in rows in the large hall,
were led by a precentor as they chanted scriptures out loud. Yet this ordinary
chanting session, usually uneventful, was abruptly disturbed that day. A few of
the front rows began to stir and the entire congregation began murmuring.
Tulku Asong (the head lama) was paying an unscheduled visit to the nuns'
hall. The chanting suddenly paused, and the well-arranged rows were instantly
muddled by a crowd of nuns running forward to get closer to their esteemed
teacher. (I doubt that this same situation would happen in the monks' assembly
hall because the monks have much more frequent meetings with their teacher.)
I was seated among the nuns in the hall that afternoon. As the congregation
scrambled in disarray, I was running, too, in hopes of figuring out and captur-
ing what was happening with my small camera. Tulku Asong soon appeared
and took a seat at the front. The chaotic crowd immediately halted its movements and became silent. Everyone was holding their breath to avoid missing a
single word coming from their most revered teacher. I kept moving slowly forward for a better view. As I did so, I recklessly stepped over a nun's scriptures
that were open on a reading stand on the floor. Because I did not touch either
the stand or the scripture, I thought there would be no problem, and I continued trying to move to the front. But I was soon stopped by a nun who grabbed
my arm. I was not fully aware of what I had done and why I was being stopped.
Holding my arm, the nun stared at me but didn't say a word.

Those wordless few seconds of silence, jumbled together with her doleful
face and dewy eyes, haunted me for a long time. I learned later that in Tibetan
Buddhist contexts, stepping over scriptures is considered an extremely disre-
spectful action. The nuns never place scriptures on the floor but always keep
them on a mounted stand and cover or wrap them with *khatak* ([*kha btags*] a
Tibetan ceremonial scarf) when they are not being used. If a scripture is acci-
dentally dropped on the floor, it is immediately picked up and touched to the
forehead, while the one who dropped it chants mantras to beg forgiveness. In
addition to scriptures, other objects related to lamas—including their clothes,
plates, bowls, furniture, vehicles, and even their leftover food—are considered

sacred. After learning this, I wished that the nun holding my arm had expressed anger or had admonished me. From her perspective, perhaps it was of little use to reprimand a careless outsider when something sacred had already been violated; paying a silent tribute to the situation might have been the only thing she could do in that disturbing situation.

This unfortunate event made me think further about how bodily gestures are one of the fundamental ways of respecting teachers, and about how thoroughly entrenched their teachers are in the lives of the nuns. In Yachen, the physical presence and absence of Tulku Asong greatly influences the general morale. Although there are no official announcements about his schedule, the nuns always carefully track his whereabouts; whether he is away, where he is traveling, and when he will return are focal topics for internal news circulation.[3] One summer, Tulku Asong's absence was extended for over three weeks because he was hospitalized in the city due to overwork. The news spread quickly among the nuns, who were extremely worried and gathered to pray every day for their beloved teacher's recovery. The changing conditions of his health were almost simultaneously transmitted to the nuns from various sources; photos of Tulku Asong in his hospital room in Chengdu, which captured him napping, eating, and smiling, were instantly circulated among the nuns. While his quick recovery was a great relief to everyone in Yachen, his extended absence continued to be the source of anxiety among the nuns. The nuns looked like nervous children waiting for a parent, even though they knew that their teacher was in the city, well taken care of, recovering, and coming home soon. The lives of the nuns in Yachen, without Tulku Asong's presence, seemed plunged into a state of emergency, with something essential missing or wrong. Tulku Asong, as he told me later, restricts himself from traveling for extended periods of time precisely for this reason.

In general, the emotional involvement of the nuns with Tulku Asong seems deeper than it is for other groups of practitioners in Yachen. Tulku Asong (it was Achuk lama before him), is almost the sole reason for the nuns to come to Yachen in the first place and then to remain there for the rest of their lives. Yachen is one of the few places in Tibet where nuns enjoy nearly full access to the highest teachings as well as to distinctive educational opportunities that few other places can offer (I will discuss this in detail later in this chapter). The nuns greatly appreciate Tulku Asong for his enormous compassion in allowing them to learn, practice, and explore these new opportunities. In addition, the geographic location of their quarters in Yachen heightens their appreciation of their encounters with Tulku Asong. Because the nuns' quarters are located farther away from the high-ranking male lamas' quarters, including Tulku Asong's, the nuns' chances of encountering these lamas in their daily lives are much lower than the monks' chances. Thus, for the nuns, unofficial encounters with Tulku Asong—for example, on the streets or when his car passes by—are treated as sacred and occult events.

Some might associate such sincere devotion and reverence toward the lamas with the tradition of "guru worship" in Tibetan Buddhism.[4] A guru, a tulku (reincarnated lama), or simply a lama (*shangshi* in Chinese) is an enlightened being who continues to appear, through reincarnation, in the world to teach and help sentient beings. Among the various Buddhist traditions across Asia, one of the distinctive features of Tibetan Buddhism is its institution of reincarnated lamas. The role of lamas in Tibetan society traditionally hasn't been merely as Buddhist teachers who reside in monasteries; lamas are at the center of all facets of the Tibetan way of life—they play the roles of educator, judge, doctor, and politician all at the same time (for example, the Dalai Lamas). In the case of Yachen, the emphasis on gurus is particularly prominent because of the dominant teaching in Yachen: Dzokchen, or Great Perfection. The success of this practice depends on the capacity of the teachers and the absolute faith of disciples toward them.[5] Given the combination of Dzokchen practice, the already important role assigned to teachers in Tibetan Buddhism, and the relative lack of opportunities for women in Tibet, it makes sense that Yachen's nuns demonstrate such profound reverence toward their teachers.

This reverence is coupled with a deep sense of awe—a complicated mix of esteem, devotion, and fear. One Tibetan nun often said to me, "Han Chinese have the guts to visit and talk to Tulku Asong all the time, but we dare not." The Tibetan nuns with whom I worked admired the head lama so profoundly that they wished to be near him and to breathe the same air as he did. At the same time, and precisely for the same reason, however, they were also deeply frightened of being near him and having a direct encounter with him. The nuns believe that their minds are too limited to fully process how wondrous a being Tulku Asong is, and being close to such a figure is an extremely nerve-racking experience. A nun once showed me a *tangka* picture from a book, saying, "This is our Tulku Asong." From my insufficient knowledge of tangka subjects, the picture depicted an image of a wrathful deity with multiple arms and standing on one leg, surrounded by many lotus petals and balls of fire. She pointed to the picture by using her entire right hand, palm side up (the nuns never use their fingers to indicate lamas and lamas' images), explaining that the actual appearance of Tulku Asong is just like this picture, but we are too ignorant to see his true form and can only see his human body. Although the figure's multiple arms symbolize his extended caring and compassion, the image is also frightening and alarming. In front of such a generous, powerful, and fearsome teacher, the mixed attitudes of wishing-to-be-near and daring-to-be-near are not surprising. Whenever the Tibetan nuns sense any sign of Tulku Asong's presence, they immediately stop whatever they are doing and bow down. For example, when Tulku Asong's white SUV approaches in the distance, the nuns move forward toward the vehicle and take off their hats, and bend deeply at the waist with their faces toward the ground until the lama passes by.

Nuns Serve Monks

Another widespread notion held in Tibetan Buddhism and Buddhism in general is the tacit acceptance of the idea that "nuns serve monks." It is a de facto long-standing gender norm in Buddhism, and most nuns in Yachen are not exempt from it. The risky trip to the hometown of Jubei (see chapter 2), a nun in the Tibet Autonomous Region (TAR), allowed me to see one such gender-bound occasion that the nuns commonly experience in their daily interactions with monks.

As I have already recounted, the time when Jubei and I traveled was politically sensitive for both of us, and our IDs and appearances could have caused trouble, so we planned to avoid towns that had stringent checkpoints, and we tried not to register in any hotels on the way that might attract unnecessary attention from towns we did pass through. Our cautious measures forced us to travel eventually in a severely roundabout way, but we both agreed that this was the right decision. As we passed through a small provincial border village between Sichuan and the TAR, we spent one night in a monastery where Jubei had a connection with a monk through her relatives back home, although she had never met him. We were allowed to unpack our heavy backpacks late that night in a room in the two-story Tibetan house led by the monk. I realized only later that this entire house was the monk's residential unit and that the monastery was made up of many such houses for individual monks.[6]

We were not fully aware until the next morning of how generous the space was that this ordinary monk owned. The room we were led to and slept in, undecorated and unfurnished, was a spare room on the second floor next to his living room, which contained a TV and an electric stove. This entire two-story, Tibetan-style house with its spacious front yard belonged solely to the monk, and each monk in this monastery had a more or less similar house for himself. Such houses indicate the amount of financial support these monks receive from their families and patrons. Based on this and other trips I took later to monasteries in Tibet, it is safe to say that such living conditions for monks are not unusual but are difficult to imagine for most nuns in Tibet.

Jubei and I went to a small market and bought vegetables and fruits to make dinner for us and the monk as a gesture of gratitude for allowing us to stay in his quarters. Upon returning from our shopping trip, Jubei began cleaning the house and making dinner in the monk's kitchen. I assisted her. The monk stopped in and saw that we were in the kitchen. A short while later, he passed a chunk of meat to us and went out again. Perhaps he thought that meat was missing from our meal and his way of treating us was to provide meat for the dinner. When dinner was almost ready, he appeared with two junior monks, similar to or younger in age than Jubei. Within an hour or so, Jubei had prepared three flavorful dishes, plus a soup and rice. This was a banquet by Yachen's standards. The three monks were seated at the center of the table and Jubei and I took the corners. Throughout dinner, Jubei served them hot tea and food, and refilled their rice bowls as soon as she saw that the bowls were empty. I again assisted her at the table in whatever way I could. The conversations took place mostly among the monks, as if we were eating at separate tables. Once dinner was over, Jubei began cleaning the table and washing the dirty plates. Jubei and I constantly checked the living room and the table to see whether there were residual chores that we needed to attend to. Meanwhile, the monks sat with their torsos against the wall, comfortably stretching out their legs in front of the TV and sipping hot tea.

Before dinner, Jubei even suggested a separate table for us. She either thought it was inappropriate to sit at the same table with the monks or simply felt shy about doing so. But because it was inconvenient to set up two dinner tables in someone else's house, she reluctantly took a seat at the edge of the table; she seemed to negotiate this inappropriate situation by playing the role of waiting on the monks. It was a family-style dinner where people share all the dishes placed at the center of the table. But during dinner, her body was bent over like a ball and her arms occasionally reached out to the one dish that was relatively close to her; she barely touched the other dishes that were close to the monks, avoiding eye contact with them and remaining almost silent except when she was asked to reply. On the other hand, the monks stretched their bodies out, their postures were relaxed, and their voices were loud and confident. The gendered bodily postures assumed by the monks and Jubei were starkly contrasting, and their gendered roles were seamlessly performed. I did not view Jubei's actions as exaggerated or unusual; any Tibetan nun would likely act in a similar way in front of monks regardless of their age or status. Such embedded attitudes, gestures, and ways of acting by the nuns and monks when encountering one another are both social and individual. They belong to a kind of habitus (Bourdieu 1977) that is inscribed in their respective bodies, a safe and structured way to reaffirm who they properly are in various situations. Given these firmly rooted gender roles, the fact that the nuns in Yachen make tea and food for the monks during rituals is not at all unusual; it is a socially expected, bodily ingrained, taken-for-granted service provided by the nuns.

Nonetheless, the nuns in Yachen do not simply and always succumb to conventional gender roles; they are no longer only submissive and supplemental in monastic activities. They appear increasingly at the center of major events, presenting authoritative knowledge and expertise of their own. While the fundamental monastic gender norms are still in operation and routinely upheld in Yachen, some occasions provocatively overturn such norms and expectations. In the following sections, I introduce two initiatives—the annual oral exam and medical nun training—that were undertaken in recent years to improve the nuns' education and welfare in Yachen. These initiatives alter significantly, albeit not yet permanently, the traditional roles, attitudes, and bodily gestures accepted as necessary for being a proper nun in the Tibetan context.

The Annual Oral Exam

Dolma's voice started trembling. Her vocal tremors were simultaneously transmitted through the microphone to a few thousand nuns in the assembly hall as well as to the several thousand more outside the hall who were listening to her oral presentation via a livestreaming radio broadcast. The quavering was so pronounced that I could vicariously feel her anxiety on the stage. The large video screen next to Dolma, a device somewhat out of place in Yachen, also doggedly captured her awkward bodily movements. The overall atmosphere of the hall was quite tense because this was the largest and most important yearly exam to take place in the presence of the head lama, Tulku Asong, along with other high-ranking lamas and khenpos.

When Dolma's turn arrived, she walked toward the stage and paid homage to the ten or more lamas who were sitting in front of her. The lamas' seats and the stage were shaped like a large rectangle, with the stage on one side and the other three sides occupied by the lamas. Outside the rectangle was the remaining space of the hall, where the audience was seated to watch the exam (figure 16). In this arrangement, the distance between Dolma and the head lama was about ten meters, which was close enough to make her extremely nervous; in addition, Tulku Asong would be focused solely on Dolma during the exam. It was one of the most glorious and blessed moments of her life and, at the same time, one of the most agitated ones.

After bowing to the lamas, the nun next to Dolma announced Dolma's full name and the subject that she was going to present at the exam. Each nun had prepared an individualized subject so that the lamas and the audience needed to be informed about what subject would be discussed on the stage. Following the announcement, Dolma began speaking phrases from the scriptures that she

FIGURE 16. The nuns taking exams. Photo by the author, 2013.

had learned by heart through the microphone. Although her voice was trembling and her face blushed, Dolma managed to continue her oral presentation for a while until she suddenly paused, at a loss for words. She seemed to be falling apart and failing to overcome the enormous pressure of public presentation, perhaps her first experience of this kind in her life. The audience held its breath. Some nuns began intoning mantras, and others began to repeat the lamas' names. Tulku Asong, while looking at Dolma breaking down on the stage, picked up a microphone and initiated some small talk with her. Dolma seemed almost frozen. He began asking her questions about her hometown and some other easy questions that Dolma couldn't fail to answer. After engaging in this back and forth for a few minutes, Dolma seemed to grow calmer, and a light smile even appeared on her face. Tulku Asong chanted briefly as he finished the conversation with her. Dolma was able to resume her presentation shortly after in a much calmer voice, and the audience shared a sense of relief.

Once a year, for about three weeks, between late August and early September (two weeks for nuns and one week for monks), Yachen is engulfed in the feverish milieu of the annual exam. The exam consists of a lively oral presentation that includes a question-and-answer period between the lamas and the exam takers.

For the nuns, it is a very special, if not the only, opportunity at an official event for them to take the stage as independent practitioners who engage in intellectual conversation with the lamas. During the exam, the usual monastic activities, such as afternoon prayers and classes, are either rearranged or suspended. Most of the androcentric arrangements made in Yachen, such as the nuns making tea and their labor mobilization for communal construction projects, are also temporarily suspended or significantly reduced (except for the task of lighting the butter lamps). Because of the extended time and attention required of the lamas for the exam, the usual daily affairs of Tulku Asong and other high-ranking lamas, such as receiving disciples, lecturing, and transmitting teachings, are also either rearranged or simply canceled. During the exam period, radios actively stream the event the entire time so that the nuns continue to listen to the performances of their fellow nuns even when they are physically away from the hall. In addition to listening to the exam, they also talk about it and share various experiences about it throughout the day: who won the prizes, the anxious moments, the mistakes the nuns made, the lamas' reactions, and so on. Stories like Dolma's are circulated widely across the community with an emphasis on the deep compassion and thoughtfulness with which their head lama so wisely handles such situations.

With the exam day approaching, the pace of the nuns' daily activities in Yachen increased. The nuns who were taking the exam were busy preparing while they also did their daily tasks such as chanting, communal labor, and taking classes. Chegga, a nun from the TAR, was one of the exam takers who was too busy to sit down for a moment to talk with me at this time of the year. One day, when she had a little spare time before her class, she opened a book, telling me that she must memorize an entire section by rote for the exam. The section was from a voluminous Buddhist scripture that she had been learning for the past few months in her small study group, and it was long enough that just reading it filled half an hour. Like Chegga, other nuns who were preparing for the exam scheduled segments of time during their hectic days to study their exam subjects. For those nuns who were taking the exam and who had to multitask to prepare for it, and because of all the general fuss around it, the exam in Yachen in fact began long before its actual dates.

Small study groups are another important initiative for the nuns in Yachen, along with official lectures, rituals, and chanting. Small study groups are tailored to the specific needs of individual nuns and include not only supplemental scriptural studies but also language studies, such as learning the Tibetan alphabet, grammar, and composition. Tibetan language training is an urgent need for many nuns in Yachen who have never been to school or have insufficient education for understanding scriptures and advanced practices. Although Yachen's focus is on personal meditation rather than textual analysis and reasoning, a full command of reading and writing in Tibetan is nevertheless considered crucial for the nuns if they are to continue advancing in their practices, which will eventually allow them to become mature, independent practitioners. Yachen's head office has recognized the lack of general educational opportunities for Tibetan girls, particularly in the rural regions from which many nuns come. Tibetan language training in Yachen has been undertaken precisely to resolve this deeply rooted problem for the nuns. Therefore, the "small" groups that focus on the Tibetan alphabet, for example, are often quite large, with hundreds of nuns in one group. More advanced language groups tend to be smaller in size, and they usually focus on grammar and composition. These groups are often led by fellow nuns who are fluent in Tibetan writing and reading. In these small language groups, nuns who have studied well and for long enough are promoted to the position of teachers and go on to lead new groups of their own.

During my stay in Yachen, small groups were usually held twice a day, one in the early morning before the main lecture by Tulku Asong at 8 a.m. and one in the late afternoon around 3 p.m. after the communal chanting session. The morning groups on Buddhist textual subjects were usually led by khenmos and khenpos, and the afternoon groups were varied and flexible, so that subjects such as language training could be included. In these groups, the nuns were required to take frequent tests and complete daily assignments. Based on their performance in the classes, the small-group teachers, usually khenpos, would recommend and select exam takers each year. Chegga was chosen for the exam two years in a row for her apparently superb performances in her small group.

Eligibility for the exam is not strict; anyone who has finished her three-year novice training is allowed to participate in the exam. Although the subjects for the exam are largely about the Buddhist scriptural knowledge that the nuns learn in their small groups, the subject matter for the tests is quite flexible. For example, in consultation with their monitor nuns, exam takers are allowed to expound on subjects of their choice, such as *tangka* paintings, *torma* making,[7] or *gyaling* performance.[8] While these subjects are highly relevant to Buddhism, I found the exams to be even more diverse and radical in their subject matter. Quite often I was asked by the nuns whether I could play the piano or speak English and, if so, whether I could teach them these subjects. Many nuns I met in Yachen sought opportunities to learn new things and saw outsiders as providing such opportunities. While the nuns saw these as open-ended learning requests, they also expressed their wish to demonstrate such newly learned skills in front of Tulku Asong at the exam. In general, learning itself is highly encouraged in Yachen; thus, whether the subjects are related to Buddhism or not, education is considered an extremely respected and valuable activity, and the exam is one platform for the nuns to achieve this value. A nun put it this way: "In the exam, we can bring up any subjects that we newly learn while we are in Yachen."

In one exam session, a nun brought out a laptop and projected its screen onto the large screen next to her. She thus demonstrated her skills of inputting Tibetan script into a word-processing program. Tulku Asong liked this. Some nuns submitted themselves to be tested in the exam on their Mandarin speaking and reading.[9] Basic English speaking was also performed, albeit only by a few nuns. The exam is the crux of the educational enthusiasm and the freedom to learn that is spread among the nuns in Yachen. It should be noted, however, that Yachen did not start this way. The improvement of the nuns' education and the accompanying rise in their status in this regard were not components of either the initial or the primary schema of those monks and practitioners who led Yachen at the beginning in the 1980s. Although Achuk lama, the inaugural head lama, allowed women to live and practice freely in Yachen, recognition of the existence of fundamental social and monastic obstacles for the nuns and systematic efforts to alter such imbalances, including gendered discrimination in (monastic) society at large, had almost never been the subject for discussion, at least not publicly, until very recently.

Since Tulku Asong took charge of the head office in 2011, several innovative projects have been instituted in Yachen. Among the many lamas I met in Yachen and elsewhere, Tulku Asong is the one who saw through and frankly articulated the real problem that Tibetan nuns have faced in Tibetan Buddhism and Tibetan society.[10] He is fully aware that the unfair treatment of nuns is a norm that exists throughout Tibetan society, and his diagnosis is that the nuns' general lack of education is one of the main causes; however, the lack of education for nuns is, in fact, caused and reinforced by the misogynistic norms throughout society. The lack of education and misogyny comprise one entangled chain. Jubei's submissive actions in front of the young monks and their treatment of her attest to this point to some extent. In most cases, a Tibetan nun, regardless of how long she has practiced and how sincere she has been as a practitioner, is not treated as having the same religious authority as a monk who has undertaken a similar or even a smaller amount of practice. To stop this vicious cycle of cause and effect, Tulku Asong has initiated several innovations to improve the educational situation of the nuns, and the annual exam is one such initiative. Since the platform was established, the individual nuns have developed and expanded it in the most dynamic and active ways. The nuns with whom I worked in Yachen proudly hung their prizes in their rooms; on these certificates, the nuns' name, the exam subject, and the type of prize are inscribed. Through the exam, the nuns take the stage in public and are also recognized officially as independent, serious practitioners for their in-depth knowledge, expertise, and intellectual capability.

But despite the remarkable progress that the exam brings to the nuns' education, it should not be forgotten that initiatives like this are still unfamiliar to many Tibetan nuns outside a community like Yachen. Even in Yachen, the exam takes up only a few weeks of the year, and the actual exam takers, around two hundred each year at the most, represent a very small portion of the entire population of nuns. Furthermore, the swirl of technological facilities set up for the exam, such as microphones, projectors, screens, and professional video cameras, enhances the sense of uncanniness since most of the nuns have never seen, much less been surrounded by, so much equipment. When the exam is over, once again the nuns make tea and food for the monks and are mobilized for communal construction projects.

This doesn't mean that the exam has little actual benefit for the nuns. During the exam at the very least, the nuns' status is de facto improved and Yachen's androcentric arrangements are temporarily dismantled. We can see the exam as a temporary overturning of gender norms that may cause other effects or transform certain contexts. Once a year, some of the nuns are hurled into an unfamiliar sphere where they perform beyond who they supposedly are and what they supposedly do in a traditional context. During this time, the nuns are no longer treated as anonymous bodies with robes and shaved heads among thousands of indistinguishable and interchangeable practitioners in a Buddhist throng. Each nun on the stage is individualized with her own name, gestures, and voice. These nuns certainly "have a part" to play (Rancière 1999). They are no longer in the background; and in fact, other bodies, including those of the male lamas, become the background instead. Dolma's body, quivering on the dais, produced an immediate sensory awareness among the audience. Her voice was transmitted through a microphone, and her subtle bodily gestures, eye contact, and the rhythm of her breathing commanded the full attention of everyone in the hall. What was being produced was a bodily inversion of what is expected from the nuns; their habitually and ethically bounded ways of being—how they act, talk, and walk, and how they embody what it is to "properly" be a nun—were upside down in that moment and in that space.

What Dolma demonstrated in the exam and what her fellow nuns witnessed was the suspension of a psychophysically embedded set of bodily techniques and the initiation of another set of techniques and relationships that were previously unimaginable. The exam therefore is not merely a temporary system implemented for the nuns but a dynamic platform that offers new possibilities and that forges and reassembles new and existing relationships and subjectivities in unexpected ways among and beyond the nuns themselves. While the exam is only a short-term event and the nuns' unusual performances only graze the boundaries of the firmly embedded androcentric mechanism of Tibetan monasteries and society, it presents a story about nuns that is rarely told and that may have rhizomatic effects (Deleuze and Guattari 1987); namely, the nuns' initiatives, actions, and participations in and beyond Yachen. It is difficult, if not impossible, to locate single causes of such effects, or to identify a master-mind behind them. But such effects may nonetheless bloom and thrive any-where and everywhere, slowly yet firmly changing norms, rules, or minds. While the rhizomatic effect of the exam may take a long time to come clearly and substantially into view, what is important is that the exam continues to take place each year. Even after the forced reduction in Yachen's size since 2017, the remaining nuns have continued improving their expertise through the exam.

Medical Nun Training

A day or two during the two weeks of the exam are usually dedicated to a spe-cial group of nuns: the medical trainees. In 2011, Yachen's head office inaugu-rated two special, long-term medical training programs for the nuns. A small number of selected nuns were dispatched to outside medical institutions for intensive medical training. Another much larger group of nuns was also chosen and assigned to medical training within Yachen under the tutelage of the monk-doctor in the main clinic. In the annual exam, some of these medical trainees presented their medical knowledge—including knowledge of the symptoms of various illnesses and their diagnoses and treatments—that they had gained over their year of training within or outside of Yachen. Given that Tibetan medicine has traditionally been part of Tibetan Buddhist knowledge and monastic education and still is in some cases, training medical nuns in Yachen may not appear special in and of itself. But monastic medical education has rarely focused on systematically training ordinary nuns. With the relative lack of interest in educating women in traditional Tibetan society, nunneries in Tibet are unlikely to be equipped with the proper resources and personnel to transmit medical knowledge. For this reason, the newly emerging group of medical nuns in Yachen who are participating in well-organized medical train-ing and clinical practice in both Buddhist and secular institutions is a distinc-tive phenomenon. It showcases how the bodily techniques of being proper nuns can once again be overturned.

For decades, Yachen had a single medical facility that served both monks and nuns. This facility is located in the monks' area and had a monk-doctor and a few monk assistants serving the patients. Although the clinic expanded

slightly over the years as the population of Yachen grew, its capacity for handling patients was far short of what it should have been. The Tibetan nuns I
worked with spoke about the limited hours at the clinic and the long waiting
times when they visited. They also told me that they felt uncomfortable seeing a
male monk-doctor when they had female-specific illnesses; for this reason, they
often postponed seeing the doctor for as long as possible. Yachen's head office
recognized the urgency of having clinics for the growing number of nuns in the
community. As soon as Tulku Asong took charge of the head office, the medical
training program for the nuns was initiated. The goal of the program was clear:
nurturing a sufficient number of qualified nun medical practitioners to provide
stable and practical medical care for the nuns in Yachen.

The medical training program has instituted two tracks: one for dispatching
select groups of nuns to outside medical institutions and the other for educating another set of select groups of nuns in Yachen itself using Yachen's own
resources.[11] Although both training programs were initiated and have been
supported by the head office, the external program has received distinctive
input from a group of devout Chinese disciples who work in medicine. For
studying outside, a few groups of nuns, four to five each, were first sent to a
southern Chinese city to study the traditional Chinese medicine (zhongyi) in
which some Chinese disciples of Yachen were involved. These disciples, who are
medical experts, helped the nuns to settle in their institutions and began teaching them medicine in informal yet systematic ways. Soon, several more groups
of nuns were sent to Tibetan medical institutions as well as to Western biomedical institutions for training. The nuns spread out to small and large towns
across the plateau as well as to other Chinese regions; they sometimes moved to
different institutions according to the changing situations of the hospitals they
were in. The educational arrangements the nuns had in these institutions varied, although they were generally designated as a special type of apprenticeship
outside regular medical education. As special trainees, the nuns did not seek
medical degrees or certificates, and they were not enrolled in any formal programs or classes for credits. Their education was focused on obtaining practical
medical knowledge that could be used immediately once their training was
completed. About four years later, between the years of 2015 and 2016, these
medical nuns were all summoned to return to Yachen.

My first meeting with Dolka was in the Tibetan hospital in Kangding (Dart-
sédo) where she was spending her final year as a trainee in the winter of 2015.
Dolka and four other nuns were being trained in this hospital, which is one of
the country's flagship institutions for Tibetan medicine. Not long ago, they had
received Tulku Asong's request to return and were finishing their four years of
training in Tibetan medicine. Dolka and other nuns were trained mainly by a

Tibetan doctor-teacher in this hospital. After years of training, Dolka was able to assist her teacher in treating various patients and even in minor surgical cases. As the years went by, she began taking some of the classes with other medical students as well, and the doctors gave her separate exams tailored for her needs and situation. The relationship between the nuns and the doctors was mutually trustful and caring; the nuns followed and respected the doctors in a way that was similar to how they followed Tulku Asong. The doctors took special care of the nuns by letting them attend with other students when examining and treating patients and by helping them sometimes with groceries and other necessities. Dolka lived in a small dormitory near the hospital with other nuns; their basic living expenses were supported by Yachen. Yet living in a larger town always cost more money than Dolka expected, and she sometimes had to rely financially on her family.

The head office had opened several clinics in the nuns' area around the time these medical nuns returned. The newly opened clinics were largely based on using Tibetan medicine to treat patients. It was practically impossible to open a separate biomedical clinic in Yachen, and the trainees from biomedical institutions began working together in some of the Tibetan medicine clinics. In addition, the Chinese disciples helped to open a larger Chinese medical clinic in the nuns' area. Since 2016, the conditions of medical care in Yachen have changed dramatically. Several medical facilities in the nuns' area provided diverse medical care options for the nuns: Tibetan medicine, Tibetan biomedicine, as well as Chinese medicine. The nuns no longer had to wait to visit the clinic on a permitted day or stand in a long queue to see a doctor, nor did they have to feel embarrassed about discussing female illnesses with a monk-doctor. Based on their own preferences, they could also choose among different types of medicine and medical practitioners. The medical nuns who were trained within Yachen transformed how the original main clinic in Yachen operates as well; since the beginning of the medical training program in Yachen, nun trainees have been studying and assisting in the main clinic, examining patients, and prescribing herbal pills and other medicines. Approximately eighty Tibetan nuns who were in the active training program in Yachen, grouped in teams of twenty or so, take turns each week rotating between the main clinic and the small clinics in the nuns' area to study clinical exercises with their monk-doctor.

In 2016, when I saw Dolka again in Yachen, she was no longer just an ordinary nun; she was also a medical practitioner. She wore maroon Buddhist robes, but during the day, she put on a white lab coat over her robes. While other nuns went to their small study groups in the afternoon, Dolka would head to her clinic to see patients. Her clinic was a small room at the corner of a two-story building in the nuns' area where Dolka and other medical nuns had

FIGURE 17. The medical nuns seeing patients in their clinic in Yachen. Photo by the author, 2016.

arranged two tables and a couple of chairs for the examination of patients. A few shelves behind the tables were used to store various Tibetan herbal medicines. These medicines were purchased with the help of the doctors in the hospital in Kangding, where they had trained. Since the opening of the clinic, a stream of patients had visited each day. Many older nuns preferred Dolka's clinic in particular because it was close to their huts and because the clinic used Tibetan medicine, which was familiar to them. Dolka's attitude to her patients also added to the popularity of the clinic. After carefully taking the patient's pulses, Dolka would explain to the patient in great detail the meanings of each different pulse. She focused on patients' own stories as well—the kind of symptoms they felt, their pains, and their dietary habits—because all this information would help her to diagnose the illness (figure 17). Dolka wrote down the basic symptoms, pulses, and other specific details about each patient and, based on her notes, she prescribed medicine and wrapped herbal pills for the patient. In large script on each pill wrapper, Dolka marked the number of pills to take so that the patients could refer to it easily. The patients were charged a fee for the medicine they bought and nothing more.

What was impressive about Dolka was that her formal education had in fact ended in the middle of primary school. For various reasons, it is not unusual in rural Tibet for girls to drop out of school after or even before finishing primary school. The nuns with whom I worked normally would never imagine or expect to resume their education in secular subjects once they joined Yachen. Dolka never imagined that she would be trained in medicine. Dolka explained that, although her formal education was brief, she had studied Chinese on her own by, for example, watching TV throughout her childhood. When the medical training program was announced in 2011, she had a fair working knowledge of Chinese and Tibetan. The basic qualifications for applying to the training program at that time were the completion of an initial three years of practice in Yachen (usually the selected nuns had practiced in Yachen a lot longer than three years) and, most important, they had a good command of both Chinese and Tibetan. Because the selected nuns would live outside Yachen for a lengthy period, the ability to speak Chinese was crucial regardless of what form of medicine they were going to be trained in. Of course, for those nuns who were to study Chinese medicine and biomedicine, working fluency in both reading and writing Chinese was essential for their training. As soon as she heard the announcement, Dolka immediately expressed interest in this program to her monitor nun. After the initial selection process, Tulku Asong interviewed each nun on the final list. Based on his decision, approximately fifty nuns were sent to various medical institutions in different regions for their multiyear medical training.

Studies have pointed out that, in medicine, unlike other domains in Tibetan society, it is relatively easy for women to enter and build a career.[12] While politics and religion have mostly blocked women's participation, women can develop and thrive in careers as medical practitioners. Medicine seems to be the most likely realm in which an ordinary nun may have a chance to etch her name into history; and there are records of several historically renowned female medical practitioners in Tibet. But these medically gifted Tibetan women were mostly born to medical families and were able to succeed through family tradition because there were no proper male heirs available. It was also convenient and acceptable for their daughters to receive medical training because of the traditional apprentice-style of learning and teaching medical knowledge in Tibet. Although the introduction of medical colleges, such as the Chakpori [lcags po ri] Medical College in Lhasa in the seventeenth century and later the Lhasa Mentsikhang [sman rtsis khang] (The Institute of Tibetan Medicine and Astrology) founded by the thirteenth Dalai Lama in the early twentieth century, provided a more standardized curriculum for students, the apprenticeship system itself has been widely adopted for transmitting knowledge about Tibetan medicine.[13] Since the 1950s, when Tibet came under Chinese rule, the standardization and secularization of medical education have rapidly accelerated. But even under Chinese rule, individuals—mostly monks who claim to be medical experts based on their handed-down medical knowledge—have accepted students on their own and taught them individually in informal settings. A nun from Yachen told me that, for years before she became a nun, she learned medicine in a private class taught by a senior monk from her village. She would have been prepared herself to be a medical practitioner in informal village settings if the class had not been shut down abruptly by the Chinese government.

This type of apprenticeship system in medical education still exists outside the standardized formal education system in Tibet, especially in smaller towns and counties where centralized medical education is absent. Yachen's medical nun program adheres to this tradition of knowledge transmission, which has produced an informal agreement in Tibet that whoever has studied with qualified teachers can be a medical practitioner. What is also clear is that, just like the other exam takers in Yachen, a group of ordinary nuns who have been medically trained and can demonstrate special expertise, knowledge, and authority on matters that have been almost exclusively owned and performed by monks and male lamas have become a novel presence in Yachen and in Tibetan Buddhism. The medical nuns are now spreading throughout the nuns' residential area, diagnosing illnesses, explaining pains and symptoms, prescribing medicines, and administering injections to their sick fellow nuns. The medical nuns are inserting their unique expertise and knowledge into the mundane and material settings of Yachen.

Coda

A nun wearing a white lab coat in Yachen certainly creates a different impression and taking the pulses of a patient is certainly a different kind of bodily performance for a nun when seen, for example, in contrast to the lives of Jubei and Dawa. A nun debating and discussing in front of high-ranking male lamas about Buddhist scriptures and the medical knowledge she has learned is also quite unfamiliar to many people who are accustomed to how Buddhist nuns usually act and what roles they usually play in monasteries and elsewhere. I do not want to exaggerate the significance of this by implying that the nuns in Yachen are completely shaking up gender norms in Tibetan Buddhism or producing significant transformations of their status in Buddhism and society. But I also do not want to downplay the effects of their initiatives and activities in Yachen. At least it is certain that the exam takers and the medical nuns are disturbing the usual distribution between bodies and the tasks assigned to those bodies. In a Rancièrean sense (1999, 2004), the nuns' activities are political activities: they are shifting from their assigned places.

It remains to be seen what further effects will be produced from these new arrangements in the lives of the nuns. I suspect that any such effects will continue to be anchored in and expand from the mundane and material settings in which the nuns practice and live because these mundane and material contexts are where robust and unchanging gender norms are repeatedly played out and reinforced. Perhaps precisely for this reason, such contexts provide a space where the nuns' bodily presentations and performances can suddenly and substantively overturn these norms.

CABBAGE, TOFU, AND SAUSAGE

Before, during, and after my field research, friends and acquaintances alike who had heard about the living conditions in Yachen would ask me about the food situation. "What did you eat there?" "What do the residents of Yachen eat?" "Are there vegetables in Yachen?" Whether these questions arose out of curiosity about the nuns and the place or out of a concern for my well-being, they reflect one of the fundamental material conditions of human beings: we must consume food to survive. But my intention to discuss food in Yachen is neither because it is so essential to human survival nor because I'd like to satisfy some curiosity about how and what the Tibetan nuns eat and cook in a remote Buddhist encampment. Instead, I would like to emphasize that food and eating, so material and so mundane in and of themselves, have generated a transformative effect regarding how Tibetan Buddhism is practiced among both Tibetans and non-Tibetans in the contemporary era. Through unassuming, nonpolitical, and makeshift assemblages, food and eating play a central role in changing not only the dietary regulations but also the ethnic relations among practitioners in and beyond Yachen.

No communal dining is provided in Yachen, so individual practitioners must spend a good deal of time each day buying vegetables in the markets and preparing their own meals in their tiny kitchens. Despite their existential significance and the time required, however, food and eating (including cooking) in Yachen are often given far less priority than the apparently loftier and more spiritual affairs such as meditating, chanting, and performing rituals. Yet it is precisely through their mundanity and materiality that food and eating pose a challenge for Buddhist practices because they foreground one of the most resilient desires and attachments: the pursuit of appetite, or the gustatory pleasures that cloud the path toward enlightenment. In a Buddhist context, in other words, food and eating, despite their "triviality," are often targeted, and thus oddly centered, as something crucial to overcome and to control fully for the integrity of one's sincere practice. To add to this complexity, Yachen's specific ethnic arrangements—with Tibetans in the majority and holding (religious) authority over Han Chinese—reveal another important yet hidden aspect of food politics: food and eating serve to categorize different ethnic groups according to distinctive senses of morality. Discourses around what to eat, what not to eat, how to eat a certain food, or how not to eat it are frequently circulated among the nuns and are often used indiscriminately to gauge the Buddhist ethics of the other group who does not or cannot follow the same criteria for dietary selection and consumption.

Anthropological studies of food have already shown that food is more than merely a material object that maintains the biological metabolism of human beings; its production, consumption, circulation, and treatment are culturally, sociopolitically, and historically bounded.[1] Food indicates and partially defines who you are in the most mundane and intimate ways, as well as through the social contexts and norms in which you are embedded. Food, as "a liminal substance" (Lupton 1996, 16), straddles nature and culture, the inside and the outside, and the physical and the spiritual. In the context of Yachen, particular food items and their proper eating methods and nutritional value have become the source of discourse about which ethnic group owns the particular knowledge and infrastructure that provide and circulate the "right" kinds of food and at the same time exclude the "wrong" kinds. The notion of "right" and "wrong" food choices and the treatment and preparation of food are subsequently attached to the right and wrong way of practicing Buddhism. I argue that the role of Chinese disciples (including lay devotees), through their distinctive devotion, networks, desires, and knowledge, has been decisive in transforming the foodscapes in Yachen and Tibetan Buddhism over time. I do not view these disciples as intentionally setting a goal to change Yachen and Tibetan Buddhism through food. But in these utterly mundane contexts, their focus on what they think is crucial to becoming the right kind of Buddhist practitioner ultimately results in their own version of a politics of tranquility.

Food in Yachen, through its essentiality and mundanity in human lives, has disturbed the assumptions about the everydayness of Buddhist practitioners both in Yachen and beyond. I discuss how banal food items such as tofu, cabbage, and sausage are brought in, consumed, and prohibited and are thereby changing the daily lives of the Tibetan nuns in Yachen. In this process, ethnic hierarchy and Buddhist morality are constantly renegotiated. The definition of what makes a proper Buddhist practitioner is constantly reset and renewed according to the Chinese standard, and the Tibetan practitioners often end up adopting this new regulation. While food primarily provides nutrition and affects metabolism, it also evokes discourses, networks, and forms of awareness that link bodies, knowledge, and power to one another. In Yachen, food often serves as a material source of moral judgment for signaling what is a good and proper way of practicing Buddhism. This "liminal substance" is neither innocent nor neutral in Yachen; it resonates with and reflects the larger sociopolitical contexts and power grids in which ethnic demarcations have long been reproduced and sustained in China.

The Foodscape of Yachen

Yachen originally had two large vegetable markets, one each located in the nuns' and monks' residential areas (figure 18). Later, several smaller vegetable shops were added in the nuns' area to accommodate their growing numbers. Yachen's head office exercises fundamental authority over all market businesses

FIGURE 18.   A vegetable market in Yachen. Photo by the author, 2013.

in Yachen, including shops, restaurants, lodgings, and so on. This means that any private vendor who wants to open even a small street shop in Yachen must seek permission from the head office and pay rent and other fees for their business. The head office also runs several main shops in Yachen to ensure a stable supply of the basic necessities for its residents. These shops are usually managed by the nuns and monks themselves. In the case of the vegetable shops, the head office consigns a couple of merchant groups, usually kin-based groups of Chinese vendors, to supply vegetables to Yachen year-round. Transporting fresh vegetables from faraway Chinese cities and towns for thousands of people each week is too much for a busy monastic head office to manage. In addition, the daily inclusion of green vegetables in ordinary meals is not part of the traditional Tibetan diet, and it was certainly not something that was provided to the practitioners when the encampment was established. It is not unusual to see solitary Tibetan practitioners who sustain themselves with a very simple diet of tsampa and hot tea. In the beginning, this was a typical diet for Tibetan practitioners in a secluded hermitage. Now, even in Yachen, very few Tibetan nuns live on only tsampa and tea; vegetables and Chinese spices have become a major part of their ordinary diet. The vegetable shops are examples of the most visible Chinese intervention in Yachen.

While the head office allows particular groups of Chinese vendors to monopolize the vegetable markets in Yachen, it also places a strict condition on their businesses: they cannot randomly increase the prices of the vegetables. If the sellers fail to abide by this condition, their contract will be nullified and they will be replaced. In this way, the head office controls the market price and secures a stable vegetable supply for the entire population of Yachen.[2] Practitioners in Yachen do not spend time cultivating land for food; this was certainly not considered a "job" they should be doing as full-time practitioners, although some Chinese nuns who had relatively spacious front yards cultivated these small plots of land and grew vegetables during the summer for their own consumption. But even in that case, cultivation remained at a modest level, and the population of Yachen relies solely on foods transported from outside. Therefore, having a monopoly on the entire vegetable supply for Yachen is a highly lucrative business, and the Chinese merchants who are chosen to do business bring in their kin members from their natal hometowns. They work and live together for an extended time by setting up tents next to the market building. They eventually leave Yachen when they have earned enough money to make other investments. When I first visited Yachen in 2010, the seller group was from a small town in the Hubei province of China; by 2014, that group had left and another group, also distant relatives of the previous group, had taken up and continued this profitable business.

As I examine the mechanism of food consumption and the food discourses circulating among the nuns in Yachen, I see more clearly the entrenched Chinese involvement in Yachen and more broadly in the contemporary Tibetan Buddhist revival. I do not only mean the handful of Chinese vegetable merchants who monopolize one of the main food staples in Yachen. The Chinese nuns, albeit only a few hundred, and the much larger number of Chinese disciples outside Yachen engage in a particular dietary practice and, in doing so, they also cultivate a moral standard of eating for the proper Buddhist practitioners. In general, the "Chinese influence" in contemporary Tibetan Buddhism has become widespread and crucial; the presence of Chinese disciples in major Tibetan monasteries is well documented, and their devotion is often expressed in the funding of new monastic structures; the lamas' active travels to Chinese cities and abroad; and the numerous self-organized, on- and offline Buddhist groups in cities.[3] All these activities are undeniably forming and transforming a significant part of the current Tibetan Buddhist revival in China.

Sino-Tibetan ethnic politics, which includes ethnic hierarchization, discrimination, and more, ceaselessly applies in the Buddhist context, even if it doesn't exhibit the same violent, obvious, or destructive elements that apply in other cases. If we think of ethnic politics in terms of the actions of one dominant group trying to change what has fundamentally defined another group, whether by force, negotiation, or assimilation, such a politics is taking place in Yachen, although in a much more nuanced manner. The Chinese disciples in Yachen and in Tibetan Buddhism focus on self-care and self-improvement as Buddhists rather than on changing others' way of life per se. In the same vein, the foodways imposed by the Chinese practitioners in Yachen are, first and foremost, intended to help them personally cultivate rightful Buddhist selves; their foodways do not belong to a political agenda intentionally aimed at demonstrating to Tibetans how to be good, self-caring Buddhist-citizen subjects in China. Nonetheless, certain political effects arise through the nonpolitical and unassuming dietary practices exercised by individuals. Through the consumption and treatment of food, the Chinese practitioners are implanting, quietly yet profoundly, their version of the ideal Buddhist subject into the daily lives of Tibetan practitioners. The Tibetan nuns in Yachen are now required to change their dietary habits based on new regulations for food consumption, instituted by the lamas, that are more and more influenced by Chinese foodways. Food and eating in Yachen aptly manifest the subtle yet enduring nature of a politics of tranquility, exercised by Chinese disciples, that is transforming the lives of the Tibetan nuns in their most mundane and material settings.

Providing concrete evidence for something that happens in such a nuanced manner is a challenging task, even for ethnographic engagements that aim to capture the subtle rhythms of individual lives. I cautiously offer the following observations, which are more "circumstantial" or "inferential" (Hastrup 2004) than concrete and evidential. In other words, I juxtapose related descriptions of food and eating across different settings in the lives of the nuns and Chinese lay disciples in Yachen and in a nearby Tibetan city to see how seemingly irrelevant, small actions, objects, and aims can usher in larger, fundamental transformations. In Yachen, a site that triangulates the material, the mundane, and the ethical, food is simultaneously nature, culture, and politics. In the following sections, I look at body-care talk, via cabbage and tofu, among the Chinese nuns; Tibetan nuns' conundrum about sausage; and stories about a vegetarian restaurant run by patrons in a Chinese city. These stories are not obviously and directly connected to one another initially but, as I show below, it would be naïve to treat them as completely unrelated.

Cabbage

The first meal I was ever offered in Yachen was a simple stir-fried green cabbage and a bowl of cold rice. On my first night, a Chinese nun, who allowed me to stay in her abandoned meditation cell, fixed me a quick meal. Without electricity, the dim bulb powered by her small solar energy panel added austerity to her already humble space. In this gloomy kitchen, she lit the portable gas stove and heated her aged wok. The cabbage sauté, seasoned with Sichuan peppercorns and salt only, was surprisingly tasty. I quickly cleaned my bowl. This simple cabbage dish, which I occasionally crave even now, was not only the first meal I had in Yachen but also the most common meal I ate there. Cabbage, along with potatoes, is the most widely available and most affordable vegetable in Yachen and is consumed by the nuns almost year-round. Based on how it was consumed and when it was consumed, this popular vegetable often became the platform for introducing a sense of moral superiority and reinforcing ethnic hierarchies and social classes among the nuns.

Cheyong, a middle-aged Chinese nun and one of my hut-mates in Yachen, liked to talk about the nutritional value of the vegetable she was cooking. Her knowledge about food came from commonly circulated wisdom in Chinese society about food and foodways as well as from her personal interest in health and bodies obtained through a wide range of reading. During the time I stayed with her, Cheyong was reading various books about general nutrition for bodies. One of her favorites at that time was a medical report written by a royal physician from ancient China who performed clinical trials on prisoners serving life sentences. The physician used these prisoners to conduct clinical tests of dietary treatments for a variety of diseases. The author then produced a grand food chart, based on his experiments, that explained various nutritional specifications, suitable cooking methods, proper eating seasons, and so on. Cheyong liked this book a lot because it was, as she told me, scientific and objective, supported by actual data from clinical cases. When she had meals with me, she kept the book at her side and often flipped through its pages to read passages to me when she found something worthy of review. Cheyong's interest in health and nutrition was not exceptional in Yachen; many Chinese nuns with whom I worked paid great attention to and were quite knowledgeable about the nutritional benefits of different food ingredients as well as basic human physiology and metabolism, or at least this is how they presented themselves.

Maintaining good health is crucial for continuing and advancing one's practices in Yachen. After spending a few years there, many Chinese nuns, even young ones, would find that their health was deteriorating. In particular, the harsh winters and high altitude posed dire challenges to the Chinese nuns, who were less familiar with the physical environment of the plateau. In addition, a relatively poor diet, lack of proper rest, and insufficient medical care tended to worsen their condition. Their failing health over the years in Yachen was often the decisive reason that drove them eventually to move back to Chinese cities. How to maintain good health and how not to lose the vital rhythm and energy of their bodies during their time in Yachen were, thus, popular themes and critical concerns among the Chinese nuns. They circulated books about health, supplemental foods, and other various health-related information and tips. Some Chinese nuns received comfort packages from their supporters (patrons, friends, and family members) that contained vitamin pills and nutritional supplements such as dried mushrooms, nuts, soybean flour, and herbal medicines, none of which were easily found in Yachen.

The Chinese nuns' vigilant attention to bodily health and their excessive dietary talk often turned to emphasizing ethnic hierarchies between Chinese and Tibetan nuns. Cheyong's deeper knowledge about nutrition and her well-regulated daily food consumption gave her a sense of superiority when she habitually compared her diet to those of the Tibetan nuns next door, who, from Cheyong's perspective, did not know or care about the importance of nutrition and health. One day, while Cheyong was cooking *dabaicai* (napa cabbage) for our dinner, she talked to me about how good *dabaicai* was for the body if it was consumed in summer but how harmful it was in winter. She often divided other vegetables between the categories of "cold" and "hot" and believed that practitioners should carefully choose the proper vegetables by following the changing of the seasons.

> You see? Those Tibetan nuns (*zangjuemu*)[4] eat *dabaicai* all winter! They don't know how harmful it is! *Dabaicai* makes your body cold! And they also use spices too much! I don't eat artificial seasoning anymore and even try to quit soy sauce as well, because they are harmful for meditation. But Tibetan nuns eat a lot of spicy foods and artificial seasoning that stimulates their stomachs! They're only concerned with *the transient happiness of their mouths and do not care about their bodies!* (emphasis added)

To Cheyong, consuming napa cabbage all winter, along with other "bad" dietary habits, revealed the Tibetan nuns' lack of crucial knowledge about human bodies and natural laws. Yet Cheyong's message did not point only to the Tibetan nuns' ignorance of certain food items, it also carried a Buddhist moral implication that, as Buddhist practitioners, what the Tibetan nuns were doing was wrong. In her remark, *the transient happiness of their mouths* was being juxtaposed and contrasted with *not caring about their bodies*. Although both mouths and bodies are part of human physiology, in a Buddhist context they convey starkly opposite ideas. *The happiness of the mouth* indicates subjection to bodily desires or bodily pleasures, while caring about the body is directed to the loftiest task of a good Buddhist, which is to seek the best bodily condition for receiving fundamental truths about life. In Cheyong's view, doing harmful things to one's body because of a lack of knowledge about food and nutrition is therefore unethical in a Buddhist sense.

The mouth here has become a contested bodily cavity, complicating the relationship between food and language. As a physical organ, the mouth absorbs substances that can generate sensory pleasure, which, to most Chinese nuns, is something to be on the alert for in their practices. The mouth's taste buds are sense organs that represent one of the most corporeal desires that any mature Buddhist practitioner should be able to recognize. In Cheyong's as well as in many other Chinese nuns' minds, the spiciness and artificial seasoning of the food that many Tibetan nuns indiscriminately consume is nothing more than a delusional, gustatory, and sensual happiness that will quickly dissipate and eventually hinder the proper way to practice Buddhism. According to Cheyong, strong seasoning often upsets the stomach and interrupts the tranquil mind, or *qi*, during meditation; such foods are signs of ignorance stemming from the mind of craving and attachment.

While the mouth is often treated by the Chinese nuns as a tantalizing physical organ that requires one's constant alertness, it also serves as a linguistic organ that produces discourses precisely for regulating, judging, and controlling such sensual desires. Many Chinese nuns with whom I worked habitually enunciated what was the "right" way of consuming foods and maintaining health in Yachen. By the time I was halfway through my fieldwork and after spending many mealtimes with Chinese nuns, I felt I had obtained a great deal of knowledge about the nutritional value of each vegetable and about the right methods and times for their consumption. By learning and incorporating specific dietary practices in their daily lives and by abstaining from gustatory desires altogether, Cheyong and many other Chinese nuns in Yachen detached themselves from what they saw as unhealthy and unethical habits and environments, and they also actively created new discourses and norms for pursuing what they believed to be the right way to practice Buddhism. The mouth is simultaneously a threat and an opportunity in this complex process.

The Chinese nuns with whom I worked transformed their concerns for health into an ethical practice by abstaining from sensory desires (savory foods) and thus turned themselves into ethical subjects through their acts of regulation. Furthermore, like Michel Foucault (1994), who understands ethics as linked to care of the self through technologies of living, Cheyong believes that taking good care of herself is an ethical action because doing so allows her to sustain herself in Yachen for a long time. Her specific food choices are thus an important part of her Buddhist practices. To Cheyong, food is not just an edible substance for maintaining her health but is also a form of technology that allows her to construct and renew herself as a proper Buddhist practitioner through the mechanism of self-regulation. Cheyong's ethical claim, expressed through the care of her body, serves as a means for transforming herself into a better person, an ethical being, and eventually a good practitioner. In Cheyong's eyes, Tibetan nuns who do not know or do not care about how to take care of their own bodies are not just culturally different others; they are also *ethically inappropriate*. They belong to the group of Others who lack the necessary knowledge to practice Buddhism properly.

By circulating health discourses and making them an ethical standard for practicing Buddhism, the Chinese nuns with whom I worked produced their own version of biopolitics and imposed it on Tibetan nuns and their bodies. The "bodies" are objects to be taken care of through universalizing tactics and knowledge that likely dismiss other particular (Tibetan) bodies. The Chinese nuns perhaps conveniently ignored the possibility that Tibetans, who were born and grew up in Tibet, might have their own techniques of body care and their own understanding about ways of living. Monopolizing knowledge in a particular and limited manner and applying it as if it were a universal standard causes serious misunderstanding about other bodies and results in pushing away, or constantly demarcating, those who do not possess the same knowledge or who are not interested in it in the same way. Many Tibetan nuns were not fully informed about and sometimes were not even aware of the implicit and explicit criticism they received from the Chinese nuns about their diet. The Tibetan nuns in general seemed less obsessed with food and health issues, at least not in the same way or with the same intensity usually shown by the Chinese nuns. Although it was in rather minor ways, the Tibetan nuns also sometimes shared a version of their own body-care talk and made comparisons between themselves and the Chinese nuns regarding tsampa, a specific food item.[5]

Tofu

For those who visit Yachen, Ganzi is usually the last stopover town before their final destination. When I did my field research between 2010 and 2016, the shuttle bus to Yachen ran once a day from Ganzi, and the bus tickets were sold a day before the departure. This arrangement forced, or rather allowed me, to stay for a whole day in the town before my departure the next morning. But on this supposedly restful day, I was in fact quite busy running "errands"—largely buying food items as gifts for the nuns. My backpack and suitcases were already loaded with sweets and instant coffee from the big cities in China and even overseas. Certain in-demand food items, however, such as tofu, had to be purchased from the closest local market. I observed that Chinese nuns brought tofu to Yachen and circulated it as gifts for fellow nuns or lamas; but they traveled infrequently, so I decided to bring tofu to Yachen whenever I could. Tofu, as a high protein substitute, is very common in Chinese markets but was extremely scarce in Yachen at that time. The vegetable markets there did not sell fresh tofu, at least not in the years I stayed in and visited Yachen. This was partially because of the inconvenience of its transportation and maintenance, but the main reason would have been the lack of market potential. Most Tibetan nuns did not seem to desire tofu as the Chinese nuns did, and Yachen's vegetable merchants could not see the monetary value in transporting tofu to this faraway highland for a relatively small number of customers.

Buying tofu and transporting it to Yachen was quite a laborious task, especially when using public transportation. Over repeated tofu deliveries, I invented my own system to deal with this tricky transportation process. There are usually three types of tofu available at the local market: dried tofu, dried roll-shape tofu, and white tofu (figure 19). White tofu seemed to be the most welcome of the three because of, I assumed, its freshness, rarity, and softer texture.

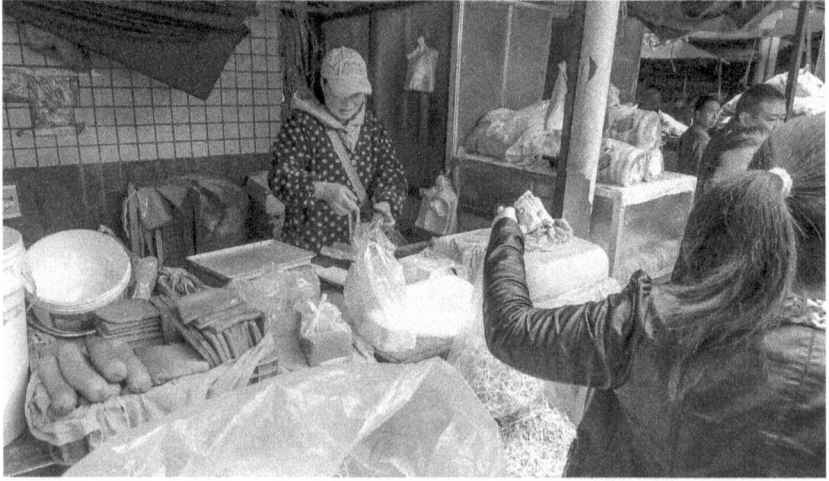

FIGURE 19.   Various types of tofu in a market stall in Ganzi. Photo by the author, 2015.

Before buying tofu, I bought a large plastic bucket that had a lid. Inside it, I carefully placed several chunks of white tofu individually wrapped in plastic bags. Then I would add the lid and tightly seal it with tape to make sure it would be safe for the five hours of bumpy travel the next morning. Because of tofu's high water content, the weight of the tofu bucket was almost the same as the weight of a bucket filled completely with water. Because of the difficulties in carrying this heavy bucket along with my other luggage the next morning, I would bring the tofu bucket to the bus stop the day before and load it onto the bus. The bus driver allowed passengers to preload their luggage on the day before departure because there was usually too much to handle in the morning, and it was more efficient to do part of the loading beforehand. The timing for transporting tofu is crucial as well; it must be transported before the sun is too high on the plateau. An early departure on the bus schedule was relatively safer for my tofu.

After I finished loading the tofu, I returned to the vegetable market to buy less delicate food products for the Tibetan nuns. The foods I bought for them, based on their preferences, were usually the spicy, saucy side dishes often sold at the street vendor stands—spicy glass noodles, Sichuan-flavored pickled vegetables, and deep-fried cookies. Although I enjoy them a lot myself, whenever I looked at these foods that were smothered and soaked in oils, artificial seasonings, and stimulating chilies, I felt a sense of moral dilemma: Should I bring these relatively unhealthy foods to the Tibetan nuns while I am bringing nutritious foods to the Chinese nuns? Because these were meant as gifts brought from outside,

I wanted to give the Tibetan nuns items that pleased them. I could not offer them "tasteless" tofu that they did not want and lecture them on how healthy it was, as the Chinese nuns often did. And I did not bring spicy street food to the Chinese nuns for fear of giving them a bad impression by presenting the wrong foods to them. It did not matter whether all Chinese nuns loved tofu and hated street foods (of course, some Chinese nuns were fond of spicy street foods, too); in this context, I wanted the gifts for the Chinese nuns to carry a positive meaning. Regardless of the specific preferences of individual Chinese nuns, tofu signified wellness, and that's what mattered. By the next morning, when the bus started, I often ended up carrying six or seven large bags of luggage filled with various food items for different groups. The ethnic demarcation in Yachen seemed to begin already in my luggage, and it reflected each group's different demands and divergent interpretations of foods and bodies as well as their different senses of taste.

Mary Douglas (1975, 249) says that food, as a code, carries messages about certain social relations: "The message is about different degrees of hierarchy, inclusion and exclusion, boundaries and transactions across the boundaries." Tofu is a bland product that has rarely been an appealing food choice for the Tibetan nuns, especially in a traditional context—it simply does not invoke *the happiness of the mouth* unless it is cooked skillfully with various seasonings and spices, which itself is difficult to do in Yachen. For the Chinese nuns, however, tofu seasoned with simple salt is a triumphant food substance that satisfies their nutritional, religious, and moral values. It is a material and nuanced code that reassures them of who they are and what Buddhist practitioners should be like. By consuming "tasteless" tofu and dissociating themselves from all artificial seasonings, including the five seasoning vegetables (*wuxincai* in Chinese),[6] Chinese nuns in Yachen have established a hierarchical as well as a moral boundary between the Tibetan nuns and themselves.

"Taste," as Pierre Bourdieu (2005, 74) puts it, is "class culture turned into nature." To the Chinese nuns with whom I worked, the ability to control gustatory desire and to practice bodily abstinence is a Buddhist moral claim; thus, to appropriate Bourdieu's expression, "taste" is "morality turned into nature." The Chinese nuns' tofu consumption, therefore, not only reflects their biological needs (protein, for example) and their preference for foods that promote good health; it is also tied to their lifestyle; cultural values; and, most of all, their moral superiority as Buddhists. It may also be a distinctive form of both subtle and strong self-identification for Chinese nuns living in a Tibetan-dominated space—a sense of class incorporated into the body and a set of moral claims that are undeniably connected to a "superior" Chinese society (in terms of knowledge, infrastructure, and technology). By taking care of their bodies through meticulous food choices and treatments, the Chinese nuns with whom I worked continued enacting ethnic hierarchization and performing cultural distinction.

We can go one step further and analyze the use of tofu from another perspective by using Michel de Certeau's (1984, 31) notion of consumption. He discusses consumption as "an entirely different kind of production. . . . [Consumption] shows itself not in its own products but in an art of using those imposed on it." Borrowing de Certeau's understanding of consumption practices, we can see that the Chinese nuns in Yachen are also producers: they use tofu to produce cultural distinction. Because of its rarity and its popularity among a select group, as well as the hardship involved in its transportation, tofu in Yachen *created* a distinctive and exclusive network in the political economy of food consumption. As I said, white tofu is a fragile, bulky, and delicate product that requires meticulous care from both sellers and consumers. Unlike the nicely packed tofu in the markets in cities, white tofu in a traditional market, such as the one in Ganzi, is usually sold unwrapped and unrefrigerated, so it must sell quickly and be stored as soon as possible in cold water or in a refrigerator. Not only does the need for prompt storage make it difficult to handle, but tofu's crumbly texture also requires particular attention. Precisely because of its delicacy and deformability, I was forced to develop the specific delivery system mentioned earlier (using the plastic bucket). To deliver tofu to Yachen in a timely manner, a certain infrastructural network was required, including cell phones and personnel who would travel frequently and preferably in their private vehicles, none of which was easily accessible or obtainable for most Tibetan nuns. This network is itself a manifestation of the very presence of "China" in Yachen, as are the larger cultural, technological, and monetary influences constantly drawn from Chinese society.

Because of the delicacy of the product and the resource-driven procurement processes, upon my arrival in Yachen, the tofu immediately began traveling. It circulated almost exclusively among Chinese nuns and sometimes was also offered to their Tibetan teachers when the shape and freshness of the tofu was well preserved. Because of its nutritional value, the enormous amount of labor required to bring it from outside, and the Chinese infrastructural power its procurement signified, tofu became a highly valued product. When tofu was offered to the Tibetan teachers, it produced subtle yet sustaining ethnic pride and self-respect; the Chinese nuns, by consuming tofu, also created a sense of confidence and inclusion that made their presence in Yachen valuable. They felt that they could bring "good" things to Tibetans who would otherwise not know or care about such items. This gave the Chinese nuns a sense of superiority, culturally, politically, and economically, within a Tibetan-dominated space.

It is an unlikely or perhaps felicitous fact to note that a Chinese nun has been included in the Tibetan head lama's main cooking team along with other Tibetan members. Chinese food, with its culturally specific values and meanings, has become entrenched in the strikingly mundane settings of the head lama's kitchen and his daily dining table.

Vegetarianism and Body Politics in Urban China

The presence of the Chinese nuns in Yachen and their distinctive foodways are not separable from the growing number of lay Chinese Buddhist practitioners in urban centers who practice the same or a similar set of dietary practices. The Chinese nuns with whom I worked in Yachen were related, in one way or another, to the active lay Buddhist society that has grown rapidly for the past few decades. The lay devotees visited Yachen to pay homage to their lamas (*shangshi*), and some also came to see the Chinese nuns and monks (*shifu*) they supported. By doing so, they not only deepened their individual practices but also continued sharing and circulating the ideas of what were the "right" ways of living as sincere Buddhists. Food consumption was a common subject in this regard. In what follows, I focus on one active lay Buddhist community in Chengdu and discuss the larger context of recent vegetarianism in urban centers in China. These centers have complex and circumstantial links to the changing dietary habits among the Tibetan nuns in Yachen and more broadly among lay Tibetans on the plateau in recent years. To explore how Buddhist vegetarianism has grown and has also been entangled in the recent Tibetan Buddhist revival occurring in Chinese urban centers, I have specifically chosen a Chinese group that has maintained long, steady relationships with the lamas from Yachen.

Among the many other roles it has played, the city of Chengdu has long been the gateway Chinese metropole to the plateau, receiving and promoting various forms of Tibetan Buddhist activities and engagements.[7] It has also been one of the popular bases for many renowned Tibetan teachers seeking access to Chinese cities and beyond. From a Buddhist perspective, Chengdu certainly has its unique merit and history, but the city has not traditionally advocated vegetarianism. Ranked as the fourth largest population center and the westernmost economic hub in China, it is well known for its abundance of foods and foodways as well as for its citizens' leisurely lifestyles.[8] The city is at the heart of the distinctive, spicy, seasoning-based Sichuan cuisine with its various meat choices and cooking methods. In particular, the spice called "mala" stimulates and slightly numbs the tongue at first; once addicted to it, one is tempted to fill every plate and bowl with mala flavor. Street food vendors and small restaurants that make light snacks such as mala potatoes; mala-grilled tofu; sour-spicy noodles; rice noodles; and various grilled, fried, and stirred mala-flavored meats have spread to every corner of the city, and they are usually open very late to attract a late-night clientele. I was often amazed to see countless small and large mala hot pot restaurants on the streets, which were always crowded with customers whether it was a weekday or a weekend. While the origins of hot pot may be traceable to Mongolia, it has now become the most representative Sichuan cuisine. It usually consists of a huge boiling mala pot that sits in the center of the table, and people put meats and vegetables of their own choosing into the boiling soup. Chengduers (residents of Chengdu) especially love to put various organ meats and other delicacies into the boiling red mala hot pot—duck tongue, beef intestines, chicken feet, and so on. Friends and families frequently gather around this boiling, savory red soup to share favorite foods and conversation about their daily lives. There is a popular saying that "Chengduers drink tea in the morning, play mahjong in the afternoon, and eat hot pot in the evening" (*Chengduren zaoshang hecha xiawu damajiang wanshang chihuoguole*).

In Chengdu, vegetarianism (*sushi* in Chinese) became something of a trend in the late 2010s, beginning with the growing number of middle-class Chengduers who started to reassess their well-being in light of this new trend. Because of its associations with being organic, clean, and thus healthy, vegetarianism has become a smart option for many citizens who want to refrain occasionally from a spicy, greasy, and unclean diet. But even in the early 2010s, a vegetarian diet was rarely a recognizable concept for ordinary people in Chengdu; vegetarianism was mainly for those in the middle-class who were either loosely or closely related to Buddhism, and vegetarian restaurants were rather high-end businesses with noticeably Buddhist-themed décor or semi-Buddhist embellishments, such as Buddhist background music, paintings, and objects. The menus in these restaurants also tended to be deliberately bland; menu items that used fewer spices and seasonings introduced diners to a new world of meditative cuisine that made one's stomach comfortable and calm. Today, however, vegetarian restaurants are multiplying in Chengdu with various price ranges and an emphasis on healthier eating habits and the concept of well-being instead of focusing on a Buddhist ethos per se. To appeal to a larger number of potential customers, these restaurants have also begun adopting the Sichuan style of vegetarian cuisine, which includes lots of mala-flavored foods.

I met Mrs. Sun for the first time in 2012 in Chengdu through the disciple-network of a Tibetan Buddhist shangshi (tulku, reincarnated lama) from Yachen. Mrs. Sun, middle-aged and of Chengdu origin, is one of the shangshi's earliest Chinese disciples who helped introduce the shangshi's Buddhist teachings to Chinese society. Mrs. Sun has served as an active local organizer for various Buddhist activities such as fish-releasing rituals (*fangsheng*), reading scriptures, inviting lecturers, and so on. As an experienced businessperson, she has also run a shop, in both on- and offline forms, that sells high priced, environmentally friendly, organic, and fair-trade items, including lots of dietary products. She has used her offline shop to promote vegetarianism to customers as part of Buddhist teachings, or, more precisely, to blend vegetarianism and well-being with Buddhism by displaying Buddhist-related books and items (prayer wheels, for example) on the shelves with other food items.

Because of the government's intensified control policies for religious activities across China in recent years, and especially in 2019, her offline shop and most of her other organized Buddhist activities have temporarily ceased. Mrs. Sun has managed to keep her online shop running, however, and has occasionally organized activities similar to those she has done before, but she has left out the Buddhist elements. The kind of activities she organizes now promote vegetarianism (for largely health and environmental reasons) and assistance for the elderly and the disabled, none of which directly invoke Buddhism itself. Her business practices have always included activities that address ethical and/or environmental concerns and that consider the benefits for the public at large. Mrs. Sun and the members of her network believe that "practicing Buddhism (*xiufo*)"—or more literally, "studying Buddhism (*xuefo*)"[9]—is not limited to meditating or reciting scriptures but includes performing socially beneficial activities that help a broader range of people.[10] This is the true meaning, as they understand it, of practicing *putixin* (*Bodhicitta* mind) that their teacher has taught them.

Maintaining and promoting a strict vegetarian diet are widely appealing— or perhaps given the restricted political environment, the safest—activities for Mrs. Sun and her group to engage in as committed lay Buddhist practitioners. Whenever I visited her shop, Mrs. Sun called other members who were available and led us to a vegetarian restaurant she adored. This was during the time when vegetarian restaurants were just beginning to spread and had not yet become popular. Visiting newly opened vegetarian restaurants had a twofold purpose for Mrs. Sun. The first was to serve her guests what she believed were pure and good foods; the second was to conduct a potential market investigation because Mrs. Sun was planning to open her own vegetarian restaurant soon. My first visit to such a restaurant occurred one afternoon with five other Buddhists; we met for a late lunch and a fish-releasing ritual afterward at a nearby brook. The restaurant was quite fancy and elegant, decorated with a Buddhist theme, and filled with the tantalizing aroma of incense and the sound of meditation music. The hall was huge and uncrowded. The six of us were led to a room and quickly served herbal tea. Mrs. Sun asked me to choose a favorite dish on the menu, which was filled with photos of colorfully embellished vegetarian dishes. I looked over the menu and was astonished at the diversity of foods and their decorative appearances, as well as the unusually high prices. Being so accustomed to a street diet and Chengdu's regular mala-flavored cuisine, I felt like I was walking into a different world where food was not for *the happiness of the mouth* or the fullness of the stomach but for well-being, self-care, and, to borrow from Bourdieu (1984), the very ways of making "distinction."

Mrs. Sun told me that the owner of the restaurant was also a devout Buddhist. "It is great to eat *qingjing* (pure and clean) food in an *anjing* (uncrowded and quiet) place once in a while," she said. I could see her point as I looked around the mostly empty main hall and the neatly presented non-red foods on the table, which posed a stark contrast to any meal in the crowded, red-colored, hot pot restaurants. I thought that ordinary, non-Buddhist Chengduers would not want to spend lots of money in a restaurant that serves only vegetables with little or no mala flavor. As the dishes were served one by one, Mrs. Sun and others recited a short scripture of gratitude toward their teachers, which is somewhat similar to saying grace in a Christian context. As we all began indulging in these unusual and exquisite Chinese vegetarian dishes, Mrs. Sun began commenting on each dish—their ingredients, nutrition, cooking methods, and so on. She emphasized that this restaurant used no artificial seasonings, and she also did not forget to mention that her shangshi has visited this place and liked it very much. While eating our late lunch, our conversations moved on to the importance and the hardship of adhering to a vegetarian diet and being a good Buddhist in a non-Buddhist environment.

Whenever I "hung out" with Chinese practitioners I was struck by their ability to produce Buddhist discourse and interpretations about almost every activity they were doing. Unless they are at the novice stage, many Chinese Buddhist practitioners with whom I have worked seem extremely capable of articulating on their own terms the meanings of their activities in relation to Buddhist practices. They can reason at each and every step about what and why they are doing such an activity in such a way. *Xuefo* ("studying" Buddhism), unlike *xinfo* ("believing" in Buddhism), perhaps allows its followers to be more prone to self-consciously making sense of their activities. The knowledge on which they base their articulations and reasoning does not come from an analysis of ancient texts but mostly from the speeches and private conversations of their Tibetan teachers as well as from their own experiences of practicing Buddhism in specific daily contexts. The kinds of discourse produced in this venue are therefore situational, practical, and alive to daily issues. Food-talk is a useful example for seeing how this discourse making takes place, how it is circulated and shared in a practical mundane setting, and how it is reinforced with more concrete meanings and values as conversation is shared.

At the lunch table, Mrs. Xue, who is Mrs. Sun's college classmate and is from Chengdu, talked about her challenge in maintaining a vegetarian diet at home. Mrs. Xue has a non-Buddhist husband and a teenage son who both support her religious faith but never practice it themselves. Mrs. Sun suggested to Mrs. Xue that she cook separate meals for the family and for herself so that she could keep her own diet "clean and pure" and thus ensure the "right" environment for her practice. In this way, the rest of her family would not go against her cooking and would eventually become interested in her diet, practices, and life as a Buddhist. On that day, people talked about what the proper foods and eating habits for Buddhist practitioners can and should be, and they shared various experiences, challenges, and tips about how to be a good practitioner in largely non-Buddhist daily contexts. Mrs. Sun and her group also actively participated in major Buddhist rituals either in Yachen or at other Tibetan monasteries; when they did so, they often provided vegetarian meals for the (Chinese) participants of the rituals, who often numbered from a few hundred to a few thousand. Such meals were regularly offered as donations, but sometimes they were sold at a modest price. Mrs. Sun used such opportunities to introduce a strict but still savory vegetarian diet that was clean, healthy, and beneficial to the environment and all sentient beings.

Vegetarianism is often a visible and instantly recognizable Buddhist marker for Chinese disciples because of its association with the core Buddhist doctrine of no killing. Vegetarianism is not an all-encompassing principle, however, that must be followed in the Buddhist world in general; it has been widely contextualized in various social settings for more than two millennia of Buddhist history.[11] Stricter vegetarianism occurred much later in specific contexts when monastics stopped wandering and settled down on land where they could cultivate food for their own consumption.[12] Both the Chinese Buddhist tradition and East Asian Buddhism (largely the Mahayana tradition) have adopted strict vegetarianism and have also banned the consumption of the five pungent vegetables (*wuxincai* in Chinese) in order to maintain the purity of their practices.[13]

Yet from its inception, Tibetan Buddhism did not develop a strict tradition of banning meat-eating practices as other Buddhist traditions in Asia have done. This is likely related to the environmental conditions of the plateau, where it is extremely challenging to survive if meat is excluded from one's diet. It could also be related to the influence of early Buddhism from India. In general, in Tibet and in the exile community in northern India, it is not unusual to see Tibetan Buddhist monks, nuns, and reincarnated lamas who consume meat with little restriction. This does not mean that Tibetan Buddhists do not value the practice of vegetarianism; they value it highly and respect those who commit to doing it. But the principle of vegetarianism in the Tibetan context is more flexibly and generously applied; seasonal vegetarianism, a refusal to eat selected meats (pork or chicken, for example) and a refusal to eat meat during a particular time of day or year are considered forms of practicing vegetarianism. Thus, vegetarianism is neither forced nor tied to a particular sense of Buddhist morality in the Tibetan context. In recent years, however, some influential Tibetan teachers have been more outspoken about vegetarianism and the issue of slaughtering animals in Tibet.[14] The teachers in Yachen have also begun emphasizing vegetarianism more often to their disciples.

Despite the flexibility in the practice of vegetarianism in Tibetan Buddhism, most Chinese devotees who follow the Tibetan Buddhist tradition nonetheless uphold strict vegetarianism. This should not be understood only in the light of their insistence on keeping a tenet of Buddhism; strict vegetarianism is also a social signal of their commitment to a particular lifestyle as a sincere Buddhist. Vegetarianism for lay practitioners is not only a defining religious identification but also reflects an ability and willingness to take care of oneself and to maintain both physical and mental purity as a practitioner and as a modern, intelligent citizen. The "care-talk" in this situation is highly mixed; discourses of pure religious devotion and discourses of neoliberal body-care techniques are almost inseparable. Avoiding a violation of the no-killing principle parallels and is joined with a refusal to eat junk food, that is, eating spicy, unhygienic street food in a noisy, unwholesome place. Thus, "where to eat," "what to eat," and "how to eat" indicate one's religious devotion and the depth and seriousness of one's commitment to the faith, and simultaneously, one's distinctive self-care and social status. Dining in a high-priced vegetarian restaurant in Chengdu can also be read as a performative or conspicuous action that distinguishes one's life from others through dietary practices. If we borrow again from Bourdieu's (1984) notion of "distinction," we can say that choosing a restaurant, food, and ways of eating generate and symbolize a distinctive lifestyle and social class. What Mrs. Sun and the others aspire to present is a sincere religious self, a good Buddhist who adheres to the basic principles of Buddhism (such as no killing) and who understands Buddhist practices from multiple aspects: mental, physical, and environmental. But less consciously, in doing so, they also present the middle-class social distinction of being equipped with specific knowledge and techniques about caring for the self.

It is not entirely clear in the vegetarian foodscape of contemporary Chengdu whether vegetarianism is becoming popular and carries with it a slight hint of Buddhism, or if Buddhism is soaking into the society disguised as discourses about vegetarianism, well-being, and self-care. Vegetarianism in Chengdu appears to be a hybrid that has a growing propensity to represent the body politics of the middle class in Chinese urban centers. Tibetan Buddhism has attracted many serious Chinese practitioners in the cities; at the same time, however, Buddhism as a *theme* also helps to produce a nonreligion-driven ethics of self-care in urban China today. Someone like Mrs. Sun and her businesses play an important part in this culture of Buddhist-mingled body care in a city like Chengdu.

The visible boom in vegetarianism in the city is not restricted, however, to urban middle-class citizens and their neoliberal Buddhist self-care. In the next section, I discuss how, *circumstantially*, this urban vegetarianism can boomerang to the core of Tibetan Buddhism and create openings for change from within.

Sausage

One of the most popular socializing processes in Yachen occurred when the nuns visited each other's living quarters and shared a meal. Mealtime, including the time spent in preparation and drinking tea before and after, was indeed a good opportunity for me to sit with the nuns in a daily setting, talking and listening to them. After years of being served by the nuns in their huts, I finally learned to carry some cooking ingredients in my luggage. With my own food products and my cooking initiative, I was occasionally able to arrange an alternative relationship with the nuns: from being served to being a server. For example, a request to use their kitchens to make a dish allowed me to position myself beyond the realm of being a mere guest or visitor. In addition, I strongly desired to reciprocate, in some modest way, the nuns' kindness over the years, and cooking and sharing food seemed perfect options. Yet I could not be extravagant in my cooking process in Yachen because of the limited conditions as well as my limited cooking skills. After serious consideration, I packed various kinds of instant ingredients such as curry flour and black bean flour in my luggage. With these, I could easily make a relatively decent dish (to my mind) with any available vegetables in a short time. In Yachen, therefore, it was my habit to carry a small bag of flour in my side bag at all times in case an unexpected cooking opportunity arose. While my quickly cooked dishes were well received among the Tibetan nuns, I was more careful about presenting my instant ingredients to the Chinese nuns, who were usually very sensitive about quick dishes with artificial seasonings.

Sangmo, one of the youngest nuns with whom I was acquainted, lived with her aunt who had joined Yachen decades ago. This cheerful nun was fond of inviting me to her hut and serving a meal to me. After being served half a dozen times by her, I insisted one day that I would like to cook something simple yet special in return. In her kitchen, I began peeling potatoes, chopping them into small cubes, and washing green cabbage. I was going to mix the vegetables with my black bean flour. While watching me, Sangmo suddenly suggested that we should put something else in the sauce that would, she insisted, make the dish even tastier. She then proudly brought me something with which I was very familiar: a low-quality, stick-type pink sausage that was once popularly consumed in China but was no longer found in fancy supermarkets in cities (one can now find alternative versions that are much improved in quality). Because she liked it so much, I didn't mind putting it into the sauce, but the problem was in fact a little bigger than we both realized.

Yachen had recently forbidden all meat consumption. At the time of my visit with Sangmo in 2013, no meat products could be brought in and sold in Yachen. Although Yachen had never sold raw meat, its shops used to sell cheap, spicy jerk products for snacks, and many Tibetan nuns enjoyed consuming them. But the head office had completely banned all these meat-based, processed food items; even the private restaurants and shops were prohibited from selling them. This change was somewhat abrupt, but it was clear to most of the nuns because Tulku Asong specifically preached about the change several times. I asked Sangmo about this recent change, and she was well aware of it. I became more curious and asked her again why she had bought boxes of meat products. She was surprised and said, "This is not meat, is it? That's what I was told." Without thinking for a second, I told her that sausage was a processed meat, and I even pointed out to her the main ingredient, which was chicken, written in Chinese on the wrap. Worse, I read the word *jirou* (chicken) out loud to her to make doubly sure that I was right about this. I regretted instantly the way I reacted to her; I was acting like a mean aunt who was pointing out and correcting the wrong behavior of her innocent niece.

I learned that Sangmo and a few other nuns had visited the nearest nomadic town called Changtai a few days earlier and bought boxes of sausage from one of the shops there. Apparently, few nuns were aware of the ingredients of sausage or familiar with the concept of such a food product. It was also possible that the local vendors had lied to the nuns, who usually could not read Chinese well, and told them that the product had no meat in it. The box was new, filled with several dozen of the sausage sticks; it would be wasteful if Sangmo threw them all away, but it was also awkward to keep eating the sausage after she became aware that it was specifically banned by the head lama. I came across more occasions in which Tibetan nuns I knew kept either sausage or fish cake on their kitchen shelves as cooking ingredients without knowing that these were meat- or fish-based products. These processed foods are quite affordable, already seasoned and cooked, and convenient for fixing a quick meal compared to other plain staples in Yachen such as tsampa or potatoes.

Tulku Asong has initiated several innovative policies since attaining the head office in 2011, and the removal of all meat products and the banning of their consumption in Yachen are part of one such initiative. His decision coincides with the recent changing notions of meat consumption on the plateau. These notions have been raised by some of the renowned Tibetan teachers, most of whom have visible influence among Chinese disciples. One rationale given by the advocates of vegetarianism in Tibet is that, unlike before, most Tibetans no longer have to rely on limited food choices created by the environmental conditions on the plateau. When various other nutritious vegetarian options are available, continuing to follow a meat-based diet is hardly justified. Apart from such practical reasoning, it was also a time when a sense of morality in Tibetan Buddhism was being reinforced in general (Caple 2019) and, thus, encouragement of vegetarianism on the plateau has seemed like a segue into this trend (see Barstow 2018). However, Tulku Asong's ban of meat consumption in Yachen, especially in its initial stage, was still somewhat too abrupt for the disciples; many Tibetan nuns like Sangmo, who had rarely been introduced to such regulatory and restrictive ideas about the food she consumed, did not seem to be entirely ready for such a change.

After Tulku Asong's ban, some Tibetan nuns maintained strict vegetarianism all the time, while others continued eating meat in a selective manner and on certain occasions whenever they returned home.[15] Products like sausage or fish cake that do not look like real pieces of meat (with flesh and bone) are still consumed by many Tibetan monastics both in monastic and lay settings, even among those who see themselves as following a strict vegetarian diet. I believe that a much more flexible, nuanced, and circumstantial approach is required to understand the vegetarian practices among both Tibetan and non-Tibetan Buddhist practitioners in contemporary China. Vegetarianism has indeed been given more emphasis in Tibetan monasteries and among practitioners in recent years. Large Buddhist encampments like Yachen and Larung Gar have officially adopted a strict rule banning meat consumption within their boundaries. However, some high-ranking Tibetan teachers in and from Yachen continue consuming meat on some occasions. These teachers' meat consumption is not widely visible but is not deliberately hidden either; some Chinese disciples who are concerned with the health of their teachers even voluntarily prepare meat dishes for them. Thus, even in those Chinese Buddhist circles where stricter vegetarianism is usually applied, strictures against eating meat are not always so straightforward. One Chinese monk from Yachen once explained how he understood "eating meat" as a Buddhist practitioner. "Eating meat means to *jieyuan* (make a karmic connection) with the animal you eat." It is not my intention or within my ability to understand the philosophical depth of what *jieyuan* means in this context; but his remark allowed me to navigate some of the ambiguity and complexity of the practices of vegetarianism in contemporary Tibetan Buddhism.

Adding to the complexity of this issue, I would like to point out a circumstantial factor involved in the recent vegetarianism of contemporary Tibetan Buddhism in China that cannot be dismissed—namely, the overlap between the time line of stricter vegetarianism that is being encouraged and more systematically applied on the plateau, and the time line of the growing visibility of Chinese disciples in Tibetan Buddhism. For example, until 2017, when the Chinese government began closing off Yachen to non-Tibetans and non-Sichuan-registered Tibetans, the number of Chinese devotees who visited Yachen and Tibetan monasteries had increased rapidly every year. Their involvement included not only visiting Tibetan monasteries with greater frequency and regularity but also, and more significantly, making generous donations and initiating various forms of exchange between Tibetan Buddhism and Chinese lay society. Even though, as I have stated, vegetarianism among Chinese disciples is not always straightforward, the majority uphold strict vegetarianism as an ethical and religious marker and are willing to spread this idea to others with little hesitation. The head office of Yachen has been forced to deal with the growing influence of Chinese disciples, most of whom are happy to propagate, or at least morally agree with propagating, strict vegetarianism and who thus might have felt quite uncomfortable when they saw the Tibetan nuns in Yachen nibbling jerky on the streets.

It is not difficult to see how the head office and Tulku Asong himself took care of the Chinese practitioners in Yachen. For instance, Tulku Asong held morning lectures for Chinese disciples at 7 a.m. every day for several months a year. This was during the brief free time he had between his dawn meditation and his regular long lecture at eight o'clock for Tibetans. He used this small window of time, presumably his break or breakfast time, to engage with the relatively small number of Chinese monks and nuns residing in Yachen and with the lay practitioners who traveled to Yachen from faraway Chinese cities.[16] His lecture was in Tibetan first and was immediately translated line-by-line into Chinese. This was considered a precious time during which the Chinese practitioners could see their "root teacher" (*genben shangshi*) up close and engage with him, however briefly, every morning. The head office also sometimes responded to the specific needs of the Chinese disciples who might have more difficulty adjusting to the highland environment in Yachen. For example, in the winter of 2013, the head office distributed bags of coal fuel exclusively to individual Chinese nuns and monks out of concern for their ability to endure the freezing winter on the plateau. Some donations were often specifically made for Chinese practitioners and their well-being in Yachen, and both small and large rituals and ceremonies with Chinese translation were separately held for Chinese practitioners. Many Chinese nuns with whom I talked said that they felt they were well looked after by Tulku Asong, and some even said that they were specially treated, better than Tibetans, by the head office.

Financial stability and independence are essential for a mammoth Tibetan Buddhist community like Yachen to maintain a "relatively" autonomous status with respect to its curriculum, practices, and personnel. The pious Chinese financial capital that has flowed into Yachen has been used to introduce many infrastructural improvements—including roads, assembly halls, and electricity. Equally important, however, is that this capital has also allowed Yachen to be less reliant on government subsidies, if any, for its activities. This is not to dismiss the existential precarity of Tibetan religious communities under Chinese rule; it has been proven even more clearly in recent years that the fate of a Tibetan religious community—no matter how influential in public— depends on what the Chinese state says and how the Chinese state envisions the future of Tibetan communities. Financial independence and stability alone cannot guarantee a Tibetan community's continued sustainability, but it is also too hasty to conclude that the Tibetan Buddhist revival in contemporary China is declining or nearly over. Although the Chinese lay practitioners' involvement in Tibetan Buddhism—their direct presence in Tibetan monasteries, for example—has been significantly reduced because of the government's recent policies, their networks and Buddhist engagements do not seem to be similarly decreasing in any permanent way. Chinese disciples' activities in cyberspace continue to expand at a rapid pace, and many Tibetan teachers who used to teach and meet with disciples in person are now engaging more actively with them online. The interactions between Chinese disciples and Tibetan teachers (and to some extent Tibetan monks and nuns) are in some ways "closer" than before.

Coda

An increasing amount of Chinese capital and its influence are flooding into Yachen as Yachen struggles to maintain its autonomy against the Chinese state. This produces a chasm that requires Tibetan practitioners to adopt and inscribe new forms of practice in their daily settings. The recent dietary restrictions in Yachen and on the plateau are good examples of how Tibetan practitioners are required to continually reinterpret, reconsider, and reapply new regulations—and their accompanying discourses and understandings about proper Buddhist subjects—in their daily lives. The look of guilt and shame on Sangmo's face that day, triggered by my reckless revelation, was a material manifestation of the kind of ambivalence that the Tibetan nuns have recently experienced and dealt with as an aspect of Tibetan Buddhism that is constantly being renewed in practice. The Chinese version—that is, the neoliberal and urban Buddhist version—of what constitutes proper eating habits and proper foods for health and well-being insidiously disturbs a long-standing part of Buddhist practice that had not been problematic, until recently, for the Tibetan nuns. Now, however, they are forced to reconsider their understanding of the regulatory ethics for being a good practitioner while, at the same time, absorbing a newer standard regarding what foods they eat.

The recent and ongoing vegetarian movement in Yachen and on the plateau has revolved around the growing inclusion of Chinese disciples, who more or less enjoy a stable economic status and pursue specific lifestyles based on their financial security. Many Chinese Buddhist practitioners travel to the far west of their country to pay homage to the lamas and to absorb the "air of sacredness" from Tibetan land. These remote travels and long-term stays require a certain amount of economic stability from the devotees, who must be able to afford long-term absences from their work and from their families (Yü 2012). Such a specific middle-class background in terms of both time and finances enables them to invest in more than the Buddhist teachings themselves; they can invest in Buddhism-compatible health-care activities such as walking into a fancy vegetarian restaurant in town and enjoying clean, unpolluted food in a quiet place. Through vegetarianism, we can catch a glimpse of the complex operations and economies of contemporary Tibetan Buddhism in urban China. Vegetarianism also shows how Chinese influence, with its financial power and attitude of cultural superiority and higher morality, has transformed from the inside the infrastructure that frames the daily lives of Tibetan practitioners.

I have provided circumstantial evidence, through stories such as Sangmo's and Mrs. Sun's, that shows how Buddhist vegetarianism is promulgated in Yachen by way of Chinese disciples. Sociopolitical changes can occur and be ingrained in material and mundane realms in ways that are not clearly and deliberately engineered by the actors themselves. Out of their sincerity about Buddhism and about themselves, the Chinese disciples associated with Yachen, in their own quiet and tenacious way, are imposing their own ideas of what constitutes a proper Buddhist subject; but in doing so, they have begun to unsettle, without knowing so, the existing dietary norms of Tibetan Buddhists on the plateau. This disturbance in the Tibetan nuns' daily lives might not be the Chinese disciples' intention, but it nonetheless produces a certain result—that the Tibetan practitioners make a deeply personal change in their daily lives. Although unexpected, ethnic politics in China, it seems, is also susceptible to the politics of tranquility.

EPILOGUE

Yachen's changed appearance after 2017 might shock those who remember how it looked before then. The most awe-inspiring feature of Yachen, the large shantytown in which thousands of nuns lived and practiced by building and repairing their tiny huts, has been bulldozed to half of its previous size. The space where the homes of so many Tibetan nuns once stood is now flattened. Along with the demolition of their huts, more than half of the nuns were also forced to leave Yachen. They were supposed to return to their natal homes, but we cannot be certain where they went and how they have been doing. In the fall of 2019, standing in the section of the nuns' residential area that was once filled with the bustling lives of the nuns and is now completely hollowed out, one can perceive, perhaps more strongly than ever and with a sense of bitterness, the Buddhist notion of impermanence. In the middle of this empty land, I remember that I built a hut of my own with the nuns during my long-term fieldwork in Yachen some years ago. I tried to locate approximately where it had been so that I could recall the lively times shared with the nuns. But there is no trace of it now. A few lonely dogs roam there instead.

In the half of the shantytown where the huts are still preserved, however, thousands of Tibetan nuns continue living and practicing Buddhism. The lives of the remaining nuns seem largely intact. The classes, prayer sessions, and exams proceed as they did before 2017; the remaining medical nuns continue providing medical services to their fellow nuns; the shops operate as usual (although some shops are closed); and the pilgrimages and circumambulations by local Tibetans continue. While everything has remained largely normal on the surface, there is also a kind of a chill in the air; not the chill of cold weather, but a mood of unusual calmness, invisible tension, or perhaps a sense of loss. Only those nuns who are from the province in which Yachen sits (Sichuan province) are allowed to stay and practice in Yachen. Those nuns whose hukou (household registration) are not from Sichuan have been evicted. Besides the nuns, only Tibetans who are hukou holders from Sichuan are allowed to visit Yachen. All non-Tibetan personnel, whether monastics, lay practitioners, pilgrims, or tourists, are prohibited from visiting. It appears that the Chinese government has reduced Yachen to a local Buddhist institution that is supervised by the local government and serves only the religious needs of local residents.

This is not the first time that the Chinese government has attempted to downsize Tibetan Buddhist communities in Tibet and Kham in particular. In 2001, Larung Gar, as the largest and fastest-growing Tibetan Buddhist institution in Tibet at that time, was directly targeted by a government demolition policy.[1] Thousands of nuns and monks were evicted, and their residential huts were demolished as well. In one sense, the destruction of Larung came as a surprise because its practitioners and the institute itself were generally law-abiding and didn't agitate over any politically sensitive issues. But in another sense, perhaps being a Tibetan Buddhist institution itself in China is already a sufficient condition for being a major target of government surveillance. Given the Sino-Tibetan political tensions since the 1950s and the Chinese government's extreme vigilance toward the collective engagements of its ethnic others, it was no surprise at all that, sooner or later, restrictive policies of some kind would be implemented in Larung. The official reason given by the Chinese government in 2001 for its demolition policy was to enhance the "modernization" of Tibet, even though this had little appeal for ordinary Tibetans. A more convincing explanation for their policy is that a rapidly growing Tibetan institution, with strong links to non-Tibetan and global societies, was seen as a potential political threat to the social harmony that the government of the PRC has so rigorously promoted and maintained. During this initial demolition in 2001, Yachen was not disturbed by the government and was not a primary target at that time.

In 2016, the Chinese government once again embarked on a policy for downsizing Tibetan monastic communities in Kham. This time, it took a more systematic and thorough approach. Yachen and Larung were both targeted because of their several similarities that make them potential trouble in the eyes of the Chinese government. These similarities include their unprecedented rates of growth, influential spiritual leaders, and the increasing number of non-Tibetan disciples associated with each, especially Han Chinese living both in Chinese metropoles and in global cities. Downsizing began first in Larung in

2016, and the same demolition and eviction measures were imposed in Yachen the following year. But I remember that, even in the summer of 2016, when I visited Yachen, nuns whom I knew from the TAR were already being ordered to leave Yachen. They were in a great hurry to pack a simple bag and quickly return to their hometowns because their families had to report in person with their daughters to the local police office for registration. When Chenco, a Tibetan nun from a small town in the TAR, was called by her father to come home immediately, she perceived it as a short-term home visit and anticipated that she would return to Yachen within a month or so. But most of the nuns who were summoned by their families at this time were not able to return to Yachen (some returned but only temporarily). The local police offices in their natal towns ordered the nuns to stay at home or to find a local nunnery and told them that if they disobeyed this order, their families would be punished (e.g., would have to forfeit their ID cards). In 2016 alone, more than a thousand nuns in Yachen whose origins were outside Sichuan were forced to leave Yachen. They were only the first group of nuns caught up in the government's grand eviction plan for Yachen.

A few hundred Chinese nuns were also living and practicing in Yachen until 2017, and some of these were long-standing members who had resided there for more than two decades. The government's policy for these Chinese nuns was much more systematic. They were offered compensation for any property (for example, for their huts) in Yachen that they would lose once they left Yachen and were also given a relocation fee once they had agreed to leave Yachen permanently. The local governments in their places of origin were also involved in their relocation and resettlement, arranging places for them to stay in local temples or in similarly secluded places under the condition that they would not return to Yachen again. The Chinese nuns did not have a choice about whether to stay in Yachen; they were ordered to leave and, regardless of their wishes, to sign a pledge stating that they would not return. The measures implemented by the government for Chinese nuns focused on resettling them in local communities close to their natal homes and preventing them from returning to Yachen or other Tibetan monasteries. A Chinese nun I spoke to finds this government policy tolerable and even quite nice because she has not been forced to abandon her nunship; she continues her practices in a place close to her hometown. Another Chinese nun with whom I spoke, however, finds the policy awful and considers it a serious prosecution of her religious freedom. She thinks that living in Yachen and being close to her teacher are crucial for her spiritual advancement, and the policy thus disrupts her spiritual practices significantly.

When the government orders large-scale demolitions and evictions, the activities and travels of the lamas are also affected. The influential lamas in

Yachen who used to travel widely, teaching and receiving new disciples in Chinese cities and beyond, can no longer travel freely without seeking a government permit. Their whereabouts and daily activities are closely monitored by the government; because of this, Chinese disciples discourage each other from contacting their teachers for fear of making their lamas an unnecessary target of even stricter surveillance. Interactions between Tibetan lamas and Chinese disciples have been put on hold. Even the disciples' online communities where they share information and experiences related to practices have been operating in standby mode. The message of the government policy is clear: by restricting the activities and travels of the lamas from Yachen who have gained international reputations, it reduces them to local figures who serve the local population. Since 2017, these lamas have remained either in Yachen or in their home monasteries, and their religious activities have been limited to those locations. Government restrictions on the mobility of both lamas and disciples have coincided with the global pandemic since 2020, which has prolonged such restrictions.

From a Tibetan perspective and from a practitioner's perspective, what has happened in monastic communities in Kham over the past few years looks quite grim. It is very difficult to learn what has happened since 2016 to the Tibetan nuns from the TAR who were forced to leave Yachen or Larung. Given the limited number and capacity of the Buddhist nunneries in the TAR, it is very challenging for the nuns who had to leave Yachen to find local nunneries in which to continue their practices. Even for those who can find a nunnery, the experience is unlikely to match the experience they had in Yachen. As I have discussed, Yachen is one of the rare places in Tibet that provide Tibetan nuns with full access to eminent teachings, various educational opportunities, and the strong companionship of other nuns all at the same time. In the TAR, many of the evicted nuns will likely fail to find an alternative nunnery. They will either become household nuns who keep their vows but stay at home and help with house chores (like Puthi in chapter 1) or face prolonged social and familial pressures to abandon their vows and return to worldly lives.

Despite the dampened atmosphere for Buddhist practices on the Tibetan plateau, outside the TAR a different story is beginning to take shape. In the Yushu region (Jyekundo) in Kham, a few hundred of the nuns evicted from Larung have begun self-organizing a community of their own. It is possible that the nuns evicted from Yachen may follow the same path and organize their own community somewhere, or they may join the nuns from Larung. A nun from Larung with whom I spoke in 2019, who is also one of the main organizers of the new encampment in Yushu, expects that their male lamas from Larung will be visiting their new community and transmitting teachings to the nuns once government surveillance becomes more relaxed in the future. It is unclear whether these nuns can return to Larung one day or whether they will have to remain in their new encampment forever, but by organizing a new community in which to live and practice, these nuns can avoid having their practices disrupted and can continue to be nuns. Although it is too early to say what these new communities of nuns will do and become, they show that the nuns possess the ability to build new spaces of their own when necessary. Their attempt to build such places may produce another concentration of local Tibetan girls who wish to be nuns. And if so, these places will become a new form of monastic establishment led by nuns and will deserve further study.

What should also not be forgotten is that, despite the government's large-scale demolition policy in Kham, several thousand nuns still live and practice in Yachen and in Larung as well. In 2017, after witnessing their fellow nuns leaving one by one and their huts brutally destroyed, the remaining nuns in Yachen understood, perhaps more clearly than ever, their precarious position as an ethnic minority. In my brief visit to Yachen in 2019, I met some nuns who had avoided the misfortune of being forced to leave Yachen. They were trying hard to maintain their peaceful Buddhist quest and to continue their daily activities as usual. There were even newcomers from Sichuan province who had joined Yachen. Despite the mood of tension and loss that still lingers over the encampment, the remaining nuns continue practicing, praying, building, repairing, decorating, and making do calmly and tenaciously. Perhaps what I saw in Yachen and in the community rebuilding in Yushu was a politics of tranquility once again unfolding, once again confounding the Chinese state's attempts to silence and dismiss the nuns' determination to create a life and community of their own.

Notes

INTRODUCTION

1. Gar [*sgar*] can be translated as "encampment." The other mega-sized encampment in Tibet is Larung Gar. At its peak, Yachen housed more than twelve thousand practitioners; of these, more than ten thousand were Tibetan nuns. Yachen Gar's official name is Yachen Orgyen Samden Ling [*ya chen o rgyan bsam gdan gling*], but few people use this name; the encampment is commonly referred to as Yachen or Yachen Gar. Among Han Chinese disciples, it is called Yaqingsi (Yaqing Monastery).

2. Yachen Gar is located in the eastern corner of Baiyu (Pelyül [*dpal yul*]) county, at the edge of Ganzi (Kardze [*dkar mdzes*]) county in Ganzi Tibetan Autonomous Prefecture in northwestern Sichuan province. Ganbai road is the abbreviation for Ganzi-Baiyu road, and Yachen is approximately 100 to 120 kilometers from both county seats, but it belongs under the jurisdiction of Baiyu. At the time of my first visit in 2010, the travel time from Ganzi township to Yachen on the shuttle bus was more than seven hours. But significant road construction and improvements on the Ganbai route have been made since then. In 2019, travel time has been reduced to less than four hours. However, the newly built road requires constant maintenance, which is often not properly attended to. The reduction in travel time sometimes disappears due to the lack of road repairs.

3. Gönpa [*dgon pa*] is used when referring to a Buddhist monastery as a formal compound. Ling [*gling*] is also similarly used to indicate a monastic compound in Tibet. Yachen's official name contains *ling* (Yachen Orgyen Samden Ling). As I indicated in note 1, *ling* has little currency in Yachen and the term has only been applied more recently as Yachen's existence becomes more officially acknowledged.

4. Chögar [*chos sgar*] means "religious encampment." It is also well known that Larung Gar, another similarly constructed encampment in Kham, was designated as a Buddhist academy by its founder, Khenpo Jigme Phuntshok. According to David Germano's research (1998) on Larung Gar, the name was coined for a political reason, namely, to minimize attention by the government. Regardless of the reasoning behind using "gar," both Yachen Gar and Larung Gar possess features that would not be representative of a traditional monastic compound in Tibet.

5. The work team (*gongzuozu*), which is specially tasked with monitoring the monastics' daily activities and any potential for disruption, belongs to the United Front Work Department (Tongyi zhanxian gongzuobu) in the Chinese Communist Party. The work team is distinct from the police force.

6. The conclusion of a governmental report, written in 2007 by a group of researchers dispatched from the central government to conduct a "survey" of Yachen, states that Yachen has not exhibited any problems and no future disturbances are anticipated; however, the report also states that the state should continue to guard against the possibility of unrest in the encampment. The full report is unavailable because it was produced and circulated only for internal review at the China Tibetology Research Center (Zhongguo zangxue yanjiu zhongxin), a government-sponsored research center in Beijing. I was only given access to a portion of the report when I visited the Center in 2012.

7. Some of the Chinese disciples with whom I worked displayed a romanticized attitude about Tibetan Buddhism and ethnic minorities in general. Tenzin Jinba (2014) and Louisa Schein (1997) discuss this as "internal orientalism."

8. Despite my foreign nationality and affiliation, my East Asian appearance gave me an advantage when entering and residing in Yachen during my fieldwork. I was often treated by the local authorities as one of the Chinese disciples on a pilgrimage visit to Yachen.

9. The term *tulku* [*sprul sku*] refers to reincarnated lamas, and *khenpo* [*mkhen po*] refers to the highest degree in the Nyingma [*rnying ma*] sect, which parallels the *geshe* [*dge bshes*] degree in the Geluk [*dge lugs*] sect in Tibetan Buddhism. There have been globally renowned, leading khenpos in the revival in Kham such as Khenpo Jigme Phuntsok, Khenpo Sodargye, and Khenpo Tsultrim Lodrö from Larung Gar.

10. Studies on the revival in Kham have largely focused on the achievements of a handful of legendary figures in individual monastic communities. Starting from David Germano's work (1998) on Khenpo Jigme Phuntsok in Larung Gar, Holly Gayley (2016), Antonio Terrone (2009, 2010), Magdalena Maria Turek (2013), and Dan Smyer Yü (2012) discuss the high figures emerging from Kham. In particular, the revival in Kham is closely associated with the visionary Buddhist movement that includes treasure revealers (*tertön* [*gter ston*]) and the treasures (*terma* [*gter ma*]) that they have revealed. In this visionary narrative, these revealers are considered to be the prophesized inheritors of Guru Rinpoche (Padmasambhava), who planted Buddhism in Tibetan soil in the eighth century. Yachen's previous head lama, Achuk Rinpoche, is also considered to be one of these revealers. For further discussion on the treasure movement, see Doctor 2005; Gayley 2007b; Germano 1998; Gyatso 1993, 1998; Terrone 2009, 2010; and Tulku Thondup Rinpoche 1986. Susumu Kawata (2015) has produced a fieldwork-based general survey of the Buddhist revival that has been taking place over the past few decades in eastern Tibet.

11. David Germano (1998) looks at this aspect, arguing that the Tibetan Buddhist revival of the 1980s is a reflection of submerged Tibetan nationalism and a Tibetan sense of cultural crisis as Tibetans face capitalistic encroachment from China. For further discussions on Tibetan nationalism, see Kolås 1996 and Terrone 2017. In a different context, Jane Caple (2019) shows that Tibetans' own sense of morality has played a significant role in the revival in Amdo, which, she argues, is independent from the explanation given by the dominant discourse that the revival is a product of state-society tension.

12. Many studies of Tibetan nuns largely follow the hagiographic model that characterizes most studies of Tibetan Buddhism; there are a few ethnographies of specific figures as well. See, for example, Allione 2000; Bessenger 2016; Chayet 1999; Diemberger 2007; Jacoby 2014; Schneider 2011, 2015; Shaw 1994; and Willis 1989, who largely discuss Tibetan female practitioners who have shown extraordinary spiritual power. Book-length anthropological accounts about the lives of Tibetan female monastics are rare, but see Grimshaw 1994; Gutschow 2004; and Havnevik 1989, all of which focus exclusively on Tibetan nuns in the Himalayan region. Sara Shneiderman (2006) and Kurtis R. Schaeffer (2004) discuss the lives of ordinary female practitioners, also with a focus on the Himalayan region. Karma Lekshe Tsomo's edited volumes (2014, 2019) address nunship and gender issues in Tibetan Buddhism. In anthropology, Charlene E. Makley (2005, 2007) discusses nunhood and gender politics in the contemporary Amdo Tibetan region and Mitra Härkönen (2023) focuses on the agency and power of Tibetan Buddhist nuns in both Tibet and the Himalayas. Overall, there are only a few studies in the English language on ordinary Tibetan nuns living in contemporary Tibet. In Chinese sources, see Baimacuo 2011 and Deji Zhuoma 2003. In particular, Baimacuo (Padma'tsho) is the first to present a scholarly discussion in the Chinese language about

the nuns in Yachen. She also has a survey chapter about Yachen (in English) in Tsomo's 2014 volume. Scholarly discussions of Yachen in China are also scarce, and the handful of essays that exist about Yachen typically deliver tourist-type romanticizations of Tibet and Tibetan Buddhism. General discussions concerning gender in Buddhism are available through the works of Byrne 2013; Cabezón 1992; Faure 1998, 2003; Findly 2000; Gross 1993, 2009; and Tsomo 2019.

13. During the time that I was doing my long-term field research in 2012 and 2013, fourteen female lamas resided in Yachen. They were considered Dolma [*sgrol ma*] (Tara, Dakini, a female bodhisattva), and some had achieved the highest degree in the Nyingma sect (*khenmo* [*mkhen mo*]), which earned them a position that was similar to being a teacher. They lived side by side with the ordinary nuns, respected by the nuns as awakened beings; however, their roles were relatively limited to helping the nuns practice and to supporting male lamas. They typically do not have Chinese disciples, do not travel to China, and do not receive extensive support like the male lamas do.

14. After the Tibetan protest in Lhasa in 2008 and the brutal crackdown by the Chinese armed forces, individual Tibetans (both monastics and laypeople) practiced self-immolation to continue protesting the Chinese government's repressive policies for Tibet. The number of Tibetan self-immolators since 2009 is 159. For further discussion, see McGranahan and Litzinger 2012. Also, for book-length discussions of self-immolation and its meanings for Tibetans and in Sino-Tibetan politics, see Shakya 2012; Sindhi and Shah 2012; Whalen-Bridge 2015; and Woeser 2016.

15. The number of studies on resistance is extremely voluminous if one includes studies that focus on bottom-up social change in global regimes and structures. A great number of anthropological and historical studies also fall into this category. Only a short representative list of works can be mentioned here, including those associated with colonial and postcolonial contexts: Comaroff 1985; Fox 1985; Guha 1983, 1997; Stoler 1985; and Taussig 1980. For "everyday forms of resistance," broadly defined, see Abu-Lughod 1990; Colburn 1989; de Certeau 1984; Mahmood 2005; Ong 1987; Scott 1985, 1990; Scott and Kerkvliet 1986; and Simpson 2014; among others. For critical analyses of the study of resistance, see, for example, Jones 2012; Mbembe 2001; Ortner 1995; Seymour 2006; and Theodossopoulos 2014.

16. For book-length discussions, see, for example, Barnett and Akiner 1994; McCarthy 1997; Schwartz 1994; Whalen-Bridge 2015; Woeser 2016; and Woeser, Wang, and Law 2014.

17. Beginning in 2010, I visited Yachen every summer through 2016 and spent over a year there between September 2012 and December 2013. I visited Yachen briefly again in 2019 and witnessed how half of the nuns' residential area had been completely bulldozed by the Chinese state. The remaining nuns (a few thousand) continue to live and practice as they did before.

18. During my residency and visits in Yachen between 2010 and 2016, the number of Chinese nuns in Yachen reached a few hundred at its peak.

19. See Osburg 2020 and Yü 2012.

1. BECOMING A BUDDHIST NUN IN POST-MAO TIBET

1. For discussions of internal migration in China, see Chan, Selden, and Pun 2020; Chang 2008; Hillenbrand 2023; Jacta 2006; Lee 1998; Loyalka 2012; Pai 2012; Pun 2005; Sun 2014; Yan 2008; Zhang 2001; and Zheng 2009.

2. It has been said that, in some cases, impoverished families send their children out of necessity to monastic communities, but the ability of monasteries to take full responsibility for the livelihoods of their practitioners is also limited. Even in a financially

stable place like Yachen, a certain amount of familial support for individual practitioners is considered essential to the maintenance of fruitful practices.

3. Current studies on the Tibetan Buddhist revival in Kham largely focus on the role of a handful of charismatic figures. See Germano 1998; Terrone 2010; Turek 2013; and Yü 2012. Despite the strikingly large number of nuns in Yachen Gar (as well as in Larung Gar), few studies recognize, let alone examine, the existence and role of the nuns in this movement.

4. Except for obvious public figures such as the lamas, all names in this book are pseudonyms to protect the identities of the figures. For the same reason, I also anonymize or shield the names of the natal townships of the nuns I discuss.

5. The website Facts and Details states that "only 78 percent of Tibetan children enter elementary school and only 35 percent enter middle school" (Facts and Details 2022). For an overview of Chinse government policies on education in Tibet, see Bass 1998. For a more recent and comprehensive discussion of the school dropout issue for Tibetan students in rural Tibet, see Postiglione, Jiao, and Gyatso 2005.

6. Tsampa [rtsam pa] is a distinctive foodstuff that serves as the main staple of the Tibetan diet. Traditionally, Tibetans often call themselves "the eaters of tsampa" (see Yeh 2007).

7. Chamdo [chab mdo] (Changdu in Chinese) is also often spelled "Qamdo."

8. After joining Yachen, nuns are not usually allowed to visit home for the first three years. During this crucial period, newcomers acquire essential daily habits and learn the proper order of tasks and procedures for living and practicing as a nun in Yachen; in addition, they are required to complete intensive practices during these first three years. Jubei's trip in 2013 was her first trip home after the completion of her initial three-year period of practices in Yachen.

9. For a discussion of the self-immolation protests in Tibet, see McGranahan and Litzinger 2012. See also Makley 2015; Whalen-Bridge 2015; and Woeser 2016. For the protests in Lhasa in 2008, see Hillman 2014 and Topgyal 2011.

10. The Tibetan New Year and the Chinese New Year are normally about one month or so apart, but in 2013 they were nearly synchronous at just one day apart.

11. Cheng and Selden 1994; Mackenzie 2002; Mallee 2000; and Zhang 2001.

12. Chan, Selden, and Pun 2020; Chang 2008; Hillenbrand 2023; Jacta 2006; Lee 1998; Loyalka 2012; Pai 2012; Pun 2005; Sun 2014; Yan 2008; Zhang 2001; and Zheng 2009.

13. For discussions about the Tibetan resistance surrounding Lhasa, see Schwartz 1994.

14. See Cresswell 2006; Sheller and Urry 2006; Uteng and Cresswell 2008; and Salazar 2014.

15. Rabjung [rab 'byung] is an abbreviation of raptu jungwa [rab tu byung ba], meaning "one who goes forth." These are the vows normally taken after the lay vows (five basic vows). The person taking rabjung vows commits to "leave behind lay clothes and signs, wear the robes of an ordained person and shave the head, and follow the teachings of the Buddha" (Lama Yeshe Wisdom Archive n.d.).

16. The discussions of female lay renunciants in Tibet are scattered. Anna Grimshaw's (1994) research on Tibetan Buddhist nuns residing at the foot of the Himalayas briefly sketches a group of women who live near nunneries but are not really nuns themselves. A decade later, Kim Gutschow (2004) remarks on "household nuns" in the Ladaki region who do not join nunneries but maintain celibacy at home. Charlene E. Makley (2005) mentions the existence of such lay female renunciants in Amdo. Sherry B. Ortner (1996) mentions the name korwa, as in "peripheral one," to indicate a female renunciant in the Himalayas. Outside the Buddhist context, the practice of female nonmarriage also exists for specific needs of society in the Tibetan cultural region of the Himalayas. Sidney Ruth Schuler's study (1987) on Chumik in the Himalayas shows that

the practice of female nonmarriage operates in a fraternal polyandry system for certain economic benefits and environmental adaptations. See also Goldstein 1971 for this line of discussion.

17. This is quite different from other Buddhist-dominated regions in Asia. For the past few decades, in Theravāda Buddhist societies in South and Southeast Asia (mostly in Sri Lanka, Burma, and Thailand), the number of female renunciants has grown. *Dsms* (Sri Lanka), *mae chi* (Thailand), and *thela shin* (or *thila shin*, "holder of precepts," Burma) are specific terms for indicating lay female renunciants in these societies. Unlike Tibet, these women have been socially visible and their presence has been semi-institutionalized in the mainstream Theravāda tradition. In particular, some say that the reason for the increasing number of lay female renunciants in these societies may be related to the interruption of the full ordination of females in the *bhiksunī* Order. Currently, the full ordination order is preserved in some of the Mahayana Buddhist traditions, for example, in China, Korea, Taiwan, and Vietnam, and in the Chinese diasporic societies of Indonesia, Malaysia, and the Philippines. Some women from Theravāda countries, especially those who can afford to travel to places such as China and Korea, where they can access full ordination, have started receiving the *bhiksunī* Order within other traditions. Because of the different lineages and traditions of Theravāda and Mahayana in these cases, there are ongoing debates around the legitimacy of such ordinations. See Bloss 1987; Mrozik 2009; and Tsomo 1996. For recent debates on nuns' full ordination in Tibetan Buddhism, see Hannah 2012 and Schneider 2012. In addition, in colloquial Tibetan, *ani* is also used to indicate an aunt or an elder female relative, but *jomo* means "nun."

18. The highest level of ordination (full ordination) for female practitioners in Tibetan Buddhism is *gelongma* [*dge long ma*] (*bhiksuni* in Sanskrit); but this opportunity is currently not available to the nuns. Some Tibetan nuns (particularly those from the exile community in India) have taken their *gelongma* statuses by being ordained in other Buddhist traditions in which female full ordination is still active (South Korea, China, Vietnam, etc.). Most nuns in Yachen take a novice nun's vow (*getsülma* [*dge tshul ma*]), but the full ordination issue was never raised in Yachen during the time I visited from 2010 to 2019. Debates around the full ordination of nuns in the Tibetan exile community have been ongoing for several decades because they involve complicated interpretations of monastic rules and traditions. The debates culminated in 2007 when the fourteenth Dalai Lama convened monastic and academic *vinaya* experts to discuss the Tibetan *bhiksunī* lineage at the Buddhist Conference in Hamburg, Germany. At the meeting, he expressed his support for female full ordination: "I am 100% sure if Buddha were here today, he would certainly give us permission for bhikshuni vows" (Foundation for the Preservation of Mahayana Tradition 2007).

19. This is true in most cases but not all. Some rituals in Yachen are forbidden for the nuns to join due to their lack of monastic status. But the nuns I talked to did not consider such restrictions as discrimination toward the nuns and their status. They genuinely believe that they receive equal opportunity and access to the highest teachings, equal to the monks' access, in Yachen.

2. BUILDING AN ENCAMPMENT

1. Antonio Terrone (2010) calls Yachen a "quasi-monastic community" for this reason.

2. As I discussed in chapter 1, the nuns take novice vows, *getsülma* in Yachen. Full ordination for the nuns is not available in Tibetan Buddhism.

3. When electricity became available after 2015, some nuns began using electric saws.

4. The work team (*gongzuozu*) is known to be a direct subunit of the United Front Work Department (Tongyi zhanxian gongzuobu); their chain of command therefore does not include the local police but is part of the central line of the Chinese

Communist Party (CCP). Most of the information I was able to obtain about the work team in Yachen comes from nuns who shared their encounters with work team members. Yet on one unexpected occasion, I was able to talk with a former work team member when I was in a nearby town. According to him, work team members received a good deal of financial compensation for their work in such an environmentally challenging and remote place. He vividly described to me the abundant amount of money he could spend for groceries and fuel each month during his time in Yachen. For information about the history and structure of the United Front Work Department in China, see Kataoka 1974 and Van Slyke 1967.

5. A voluminous government report on Yachen that was written in 2007 concludes with an overall assessment and advice regarding Yachen: Yachen is generally stable with no serious political disturbances being reported, but the government still should not let down its guard. In 2007, the government dispatched a team of officials and researchers from Beijing to Yachen and had them conduct a thorough examination of Yachen. The team produced this report after their trip. The document has been restricted and is meant for internal circulation only. Nonetheless, to my good fortune, I was allowed to read a few selected pages of this document, including the conclusion mentioned above, when I visited the China Tibetology Research Center (Zhongguo zangxue yanjiu zhongxin) in Beijing in 2012.

6. In Yachen, all hut transactions are strictly monitored and regulated by Yachen's head office (not the police or the work team). The price of a hut is calculated by the head office based on its examination of the individual hut being transacted. In the case of a prefabricated structure, the head office requires the nuns to pay half of the price of the unit (about 10,000 RMB, equivalent to around 1,500 USD) when they move in. They can stay there without making further payments as long as they maintain their nunship in Yachen. But if a nun decides to leave Yachen, she must pay the rest of the price.

7. Electricity arrived in the nuns' area around 2015, and public toilets have been built and renovated since 2015.

8. I asked about labor mobilization in Yachen many times over and to different personnel during my fieldwork. However, I failed to receive any straight answers. Chinese practitioners, whether monastics or laypersons, were exempt from larger labor obligations except for small physical tasks that were directly related to their own master (repairing the master's house, for example). I never witnessed any monks engaging in communal labor, regardless of their monastic status. In a regular monastery in Tibet, novice monks serve senior monks by providing various services for the monastery, but in Yachen, with its large number of nuns, all physical tasks, even heavy duties such as construction, fall to the nuns' daily duties. The nuns with whom I worked didn't think of such labor mobilization as burdensome or meaningless. Many nuns appreciated such opportunities to serve the community (see also chapter 4).

9. Padmasambhava's demon-taming stories often appear in introductory materials on the history of Tibetan Buddhism; see, for example, Powers 2007. The Nyingma sect of Tibetan Buddhism, as the oldest tradition, sees Padmasambhava and his teachings as particularly important in their lineage. Achuk lama is considered to be one of the revealers (tertön), a bearer of Padmasambhava's teachings. For other taming accounts of demons and wrathful deities in Tibetan Buddhism, see Dalton 2011.

10. Dzokchen [rdzogs chen] (a shortened term for dzokpa chenpo [rdzogs pa chen po]) is the highest meditative practice in the Nyingma sect that focuses on illuminating the primordial status of a being. Because of the influence of the two large, leading Buddhist encampments (Yachen and Larung) in Kham, both of whose main teachings are Dzokchen, many Chinese disciples who follow Yachen and Larung practice Dzokchen widely and systematically in the name of Dayuanmanfa (the Great Perfection).

For introductory information on Dzokchen practices, see Tulku Thondup Rinpoche 1986; van Schaik 2004; and Higgins 2012. The fourteenth Dalai Lama is known to be a serious Dzokchen practitioner himself despite the fact that his lineage belongs to the Geluk order. He taught Dzokchen on his teaching trips to the West in the 1990s. His Dzokchen teaching for Western audiences was recorded and turned into a book. See Dalai Lama XIV 2004.

11. Jane Caple's (2013, 2019) ethnographic work shows how Tibetan monasticism and monastic architecture have been restored in contemporary Amdo. She argues that it is unfair to see the revival of Tibetan Buddhism in Amdo entirely within the umbrella of the changing political climate or state policies in the 1980s. She argues that the revival has more to do with the struggles of individuals who secretly preserved traditions, teachings, morality, and education throughout the Maoist era.

12. For more information about the treasure movement, see Doctor 2005; Germano 1998; Gyatso 1993, 1998; Terrone 2002, 2010; and Tulku Thondup Rinpoche 1986.

13. Rita Gross's works focus on providing alternative understandings of early Buddhist texts with regard to gender issues. See Gross 1993, 2009 and Tsomo 2000, 2014, 2019.

14. There are few studies in the English language on Tibetan nuns in contemporary Tibet. A handful of book-length anthropological accounts about the lives of Tibetan female practitioners are available, but these focus largely on the Himalayan region. See Havnevik 1989; Härkönen 2023; Grimshaw 1994; and Gutschow 2004.

15. I do not mean to suggest that all Tibetan women at home are mistreated and miserable or that all Tibetan men are mistreating their wives and daughters. The point is that the groups of nuns with whom I associated in Yachen seemed to agree unanimously that, for them, becoming a nun and joining a community like Yachen brought them a far more blessed life than being a mother and wife at home.

16. Carole McGranahan's (2010) insight may be helpful in our search for clues to understanding this perspective; she shows how Tibetan women can become "dispossessed" of their own personal stories by locating themselves within a larger institutional framework and narrative. In her research on Tibetan women in the exile community, these women always narrated their own stories by situating themselves within a larger Tibetan national history; in doing so, they locate themselves in a niche within the solemn resistance of Tibetan nationalism. She finds that these women do not narrate their stories as being about purely personal matters but as part of a grand national narrative; individual stories are "dispossessed" by the story owners. Similarly, the nuns with whom I worked in Yachen narrate their stories almost only in relation to Buddhist accounts.

3. INTIMATE THINGS

1. Chinese nuns usually have some leeway to circumvent the curfew. For the early morning lectures that were initiated by the head lama for the Chinese practitioners, the Chinese nuns could attend the lecture every day without following the curfew.

2. The areas for the monks' and lamas' quarters were wired for electricity much earlier than the nuns' area and had a much more reliable supply. Even after its arrival, the electrical supply in the nuns' area has often been unstable, with blackouts that can last for a few days to a week at a time.

3. This is not meant to be a generalization about all Tibetan nuns' attitudes toward their practices. Some Tibetan nuns are also rigid about their individual practices. From my observations, however, and for various reasons that I will elaborate on further in this chapter, the Tibetan nuns usually have a relatively more relaxed and flexible approach to their individual practices than the Chinese nuns have.

4. The word "boyfriend" must be contextualized here. At the very least, the term did not seem to convey the kind of relationship or commitment between boyfriends and

girlfriends as it is usually understood in Western societies. At the time when I discovered this word in Yachen, the connotations associated with the term had to do with platonic and nonsexual relationships. But even though the term doesn't imply the existence of sexual interactions (at least not in the group of nuns I was associated with), it does leave open the possibility of such a relationship in the future.

5. This so-called punishment is performed verbally and individually (by the monitor or senior nuns) rather than physically or institutionally. As a result of the punishment, the nun's mobility is sometimes restricted; for example, she is not allowed to go outside the community to visit her hometown or go to local markets. Such punishments are mainly intended to help the nuns by giving them time to reflect on and rectify inappropriate behaviors so that they can continue to practice and advance as nuns. The punishment does not usually result in expulsion from Yachen.

6. These relationships were platonic rather than physical. If a relationship becomes physical, the nun and the monk will likely decide to disrobe (i.e., to renounce their practice and return to lay life) and leave the monastic community together.

7. Yachen's head office is in fact quite aware of the affairs occurring between young nuns and monks that will derail them from solitary practices. Therefore, a special team consisting of several monitor nuns regularly patrols hidden corners of Yachen to look for secret meetings.

8. See Keyes and Daniel 1983.

4. NEW GESTURES

1. The Tibetan term for a fully ordained nun is *gelongma* (*bhiksuni* in Sanskrit). The nuns in the Tibetan exile community in northern India have recently been allowed to take the *gelongma* exam, which means that they can obtain full ordination status, but this hasn't been the case in Tibet. There has been a wide range of debates and discussions regarding the establishment of the full ordination tradition for nuns in Tibetan Buddhism. See Gyatso 2010; Hannah 2012; Schneider 2012; and Tsomo 1999, 2003.

2. Yachen has set up a small office for collecting the prayer lists of individuals. In this office, monks write down prayers from individuals and collect money from them as well. The amount of money submitted by individuals to the office is discretionary, contingent on the situations of the donors each time. This list of prayers is transferred to the daily chanting sessions, where the nuns and monks pray communally for the petitioners. Based on their attendance at the daily sessions, the nuns receive compensation every month or so.

3. This is in contrast to Larung Gar, another large monastic encampment in Kham. The practitioners in Larung Gar seem less attentive to the absence of their lamas, partially because the lamas from Larung travel actively throughout the year in China and in other foreign countries to spread Buddhist teachings. Their frequent travels limit their time of residence in Larung, and thus the practitioners are accustomed to not having their teachers in residence all the time. I failed to meet two of the most famous teachers from Larung, Kenpo Tsultrim Lodro and Khenpo Sodargye, when I visited Larung myself three times during my field research in Tibet. Ironically, I met them both later in the United States when they each separately visited Columbia University in New York City.

4. The term "worship" should not be read as having the same connotation as in Christianity: worship of God. Buddhism does not feature an omnipotent god figure; Shakyamuni Buddha was a historic figure who reached enlightenment and transmitted the path to enlightenment to his followers. The ultimate salvation from *samsara* is therefore fundamentally up to individual practice and perseverance. The role of the guru, just as with Shakyamuni himself, is essentially to be a guide or a helper rather than a creator or a source of universal power. I admit, however, that sometimes it is difficult to separate clearly the roles of guru as guide and guru as god when seeing how

Tibetan lamas are treated by their disciples. In Yachen, stories of the supernatural powers of the lamas—for example, healing a terminal disease and walking through the walls—are popularly shared, and many disciples expect or believe their teachers to be more than just guides. Any object used or simply touched by a renowned lama is treated as sacred; leftover food and even excreta from the lamas are not exempt from this list. Belief in the supernatural powers of the lamas tends to be stronger among Chinese Buddhist disciples.

5. In Yachen, Dzokchen is transmitted only and directly through the verbal messages (direct transmission) of teachers, who possess all-inclusive power and insight into the disciple's state of mind and her readiness to receive and advance in her practice. Teachers observe the development of individual disciples' progress and decide whether the next level of practice can be initiated. This is why one can often see a long line of nuns in the head lama's yard in Yachen as they wait their turn to visit the lama and receive instructions. In an ideal situation, the teachings are transmitted during one-on-one interactions between a teacher and a disciple, but the number of practitioners (over twelve thousand) in Yachen makes this arrangement almost impossible. Therefore, nuns who are in the same or a similar stage of practice form a group and seek instructions together at a single session; any teachings transmitted during the meeting with the lama, either individually or collectively, are not shared with outsiders. For a general introduction to the Nyingma tradition in Tibetan Buddhism, see chapters in Powers 2007 and Samuel 1993. For the Dzokchen practice and the Nyingma school more broadly, see Karmay 1988 and Pelzang 2004.

6. When we desperately looked for a place to sleep for the night, I did not see clearly where we were being led to stay. The house looked like a traditional Tibetan house where a family might live rather than a monastic residential unit for an individual monk. I realized only later how inappropriate it would be for two females to stay in a monk's unit (even though the room was separate) and to dine with monks at the same table.

7. *Torma* [*gtor ma*] is a ritualistic figure made of barley flour and butter. It has various sizes and colors depending on the type of tantric ritual.

8. *Gyaling* [*rgya gling*] is a musical instrument used during puja in Tibetan monasteries, and a group of selected nuns in Yachen are specifically trained to play it when rituals are performed.

9. To an increasing extent, Tibetan nuns as well as the head office have realized that speaking Chinese is important for being fully functional in dealing with ordinary matters in contemporary Tibetan society. As the overall Chinese influence in small and large Tibetan towns is increasing, the inability to understand Chinese is no longer just an inconvenience but a disadvantage. For this reason, some Tibetan nuns with whom I worked organized themselves into a small group to learn Chinese from a fellow nun who spoke fluent Chinese. In their spare time, approximately six nuns gathered infrequently at a nun's hut and learned the most useful colloquial Chinese phrases, such as those they need at hospitals, shops, bus stations, and so on. Although these self-organized studies were not meant as preparation for the exam but to fulfill the nuns' practical needs, they signal the general zeal for learning among the Tibetan nuns in Yachen.

10. Tulku Asong also emphasized the importance of education for lay Tibetans. Many Tibetans in remote nomadic regions are reluctant to send their children to schools in towns because, as Tulku Asong observed, the parents did not want to be separated from their children. The parents also concluded that school education was not very useful for a traditional nomadic life. Tulku Asong strongly objected to this conclusion, emphasized the importance of education during his lectures for nomads who visited Yachen, and encouraged parents to send their children to schools even if just for twenty days a year.

11. I thank Nicola Schneider (2013, 151) for pointing out that a similar medical training program existed in Tashi Gönsar.

12. See Tashi Tsering 2005.

13. For a more thorough explanation of the development of Tibetan medicine since the 1950s, see Adams 2001; Craig 2012; Janes 1995; and Samuel 2013.

5. CABBAGE, TOFU, AND SAUSAGE

1. See Bourdieu 2005; Counihan and Van Esterik 2013; Douglas 1975; Goody 1982; Karrebæk, Riley, and Cavanaugh 2018; Lupton 1996; and Mintz 1985.

2. The merchants, however, sometimes cheat the customers (the nuns) by bundling vegetables into plastic bags when they sell them. In the prepacked bundles sold in the market, the nuns often found rotten vegetables hidden inside. This kind of behavior by the sellers is difficult for the head office to catch because the sellers are not technically violating the condition of not raising the price of the vegetables.

3. For a discussion on Chinese involvement in the Tibetan Buddhist revival, see Jones 2011; Osburg 2020; Yü 2008, 2012; and Zhang 2012.

4. *Zangjuemu* is the term used by Chinese nuns and Chinese disciples to refer to Tibetan nuns. It is a combination of the Chinese terms *zang* (Tibetan) and *juemu* (*jomo*, nun).

5. As a shorthand, I call this tsampa-talk. The Tibetan nuns with whom I worked often used a specific category of food, tsampa, to differentiate the Chinese nuns and their bodily capability from their own. They described Chinese nuns as being pale and weak, meaning the Chinese nuns' complexions were whiter and their physical power was weak. The main reason for the "weaker" Chinese bodies, according to the Tibetan nuns, is that the Chinese nuns do not eat tsampa. For many of the Tibetans I met, tsampa was almost a national moral food that good, real Tibetans should eat daily, and those young Tibetans who avoided tsampa would likely have more disease and weaker stamina.

6. These are garlic, green onion, chive, wild chive, and scilla. This rule is widely practiced in the Chinese Buddhist tradition but not in Tibetan Buddhism. However, Chinese nuns who practice in the Tibetan tradition continue by choice to keep this rule strictly in Yachen.

7. For a discussion of active Buddhist businesses and exchanges in Chengdu, see Brox 2017, 2019.

8. For a description of elites' lives in Chengdu and an introduction to the city, see Osburg 2013.

9. *Xuefo* ("studying" Buddhism) and *xiufo* ("practicing" Buddhism) are often used interchangeably by Chinese disciples to indicate the fact that they are Buddhists. On the other hand, *xinfo* ("believing" Buddhism) is used at times when faith in Buddhism needs to be emphasized.

10. One employee of Sun's business, who was also a Buddhist devotee herself, told me that their business is similar to the corporate social responsibility (CSR) model: they pursue profits in a way that is helpful to other people and the environment. Her interpretation of Buddhist teachings is broad, flexible, and practical; she believes that those who are studying Buddhism should care not only about their own benefits and wealth but also must always consider the broader beneficial impact for others.

11. For instance, the Buddha Shakyamuni himself is known to have died of food poisoning from pork that he was served. In his time, the sangha population was mostly on the move and relied on the food they collected from their lay supporters. For whatever food was poured into their bowls by the laity, they received it with gratitude and prayed for their supporters. Thus, in this early Buddhist context, it hardly made any sense for Buddhist monks and nuns to choose or regulate their diet.

12. John Kieschnick (2005) argues that the concept of vegetarianism existed before Buddhism was imported into China, and the vegetarian diet among Chinese laity connoted a sense of morality that is contrasted with the prevailing habit of voracious meat eating.

13. Kieschnick (2005) also mentions the "five pungent plants" that have been banned for Buddhist practitioners. These vegetables were banned initially because of their smell, but later, the additional meaning was attached that they hinder the flow of "passion" in the bodies of the practitioners.

14. The most prominent figure for advocating vegetarianism in recent years is Khenpo Trültrim Lodrö of Larung Gar. His 2003 plea to Tibetan audiences that they take up vegetarianism and his problematizing of animal slaughter initiated a wide range of debates among and beyond Tibetans. See Barstow 2018; Gayley 2017; and Kabzung 2015.

15. Refusal to consume meat altogether is not yet a solid principle upheld in many Tibetan monasteries. Meat consumption has remained mostly a matter of individual choice for both laity and nonlaity, based on flexible applications of the principle. Meat has long been at the center of the regular Tibetan diet, and it has also been offered when greeting guests, performing rituals, joining festivals, and so on. Meat dishes, including dried beef (*sha kam* [*sha skam*]) remain popular in traditional Tibetan households. Monastics also consume meat; monks cook and serve it regularly, although they use specific prayers when they do so.

16. The number of Chinese practitioners, consisting of both laity and nonlaity, in Yachen was estimated to be a couple of hundred at most.

EPILOGUE

1. A special report was published on the destruction on Larung Gar by the Tibetan Center for Human Rights and Democracy (2001).

References

Abu-Lughod, Lila. 1990. "The Romance of Resistance: Tracing Transformations of Power through Bedouin Women." *American Ethnologist* 17 (1): 41–55. https://doi .org/10.1525/ae.1990.17.1.02a00030.

Abu-Lughod, Lila. 1993. *Writing Women's Worlds: Bedouin Stories*. Berkeley: University of California Press.

Adams, Vincanne. 2001. "The Sacred in the Scientific: Ambiguous Practices of Science in Tibetan Medicine." *Cultural Anthropology* 16 (4): 542–75. https://doi.org /10.1525/can.2001.16.4.542.

Allione, Tsultrim. 2000. *Women of Wisdom*. Ithaca, NY: Snow Lion.

Baimacuo (Padma'tsho). 2011. "Dangdai Zangzu Nüni de Juese yu Rentong—Yikangqu Yaqingsi weili" ("The Role and Recognition of Contemporary Tibetan Buddhist Nuns by Focusing on Yachen"). *Religious Studies (China)* 3: 165–71.

Barnett, Robert, and Shirin Akiner, eds. 1994. *Resistance and Reform in Tibet*. Bloomington: Indiana University Press.

Barstow, Geoffrey. 2018. *Food of Sinful Demons: Meat, Vegetarianism, and the Limits of Buddhism in Tibet*. New York: Columbia University Press.

Bass, Catriona. 1998. *Education in Tibet: Policy and Practice since 1950*. London: Tibet Information Network.

Bessenger, Suzanne M. 2016. *Echoes of Enlightenment: The Life and Legacy of the Tibetan Saint Sonam Peldren*. New York: Oxford University Press.

Bloss, Lowell W. 1987. "The Female Renunciants of Sri Lanka: The Dasasilmattawa." *Journal of the International Association of Buddhist Studies* 10: 7–32.

Bourdieu, Pierre. 1977. *Outline of a Theory of Practice*. New York: Cambridge University Press.

Bourdieu, Pierre. 1984. *Distinction: A Social Critique of the Judgement of Taste*. Cambridge, MA: Harvard University Press.

Bourdieu, Pierre. 2005. "Taste of Luxury, Taste of Necessity." In *The Taste Culture Reader: Experiencing Food and Drink*. Edited by Carolyn Korsmeyer, 72–78. Oxford: Berg.

Brox, Trine. 2017. "Tibetan Minzu Market: The Intersection of Ethnicity and Commodity." *Asian Ethnicity* 18 (1): 1–21. https://doi.org/10.1080/14631369.2015.1013175.

Brox, Trine. 2019. "Landscapes of Little Lhasa: Materialities of the Vernacular, Political and Commercial in Urban China." *Geoforum* 107 (December): 24–33. https://doi .org/10.1016/j.geoforum.2019.10.017.

Butler, Judith. 2005. *Giving an Account of Oneself*. New York: Fordham University Press.

Byrne, Jean. 2013. "Why I Am Not a Buddhist Feminist: A Critical Examination of 'Buddhist Feminism.'" *Feminist Theology* 21 (2): 180–94. https://doi.org/10.1177 /0966735012464149.

Cabezón, José Ignacio, ed. 1992. *Buddhism, Sexuality, and Gender*. Albany: State University of New York Press.

Caple, Jane. 2013. "Remembering Monastic Revival: Stories from Reb Kong and Western Ba Yan." In *Monastic and Lay Traditions in North-Eastern Tibet*. Edited by Yangdon Dhondup, Ulrich Pagel, and Geoffrey Samuel, 23–48. Leiden: Brill.

Caple, Jane. 2019. *Morality and Monastic Revival in Post-Mao Tibet*. Contemporary Buddhism. Honolulu: University of Hawai'i Press.

Chan, Jenny, Mark Selden, and Ngai Pun. 2020. *Dying for an iPhone: Apple, Foxconn, and the Lives of China's Workers*. Chicago: Haymarket.

Chang, Leslie T. 2008. *Factory Girls: From Village to City in a Changing China*. New York: Spiegel & Grau.

Chayet, Anne. 1999. "Women and Reincarnation in Tibet: The Case of the Gung Ru mKha' 'gro Ma." In *Facets of Tibetan Religious Tradition and Contacts with Neighbouring Cultural Areas*. Edited by Ester Bianchi and Alfredo Cadonna, 65–82. Firenze: Leo S. Olschki Editore.

Cheng, Tiejun, and Mark Selden. 1994. "The Origins and Social Consequences of China's Hukou System." *China Quarterly* 139: 644–68.

Colburn, Forrest D., ed. 1989. *Everyday Forms of Peasant Resistance*. Armonk, NY: M. E. Sharpe.

Comaroff, Jean. 1985. *Body of Power, Spirit of Resistance: The Culture and History of a South African People*. Chicago: University of Chicago Press.

Counihan, Carole, and Penny Van Esterik, eds. 2013. *Food and Culture: A Reader*. New York: Routledge.

Craig, Sienna R. 2012. *Healing Elements: Efficacy and the Social Ecologies of Tibetan Medicine*. Berkeley: University of California Press.

Cresswell, Tim. 2006. *On the Move: Mobility in the Modern Western World*. New York: Routledge.

Dalai Lama XIV. 2004. *Dzokchen: The Heart Essence of the Great Perfection*. Ithaca, NY: Snow Lion.

Dalton, Jacob P. 2011. *The Taming of the Demons: Violence and Liberation in Tibetan Buddhism*. New Haven, CT: Yale University Press.

de Certeau, Michel. 1984. *The Practice of Everyday Life*. Berkeley: University of California Press.

Deji Zhuoma. 2003. *Zangchuanfojiao Chujianüxing Yanjiu* (Research on Nuns in Tibetan Buddhism). Beijing: Social Sciences Academic Press.

Deleuze, Gilles, and Félix Guattari. 1987. *A Thousand Plateaus: Capitalism and Schizophrenia*. Minneapolis: University of Minnesota Press.

Diemberger, Hildegard. 2007. *When a Woman Becomes a Religious Dynasty: The Samding Dorje Phagmo of Tibet*. New York: Columbia University Press.

Doctor, Andreas. 2005. *Tibetan Treasure Literature: Revelation, Tradition, and Accomplishment in Visionary Buddhism*. Ithaca, NY: Snow Lion.

Douglas, Mary. 1975. *Implicit Meanings: Essays in Anthropology*. London: Routledge & Kegan Paul.

Facts and Details. 2022. "Education in Tibet." http://factsanddetails.com/china/cat6/sub37/item201.html. Last updated September 2022.

Faure, Bernard. 1998. *The Red Thread: Buddhist Approaches to Sexuality*. Princeton, NJ: Princeton University Press.

Faure, Bernard. 2003. *The Power of Denial: Buddhism, Purity, and Gender*. Princeton, NJ: Princeton University Press.

Fehérváry, Krisztina. 2013. *Politics in Color and Concrete: Socialist Materialities and the Middle Class in Hungary*. Bloomington: Indiana University Press.

Findly, Ellison Banks, ed. 2000. *Women's Buddhism Buddhism's Women: Tradition, Revision, Renewal*. Boston: Wisdom.

Flaubert, Gustave. 1979. *Flaubert in Egypt: A Sensibility on Tour*. Edited by Francis Steegmuller. Chicago: Academy Chicago.

Foucault, Michel. 1993. "About the Beginning of the Hermeneutics of the Self: Two Lectures at Dartmouth." *Political Theory* 21 (2): 198–227. https://doi.org/10.1177 /0090591793021002004.

Foucault, Michel. 1994. *Ethics: Subjectivity and Truth.* New York: New Press.

Foundation for the Preservation of the Mahayana Tradition (FPMT). 2007, October– November. "Dalai Lama Urges Introduction of Bhikshuni Vows into Tibetan Tradition." https://fpmt.org/mandala/archives/mandala-issues-for-2007/october /buddhist-women-a-mandala-special-report/.

Fox, Richard G. 1985. *Lions of the Punjab: Culture in the Making.* Berkeley: University of California Press.

Gayley, Holly. 2007a. "Ontology of the Past and Its Materialization in Tibetan Trea- sures." In *The Invention of Sacred Tradition.* Edited by James R. Lewis and Olav Hammer, 213–40. Cambridge: Cambridge University Press.

Gayley, Holly. 2007b. "Soteriology of the Senses in Tibetan Buddhism." *Numen* 54 (4): 459–99.

Gayley, Holly. 2016. *Love Letters from Golok: A Tantric Couple in Modern Tibet.* New York: Columbia University Press.

Gayley, Holly. 2017. "The Compassionate Treatment of Animals." *Journal of Religious Ethics* 45 (1): 29–57. https://doi.org/10.1111/jore.12167.

Germano, David. 1998. "Re-Membering the Dismembered Body of Tibet: Contempo- rary Tibetan Visionary Movements in the People's Republic of China." In *Bud- dhism in Contemporary Tibet: Religious Revival and Cultural Identity.* Edited by Melvyn C. Goldstein and Matthew T. Kapstein, 53–94. Berkeley: University of California Press.

Germano, David, and Nicolas Tournadre. 2003. "THL Simplified Phonetic Transcrip- tion of Standard Tibetan." http://www.thlib.org/reference/transliteration/#!essay =/thl/phonetics/.

Goldstein, Melvyn C. 1971. "Stratification, Polyandry, and Family Structure in Central Tibet." *Southwestern Journal of Anthropology* 27 (1): 64–74. https://doi.org/10.1086 /soutjanth.27.1.3629185.

Goody, Jack. 1982. *Cooking, Cuisine and Class: A Study in Comparative Sociology.* Lon- don: Cambridge University Press.

Grimshaw, Anna. 1994. *Servants of the Buddha: Winter in a Himalayan Convent.* Cleve- land, OH: Pilgrim.

Gross, Rita M. 1993. *Buddhism after Patriarchy: A Feminist History, Analysis, and Reconstruction of Buddhism.* Albany: State University of New York Press.

Gross, Rita M. 2009. *A Garland of Feminist Reflections: Forty Years of Religious Exploration.* Berkeley: University of California Press.

Guha, Ranajit. 1983. *Elementary Aspects of Peasant Insurgency in Colonial India.* Delhi: Oxford University Press.

Guha, Ranajit. 1997. *A Subaltern Studies Reader, 1986–1995.* Minneapolis: University of Minnesota Press.

Gutschow, Kim. 2004. *Being a Buddhist Nun: The Struggle for Enlightenment in the Himalayas.* Cambridge, MA: Harvard University Press.

Gyatso, Janet. 1993. "The Logic of Legitimation in the Tibetan Treasure Tradition." *History of Religions* 33 (2): 97–134. https://doi.org/10.1086/463360.

Gyatso, Janet. 1998. *Apparitions of the Self: The Secret Autobiographies of a Tibetan Visionary.* Princeton, NJ: Princeton University Press.

Gyatso, Janet. 2010. "Female Ordination in Buddhism: Looking into a Crystal Ball, Making a Future." In *Dignity and Discipline: Reviving Full Ordination for*

Buddhist Nuns. Edited by Thea Mohr and Venerable Jampa Tsedroen, 1–22. Somerville, MA: Wisdom.

Hannah, Michelle. 2012. "Colliding Gender Imaginaries: Transnational Debates about Full Ordination for Tibetan Buddhist Nuns." *Asian Journal of Women's Studies* 18 (4): 7–44. https://doi.org/10.1080/12259276.2012.11666134.

Härkönen, Mitra. 2023. *Power and Agency in the Lives of Contemporary Tibetan Nuns: An Intersectional Study*. Sheffield, UK: Equinox.

Hastrup, Kirsten. 2004. "Getting It Right: Knowledge and Evidence in Anthropology." *Anthropological Theory* 4 (4): 455–72. https://doi.org/10.1177/1463499604047921.

Havnevik, Hanna. 1989. *Tibetan Buddhist Nuns: History, Cultural Norms, and Social Reality*. Oslo: Norwegian University Press.

Higgins, David. 2012. "An Introduction to the Tibetan Dzokchen (Great Perfection) Philosophy of Mind." *Religion Compass* 6 (10): 441–50.

Hillenbrand, Margaret. 2023. *On the Edge: Feeling Precarious in China*. New York: Columbia University Press.

Hillman, Ben. 2014. "Interpreting the Post-2008 Wave of Protest and Conflict in Tibet." *Far East* 4: 50–60.

Jacoby, Sarah. 2014. *Love and Liberation: Autobiographical Writings of the Tibetan Buddhist Visionary Sera Khandro*. New York: Columbia University Press.

Jacta, Tamara. 2006. *Rural Women in Urban China: Gender, Migration, and Social Change*. New York: M. E. Sharpe.

Janes, Craig R. 1995. "The Transformations of Tibetan Medicine." *Medical Anthropology Quarterly* 9 (1): 6–39. https://doi.org/10.1525/maq.1995.9.1.02a00020.

Jinba, Tenzin. 2014. *In the Land of the Eastern Queendom: The Politics of Gender and Ethnicity on the Sino-Tibetan Border*. Seattle: University of Washington Press.

Jones, Alison Denton. 2011. "Contemporary Han Chinese Involvement in Tibetan Buddhism: A Case Study from Nanjing." *Social Compass* 58 (4): 540–53. https://doi.org/10.1177/0037768611421134.

Jones, Reece. 2012. "Spaces of Refusal: Rethinking Sovereign Power and Resistance at the Border." *Annals of the Association of American Geographers* 102 (3): 685–99. https://doi.org/10.1080/00045608.2011.600193.

Kabzung, Gaerrang. 2015. "Development as Entangled Knot: The Case of the Slaughter Renunciation Movement in Tibet, China." *Journal of Asian Studies* 74 (4): 927–51. https://doi.org/10.1017/S0021911815001175.

Karmay, Samten Gyaltsen. 1988. *The Great Perfection: A Philosophical and Meditative Teaching of Tibetan Buddhism*. Leiden: Brill.

Karrebæk, Martha Sif, Kathleen C. Riley, and Jillian R. Cavanaugh. 2018. "Food and Language: Production, Consumption, and Circulation of Meaning and Value." *Annual Review of Anthropology* 47 (1): 17–32. https://doi.org/10.1146/annurev-anthro-102317-050109.

Kataoka, Tetsuya. 1974. *Resistance and Revolution in China: The Communists and the Second United Front*. Berkeley: University of California Press.

Kawata, Susumu. 2015. *Higashi Chibetto No Shūkyō Kūkan: Chūgoku Kyōsantō No Shūkyō Seisaku to Shakai Hen'yō (The Religious Space of Eastern Tibet: Religious Policies and Social Transformation of the Chinese Communist Party)*. Sapporo-shi: Hokkaidō Daigaku Shuppankai.

Keyes, Charles F., and E. Valentine Daniel, eds. 1983. *Karma: An Anthropological Inquiry*. Berkeley: University of California Press.

Kieschnick, John. 2005. "Buddhist Vegetarianism in China." In *Of Tripod and Palate: Food, Politics, and Religion in Traditional China*. Edited by Roel Sterckx, 186–212. New York: Palgrave Macmillan.

Kolås, Åshild. 1996. "Tibetan Nationalism: The Politics of Religion." *Journal of Peace Research* 33 (1): 51–66. https://doi.org/10.1177/0022343396033001004.

Lama Yeshe Wisdom Archive. n.d. "Rabjung (Tib)." https://www.lamayeshe.com/glossary /rabjung-tib.

Larkin, Brian. 2013. "The Politics and Poetics of Infrastructure." *Annual Review of Anthropology* 42 (1): 327–43. https://doi.org/10.1146/annurev-anthro-092412-155522.

Lee, Ching Kwan. 1998. *Gender and the South China Miracle: Two Worlds of Factory Women.* Berkeley: University of California Press.

Loyalka, Michelle. 2012. *Eating Bitterness: Stories from the Front Lines of China's Great Urban Migration.* Berkeley: University of California Press.

Lupton, Deborah. 1996. *Food, the Body and the Self.* London: Sage.

Mackenzie, Peter W. 2002. "Strangers in the City: The Hukou and Urban Citizenship in China." *Journal of International Affairs* 56 (1): 305–22.

Mahmood, Saba. 2005. *Politics of Piety: The Islamic Revival and the Feminist Subject.* Princeton, NJ: Princeton University Press.

Makley, Charlene E. 2005. "The Body of a Nun: Nunhood and Gender in Contemporary Amdo." In *Women in Tibet.* Edited by Janet Gyatso and Hanna Havnevik, 259–84. New York: Columbia University Press.

Makley, Charlene E. 2007. *The Violence of Liberation: Gender and Tibetan Buddhist Revival in Post-Mao China.* Berkeley: University of California Press.

Makley, Charlene E. 2015. "The Sociopolitical Lives of Dead Bodies: Tibetan Self-Immolation Protest as Mass Media." *Cultural Anthropology* 30 (3): 448–76. https://doi.org/10.14506/ca30.3.05.

Mallee, Hein. 2000. "Migration, Hukou and Resistance in Reform China." In *Chinese Society: Change, Conflict and Resistance.* Edited by Elizabeth J. Perry and Mark Selden, 140–61. London: Routledge.

Manning, Erin. 2016. *The Minor Gesture.* Durham, NC: Duke University Press.

Mauss, Marcel. 2006 [1935]. "Techniques of the Body." In *Techniques, Technology and Civilisation.* Edited by Nathan Schlanger, 77–96. New York: Durkheim.

Mbembe, Achille. 2001. *On the Postcolony.* Studies on the History of Society and Culture 41. Berkeley: University of California Press.

McCarthy, Roger E. 1997. *Tears of the Lotus: Accounts of Tibetan Resistance to the Chinese Invasion, 1950–1962.* Jefferson, NC: McFarland.

McGranahan, Carole. 2010. "Narrative Dispossession: Tibet and the Gendered Logics of Historical Possibility." *Comparative Studies in Society and History* 52 (4): 768–97. https://doi.org/10.1017/S0010417510000460.

McGranahan, Carol, and Ralph Litzinger. 2012. "Self-Immolation as Protest in Tibet." *Cultural Anthropology Hot Spots.* April 9, 2012. http://www.culanth.org/fieldsights/93 -self-immolation-as-protest-in-tibet.

Merleau-Ponty, Maurice. 2002. *Phenomenology of Perception.* Routledge Classics. London: Routledge.

Mintz, Sidney W. 1985. *Sweetness and Power: The Place of Sugar in Modern History.* New York: Penguin.

Mrozik, Susanne. 2009. "A Robed Revolution: The Contemporary Buddhist Nun's (Bhiksuni) Movement." *Religion Compass* 3 (3): 360–78. https://doi.org/10.1111 /j.1749-8171.2009.00136.x.

Ong, Aihwa. 1987. *Spirits of Resistance and Capitalist Discipline: Factory Women in Malaysia.* Albany: State University of New York Press.

Ortner, Sherry B. 1995. "Resistance and the Problem of Ethnographic Refusal." *Comparative Studies in Society and History* 37: 173–93. https://doi.org/10.1017 /S0010417500019587.

Ortner, Sherry B. 1996. *Making Gender: The Politics and Erotics of Culture*. Boston: Beacon.

Osburg, John. 2013. *Anxious Wealth Money and Morality among China's New Rich*. Stanford, CA: Stanford University Press.

Osburg, John. 2020. "Consuming Belief: Luxury, Authenticity, and Chinese Patronage of Tibetan Buddhism in Contemporary China." *HAU: Journal of Ethnographic Theory* 10 (1): 69–84. https://doi.org/10.1086/708547.

Pai, Hsiao-Hung. 2012. *Scattered Sand: The Story of China's Rural Migrants*. London: Verso.

Pelzang, Khenpo Ngawang. 2004. *A Guide to the Words of My Perfect Teacher*. Boston: Shambhala.

Postiglione, Gerard, Ben Jiao, and Sonam Gyatso. 2005. "Education in Rural Tibet: Development, Problems and Adaptations." *China (National University of Singapore. East Asian Institute)* 3 (1): 1–23. https://doi.org/10.1353/chn.2005.0004.

Powers, John. 2007. *Introduction to Tibetan Buddhism*. Ithaca, NY: Snow Lion.

Powers, John. 2017. *The Buddha Party: How the People's Republic of China Works to Define and Control Tibetan Buddhism*. New York: Oxford University Press.

Pun, Ngai. 2005. *Made in China: Women Factory Workers in a Global Workplace*. Durham, NC: Duke University Press.

Rancière, Jacques. 1999. *Disagreement: Politics and Philosophy*. Translated by Julie Rose. Minneapolis: University of Minnesota Press.

Rancière, Jacques. 2004. *The Politics of Aesthetics: The Distribution of the Sensible*. Translated by Gabriel Rockhill. London: Continuum.

Salazar, Noel B. 2014. "Anthropology." In *The Routledge Handbook of Mobilities*. Edited by Peter Adey et al., 55–63. New York: Routledge.

Samuel, Geoffrey. 1993. *Civilized Shamans: Buddhism in Tibetan Societies*. Washington, DC: Smithsonian Institution Press.

Samuel, Geoffrey. 2013. "Introduction: Medicine and Healing in Tibetan Societies." *East Asian Science, Technology and Society: An International Journal* 7: 335–51. https://doi.org/10.1215/18752160-2333224.

Schaeffer, Kurtis R. 2004. *Himalayan Hermitess: The Life of a Tibetan Buddhist Nun*. Oxford: Oxford University Press.

Schein, Louisa. 1997. "Gender and Internal Orientalism in China." *Modern China* 23 (1): 69–98. https://doi.org/10.1177/009770049702300103.

Schneider, Nicola. 2011. "The Third Dragkar Lama: An Important Figure for Female Monasticism in the Beginning of Twentieth Century Kham." *Revue d'Etudes Tibétaines* 21: 45–60.

Schneider, Nicola. 2012. "The Ordination of Dge Slong Ma: A Challenge to Ritual Prescriptions?" *Revisiting Rituals in a Changing Tibetan World*, January 2012, 109–35.

Schneider, Nicola. 2013. *Le Renoncement Au Féminin: Couvents et Nonnes dans le Bouddhisme Tibétain*. Paris: Presses Universitaires de Paris Nanterre.

Schneider, Nicola. 2015. "Self-Representation and Stories Told: The Life and Vicissitudes of Khandro Choechen." *Revue d'Etudes Tibétaines* 34: 171–88.

Schuler, Sidney Ruth. 1987. *The Other Side of Polyandry: Property, Stratification, and Nonmarriage in the Nepal Himalayas*. Boulder, CO: Westview.

Schwartz, Ronald D. 1994. *Circle of Protest: Political Ritual in the Tibetan Uprising*. New York: Columbia University Press.

Scott, James C. 1985. *Weapons of the Weak: Everyday Forms of Peasant Resistance*. New Haven, CT: Yale University Press.

Scott, James C. 1990. *Domination and the Arts of Resistance: Hidden Transcripts*. New Haven, CT: Yale University Press.

Scott, James C. 2009. *The Art of Not Being Governed: An Anarchist History of Upland Southeast Asia*. Yale Agrarian Studies. New Haven, CT: Yale University Press.

Scott, James C., and Benedict J. Tria Kerkvliet, eds. 1986. *Everyday Forms of Peasant Resistance in Southeast Asia*. London: Franck Cass.

Seymour, Susan. 2006. "Resistance." *Anthropological Theory* 6 (3): 303–21. https://doi.org/10.1177/1463499606066890.

Shakya, Tsering. 2012. "Self-Immolation, the Changing Language of Protest in Tibet." *Revue d'Études Tibétaines* 25: 19–39.

Shaw, Miranda. 1994. *Passionate Enlightenment: Women in Tantric Buddhism*. Princeton, NJ: Princeton University Press.

Sheller, Mimi, and John Urry. 2006. "The New Mobilities Paradigm." *Environment and Planning A: Economy and Space* 38 (2): 207–26. https://doi.org/10.1068/a37268.

Shneiderman, Sara. 2006. "Living Practical Dharma: A Tribute to Chomo Khandru and the Bonpo Women of Lubra Village, Mustang, Nepal." In *Women's Renunciation in South Asia: Nuns, Yoginis, Saints, and Singers*. Edited by Meena Khandelwal, Sondra L. Hausner, and Ann Grodzins Gold, 69–94. New York: Palgrave Macmillan.

Simpson, Audra. 2014. *Mohawk Interruptus: Political Life across the Borders of Settler States*. Durham, NC: Duke University Press.

Sindhi, Swaleha A., and Adfer Rashid Shah. 2012. "Life in Flames: Understanding Tibetan Self Immolations as Protest." *Tibet Journal* 37 (4): 34–53.

Stewart, Kathleen. 2014. "Road Registers." *Cultural Geographies* 21 (4): 549–63. https://doi.org/10.1177/1474474014525053.

Stoler, Ann Laura. 1985. *Capitalism and Confrontation in Sumatra's Plantation Belt, 1870–1979*. New Haven, CT: Yale University Press.

Sun, Wanning. 2014. *Subaltern China: Rural Migrants, Media, and Cultural Practices*. Lanham, MD: Rowman & Littlefield.

Tashi Tsering. 2005. "Outstanding Women in Tibetan Medicine." In *Women in Tibet: Past and Present*. Edited by Janet Gyatso and Hanna Havnevik, 169–94. New York: Columbia University Press.

Taussig, Michael. 1980. *The Devil and Commodity Fetishism in South America*. Chapel Hill: University of North Carolina Press.

Terrone, Antonio. 2002. "Visions, Arcane Claims, and Hidden Treasures: Charisma and Authority in a Present-Day Gter Ston." In *Tibet, Self, and the Tibetan Diaspora: Voices of Difference*. Edited by P. Christiaan Klieger, 213–28. PIATS 2000: Tibetan Studies: Proceedings of the Ninth Seminar of the International Association for Tibetan Studies, Leiden 2000. Leiden: Brill.

Terrone, Antonio. 2009. "Householders and Monks: A Study of Treasure Revealers and Their Role in Religious Revival in Contemporary Eastern Tibet." In *Buddhism Beyond the Monastery: Tantric Practices and Their Performers in Tibet and the Himalayas*. Edited by Sarah Jacoby and Antonio Terrone, 73–110. Leiden: Brill.

Terrone, Antonio. 2010. "*Bya Rog Prog Zhu, The Raven Crest: The Life and Teachings of BDe Chen' Od Gsal Rdo Rje, Treasure Revealer of Contemporary Tibet*." PhD diss., Leiden: University of Leiden.

Terrone, Antonio. 2017. "Nationalism Matters: Among Mystics and Martyrs of Tibet." In *Religion and Nationalism in Chinese Societies*. Edited by Cheng-tian Kuo, 279–308. Amsterdam: Amsterdam University Press.

Theodossopoulos, Dimitrios. 2014. "On De-Pathologizing Resistance." *History and Anthropology* 25 (4): 415–30. https://doi.org/10.1080/02757206.2014.933101.

Tibetan Center for Human Rights and Democracy. 2001. "*Destruction of Serthar Institute: A Special Report*." Dharamsala, India: Tibetan Center for Human Rights and Democracy.

Topgyal, Tsering. 2011. "Insecurity Dilemma and the Tibetan Uprising in 2008." *Journal of Contemporary China* 20 (69): 183–203. https://doi.org/10.1080/10670564 .2011.541627.

Tsomo, Karma Lekshe. 1996. *Sisters in Solitude: Two Traditions of Buddhist Monastic Ethics for Women*. Albany: State University of New York Press.

Tsomo, Karma Lekshe, ed. 1999. *Buddhist Women across Cultures: Realizations*. Albany: State University of New York Press.

Tsomo, Karma Lekshe, ed. 2000. *Innovative Buddhist Women: Swimming against the Stream*. Richmond, Surrey: Curzon.

Tsomo, Karma Lekshe. 2003. "Tibetan Nuns: New Roles and Possibilities." In *Exile as Challenge: The Tibetan Diaspora*. Edited by Hubertus von Welck and Dagmar Bernstorff, 342–66. Hyderabad, India: Orient Longman.

Tsomo, Karma Lekshe, ed. 2014. *Eminent Buddhist Women*. Albany: State University of New York Press.

Tsomo, Karma Lekshe, ed. 2019. *Buddhist Feminisms and Femininities*. Albany: State University of New York Press.

Tulku Thondup Rinpoche. 1986. *Hidden Teachings of Tibet: An Explanation of the Terma Tradition of Tibetan Buddhism*. Edited by Harold Talbott. London: Wisdom.

Turek, Magdalena Maria. 2013. "'In This Body and Life': The Religious and Social Significance of Hermits and Hermitages in Eastern Tibet Today and During Recent History." PhD diss., Humboldt-Universität zu Berlin.

Uteng, Tanu Priya, and Tim Cresswell. 2008. *Gendered Mobilities*. Aldershot, UK: Ashgate.

van Schaik, Sam. 2004. *Approaching the Great Perfection: Simultaneous and Gradual Approaches to Dzokchen Practice in Jigme Lingpa's Longchen Nyingtig*. Studies in Indian and Tibetan Buddhism. Boston: Wisdom.

Van Slyke, Lyman P. 1967. *Enemies and Friends: The United Front in Chinese Communist History*. Stanford, CA: Stanford University Press.

Whalen-Bridge, John. 2015. *Tibet on Fire: Buddhism, Protest, and the Rhetoric of Self-Immolation*. Houndmills, Basingstoke, Hampshire: Palgrave Macmillan.

Willis, Janice Dean, ed. 1989. *Feminine Ground: Essays on Women and Tibet*. Ithaca, NY: Snow Lion.

Wiskus, Jessica. 2013. *The Rhythm of Thought: Art, Literature, and Music after Merleau-Ponty*. Chicago: University of Chicago Press.

Woeser, Tsering. 2016. *Tibet on Fire: Self-Immolations against Chinese Rule*. London: Verso.

Woeser, Tsering, Lixiong Wang, and Violet S. Law. 2014. *Voices from Tibet: Selected Essays and Reportage*. Honolulu: University of Hawai'i Press.

Yan, Hairong. 2008. *New Masters, New Servants: Migration, Development, and Women Workers in China*. Durham, NC: Duke University Press.

Yeh, Emily T. 2007. "Exile Meets Homeland: Politics, Performance, and Authenticity in the Tibetan Diaspora." *Environment and Planning D: Society & Space* 25 (4): 648–67. https://doi.org/10.1068/d2805.

Yeh, Emily T. 2013. *Taming Tibet: Landscape Transformation and the Gift of Chinese Development*. Ithaca, NY: Cornell University Press.

Yü, Dan Smyer. 2008. "Living Buddhas, Netizens, and the Price of Religious Freedom." In *Privatizing China: Socialism from Afar*. Edited by Li Zhang and Aihwa Ong, 197–213. Ithaca, NY: Cornell University Press.

Yü, Dan Smyer. 2012. *The Spread of Tibetan Buddhism in China: Charisma, Money, Enlightenment*. London: Routledge.

Zhang, Li. 2001. *Strangers in the City: Reconfigurations of Space, Power, and Social Networks within China's Floating Population.* Stanford, CA: Stanford University Press.

Zhang, Yinong. 2012. "Between Nation and Religion: The Sino-Tibetan Buddhist Network in Post-Reform China." *Chinese Sociological Review* 45 (1): 55–69. https://doi.org/10.2753/CSA2162-0555450103.

Zheng, Tiantian. 2009. *Red Lights: The Lives of Sex Workers in Postsocialist China.* Minneapolis: University of Minnesota Press.

Index

abstinence, 121
Achuk lama, 5, 39–41, 56, 60, 89, 101
ani and *jomo*, 35
anthropological studies of food, 111
assemblages, 90, 110

ban on meat consumption, 15
being political, 10
bodily gestures and attitudes, 91
body-care talk, 115, 119; bodily desires or
  bodily pleasures, 117; care-talk, 128;
  techniques of body care, 118, 128
border checkpoints, 24; border restrictions,
  26; checkpoint office, 27; checkpoints, 24,
  26, 30, 95
Bourdieu, Pierre, 96, 121, 126
Buddhist ethics, 111, 134; ethical standard, 118
Buddhist monastery, 4
Buddhist practitioners, 4–6, 39, 111, 114, 117,
  121, 123, 125, 127; female practitioners, 8,
  11, 54. *See also* Chinese practitioners;
  Tibetan practitioners
Buddhist temples, 29
Butler, Judith, 82

capitalistic upward mobility, 16
cause and effect (*gyu* and *dré*), 83
Chamdo (Changdu), 21
Chegga, 99–100
Chengdu, 4, 123–124, 127–129
Cheyong, 115–118
Chinese Communist Party (CCP), 28, 46
Chinese infrastructural power, 122
Chinese markets, 119; Chinese vegetable
  merchants, 114
Chinese medicine, 105; Chinese medicine and
  biomedicine, 107; traditional Chinese
  medicine (*zhongyi*), 104
Chinese nuns, 14, 68, 73, 113–123, 129,
  133, 138
Chinese people, 11; Chinese disciples, 11,
  14–15, 70, 104–105, 111, 114, 124, 127,
  131–135, 139; Chinese practitioners, 15, 54,
  114, 126, 129, 132–133; role of Chinese
  disciples, 111

Chinese police, 24–25, 29, 45; armed force, 30;
  armed police (*wujing*), 30
Chinese state, 2, 5, 10, 17, 24, 28, 75, 133;
  Chinese government, 6, 12, 41, 108, 132, 137;
  Chinese rule, 10–11, 17, 27–28, 107–108, 133;
  Chinese state apparatus, 8; Chinese state's
  control, 41; Chinese state's ongoing controls
  of Tibetan Buddhism, 6; Chinese state's
  policy directives, 49; state power, 13, 41
codes of conduct, 58, 90–91
communal building assignments, 54;
  communal labor, 87, 99; communal
  projects, 54, 102; communal construction
  projects, 59
confession, 81–82; significance of confessions,
  81; technique of confession, 84
contemporary Chinese society, 11
converting to Buddhism, 71
Cultural Revolution, 71

Dalai Lamas, 94; current Dalai Lama, 75;
  fourteenth Dalai Lama, 25, 63; thirteenth
  Dalai Lama, 107
Dawa, 86–88, 90, 108
decoration, 64–65, 67–74, 85; arranging indoor
  space, 64; decorating practices, 65, 68, 75
Dekyi, 78–81
Deshi, 18–23, 32, 37
diet, 14, 113, 116, 119, 124–127, 131; dietary
  habits, 106, 114, 117, 123; dietary practices,
  110–111, 114, 116–118, 123, 125, 128, 134–135
discrimination against ethnic minorities, 23
Dolka, 104–107
Dolma, 97–99, 102
dominant norms and morality, 84
Douglas, Mary, 121
Dzokchen (the Great Perfection), 55, 58;
  Dzokchen practice, 58–59, 94; teacher-
  disciple relationship, 58

electricity, 5, 20, 33, 48, 51, 68, 115, 133
encampment, 1–2, 4–5, 9, 13, 16, 39–41, 46, 52,
  55–56, 60, 64, 110, 113, 131, 139–140;
  quasi-monastic religious encampment
  (*chögar*), 5; Tibetan Buddhist encampments, 12

www.ingramcontent.com/pod-product-compliance
Lightning Source LLC
Chambersburg PA
CBHW030846270326
41928CB00007B/1241